Understanding, designing and conducting qualitative research in education

Conducting educational research

Series Editor: Harry Torrance, University of Sussex.

This series is aimed at research students in education and those under-taking related professional, vocational and social research. It takes current methodological debates seriously and offers well-informed advice to students on how to respond to such debates. Books in the series review and engage with current methodological issues, while relating such issues to the sorts of decisions which research students have to make when designing, conducting and writing up research. Thus the series both contributes to methodological debate and has a practical orientation by providing students with advice on how to engage with such debate and use particular methods in their work. Series authors are experienced researchers and supervisors. Each book provides students with insights into a different form of educational research while also providing them with the critical tools and knowledge necessary to make informed judgements about the strengths and weaknesses of different approaches.

Current titles:
Tony Brown and Liz Jones: *Action Research and Postmodernism*
John Schostak: *Understanding, Designing and Conducting Qualitative Research in Education*

Understanding, designing and conducting qualitative research in education
Framing the project

John F. Schostak

Open University Press
Buckingham · Philadelphia

Open University Press
Celtic Court
22 Ballmoor
Buckingham
MK18 1XW

email: enquiries@openup.co.uk
world wide web: www.openup.co.uk

and

325 Chestnut Street
Philadelphia, PA 19106, USA

First Published 2002

Copyright © John Schostak, 2002

A catalogue record of this book is available from the British Library

ISBN   0 335 20509 7 (pb)   0 335 20510 0 (hb)

Library of Congress Cataloging-in-Publication Data
Schostak, John F.
   Understanding, designing, and conducting qualitative research in education: framing the project/John F. Schostak.
      p. cm. – (Conducting educational research)
   Includes bibliographical references and index.
   ISBN 0-335-20510-0 – ISBN 0-335-20509-7 (pbk.)
   1. Education–Research. I. Title. II. Series.

LB1028 .S28 2001
370′.7′2–dc21   2001032140

Typeset by Graphicraft Limited, Hong Kong
Printed in Great Britain by St Edmundsbury Press Limited,
Bury St Edmunds, Suffolk

Contents

List of figures

Introduction

A doctoral student writes:

> The aim of this thesis is to go beyond seeking pupils' views on curriculum and to look at some implications of pupils' views for curriculum reform. In this way, we might learn about the educational values held by these pupils that may be able to inform practical and reliable indicators for curriculum theorising. Thus, I hope to generate several criteria for curriculum theorising. Although these criteria are not exhaustive, they will provide an analytical framework for thinking about curriculum change and development. The primary justification for this study is social justice in that it hopes to provide a forum for pupils as a marginalised group to express their views on curriculum. This is advanced as a form of distributive justice based on Rawls's theory of justice, for the academically weak pupils who become a disadvantaged group and, therefore, rarely have their points of view taken into consideration.
>
> (Meng 1999: 3)

In a few words the writer's ambition to contribute to social justice in relation to curriculum reform and theory, and the specific focus on pupils as a marginalized group, is clearly outlined. Like others doing doctoral research, the project themes were something he cared greatly about. The thesis was the outcome of a personal journey drawing on, for example, philosophies of knowledge and understanding; ethical, political, social, cultural, historical and psychological critiques; data collection methods; and the intentions, hopes, ambitions of the individual and/or group carrying out the project.

This book is also the outcome of my own experience in doing numerous projects, being a supervisor and working with colleagues and students as they accomplished their own personal journeys. Based on this experience, a project cannot be conceived as a mechanical application of research techniques culled from the many textbooks available. The aim of this book is to help the beginning researcher to think about the stages of doing research from initial idea to writing up. There is no single solution to cover the range of roles and circumstances of the first-time researcher who may be:

- a full- or part-time student;
- an overseas student (both full-time and distance learning circumstances will be considered) who faces cultural as well as language issues;
- a workplace-based researcher/student undertaking a project to guide professional or more general organizational analysis and development;
- the individual, voluntary group, or consultant who wants to explore issues in a rigorous manner for publication, reports, or influencing decision making.

The project may be undertaken in the context of a full-time job; or there may be those who are engaged in delivering a professional service which requires research-based support such as an evaluation of the effectiveness of those services. Each of these circumstances focuses attention on particular needs, problems and opportunities. In all these different circumstances that researchers may find themselves occupying, what is it about a project that makes it worth engaging with? The answer cannot be summed up simply; rather it is an experience, a journey that has to be lived, not read. Completing a successful project, getting the doctorate and achieving publication demands much more than the rote application of methods or other research recipes. It demands identifying one's own critical edge and turning broad ambitions into action. The issues to be explored in doing this are the subject of the book.

Making a start

So here is the paradox: the lived always seeks to be represented in some way and thus sacrifices the sense of life for the sense of words and meanings in order to relive. The journey is thus a double structure: one track is the life of bodily engagement with the world; the other track is the life of reflection in order to re-present textually, through images, through signs of all kinds, the experience of the journey. The double tracked journey demands commitment, is often uncomfortable, takes too long and yet opens up new vistas, gives glimpses into different lives and can offer new possibilities for changes in direction, self-growth. Decisions taken on the way are not only personal but also impact on the lives of others. For some, their journey takes them into political, even hostile environments where they hope to change the circumstances of people's lives. For others it is a journey of wonder where strange worlds are encountered and where they hope only to describe, explore and understand. In each case, what is seen, heard, touched, tasted, smelt on the journey forms the essential data of experience. How an individual perceives the world is never a simple matter of just opening the eyes and looking – the data of the senses are always pre-organized culturally, psychologically. The biography of the researcher is always implicated. And the biography is never just a personal matter: the biography is always the ready-to-wear coat created way before an individual's birth and tailored by parents to fit whatever projects they may in some shared family and social fantasy hold on behalf of their expected child. Similarly, the research project is always embedded in projects long since constructed, some of which lie like remnants of old civilizations available to be rediscovered by archaeologists of the mind and others which are like the clothing of some seductive dancer, there to be discarded in the interests of some hidden, unsaid, or forbidden plan.

Starting out, it would be helpful if there were a road map or a set of instructions. Being the first to explore new territory means having to create your own as you go along. Strategies for this exist and can be learnt. Now for the bad news: trying to formulate a project is typically one step back from this; the territory itself is not yet formed, and there is no recipe for trying to visualize or realize it. There is no safe and secure journey through what is essentially the unknown. There are no formulae to scatter upon the data that will turn a fragmented mess of interview transcripts, recorded observations and piles of notes, official and unofficial documentation and an assorted array of material objects into 'findings'. If only it were that simple, it would have all been done by now and there would be nothing left to research, debate and fight about. For any researcher, then, no matter how experienced, the starting point is in a sense a process of making maps without at first knowing what the project is to be a map of; the appropriate format of a map; and whether or not a map constrains, biases, leads one astray or opens up possibilities where none had previously been seen. The initial question to be explored is: how does one find one's bearings in order to make a 'project', that is, project a course of reflection and action sufficient to map, describe and generate debate about an area of interest and concern?

Finding one's bearings

Take the familiar example of the gestalt[1] object that can be seen either as a duck or a rabbit. One project enables the seeing of the duck as a central subject against a background. Another project enables the seeing of a rabbit. Researchers who explore the duck project will no doubt be in continual battle with those who explore the rabbit project. Each will try to refine their researches to prove that either the duck or the rabbit is the 'reality'; but not both. Both find their bearings first, in relation to the task of proving their preferred gestalt picture of reality is correct, and hence, second, each person finds their bearings in relation to the other who disagrees with them. If this sounds far-fetched read Kuhn's (1970) or Feyerabend's (1975) accounts of the various paradigm battles that have taken place in science. The project, then, defines what is seen, what counts as 'real', the community of believers and the community of disbelievers. In this context, the project has to find its bearings in relation to:

1 the Self and
2 the subjective organization of experience,
3 other people and
4 the intersubjective organization of experience, through
5 symbolic frameworks involving the values, permissions and prohibitions of religions, the laws of society, political and economic order, the values and traditions of communities, the codes of language, as well as the formal laws of mathematics, sciences and so on, and
6 the material world.

In their different ways each chapter of the book takes a particular stance to one or more of these dimensions of project activity. Chapter 1 takes an initial overview or preview. Chapter 2 focuses on the self and its subjective organization. Chapter 3 moves to the level of intersubjectivity, that is, the field of others and the Other. The methods employed in finding one's bearings – self-reflection, interviews, observations, analyses of texts, discourses, images and the built environment and so on – are not key to the creation of the project but are merely tools (albeit not neutral tools) to be employed one way or another. By defining what counts as 'real' or as 'fact' the research project combines with other projects to generate a sense not just of 'knowledge' about 'reality' but of Reality itself that is somehow inclusive of self and Other yet not reducible to them. Similar to a kind of theatre production, the project could be said to 'stage reality'. Returning to the double track metaphor, the staging is a form of living and re-presenting as if Real, indeed, crossing out the 'as if', it is staged *as* Real. This is what makes a project both critical and dangerous. It is here that the politics of research, or research as a political process, engages so much energy, and produces so much passion and vitriol between protagonists. The politics begin as the twin tracked notion of research starts to twist, and derail the lives of participants. Any sense of straightforward direction becomes complicated by the considerations of postmodernism. Broaching complexity, Chapter 4 commences this process of derailment and it is continued by Chapter 5 into its logical graveyard where sense and nonsense fuse and meanings are loosened from their anchorage in master narratives. What then of Truth? Chapter 6 explores whether any hope remains following the seductive makeovers of postmodernism. Chapter 7 analyses and deconstructs the textual tracks of representational processes. It focuses on the power of possibility and the construction and use of evidence as a basis for framing 'the message' of the project. Alternative messages mean alternative frameworks for justifying and taking action. Chapters 8 and 9 explore the ethical and political dimensions to action. All of these discussions then have to be incorporated in some way in a final report, thesis, book or paper. Chapter 10 explores what is at stake in writing up.

Making paradigm tracks

Returning to the theme of the project as journey, the choice of travelling by car (material vehicle) means, first, that one needs to know how to drive (social, cultural, professional practices) if one does not employ a chauffeur; second, that one is committed to the roadways. All that can be seen is what appears at the window. To see more necessitates getting out and walking (change of vehicle, change of practices). Here one can more easily stray from the pre-designed pathway. But to climb mountains or swim rivers requires time and training. Then from the mountain top one can perhaps gaze across the panoramic vista, then, descending, gain a close-up look at the detail on the facade of a historic building. However, no matter how intensively one observes from a distance or close up, to understand the lives of the people who dwell in the houses and walk the streets contact has to be made. How does one get to know the people? It requires more than just looking. You have to engage people in conversations in order to learn their ways, their biographies, their ways of seeing the world about. This is made obvious when abroad. In order to ask one's way, a certain knowledge of the local language is required. To know more about the lives (culture, philosophy, ideas, values) of those encountered demands more than a smattering of the local language. It requires fluency. Paradigms underlying scientific endeavour are similarly structured.

Kuhn (1970) describes throughout his book how theory or philosophy, practices and material realities are so interwoven as to be utterly interdependent:

In the development of any science, the first received paradigm is usually felt to account quite successfully for most of the observations and experiments easily accessible to that science's practitioners. Further development, therefore, ordinarily calls for the construction of elaborate equipment, the development of an esoteric vocabulary and skills, and a refinement of concepts that increasingly lessens their resemblance to their usual commonsense prototypes. That professionalisation leads, on the one hand, to an immense restriction of the scientist's vision and to a considerable resistance to paradigm change. The science has become increasingly rigid. On the other hand, within those areas to which the paradigm directs the attention of the group, normal science leads to a detail of information and to a precision of the observation–theory match that could be achieved in no other way. Furthermore, that detail and precision-of-match have a value that transcends their not always very high intrinsic interest. Without the special apparatus that is constructed mainly for anticipated functions, the results that lead ultimately to novelty could not occur. And even when the apparatus exists, novelty ordinarily emerges only for the man who, knowing *with precision* what he should expect, is able to recognise that something has gone wrong.

(Kuhn 1970: 64–5)

The passage describes how paradigms act paradoxically as road map, constraint and liberation. Novelty, interestingly, is linked to something going wrong, a kind of derailment. This curious search for dilemmas and anomalies is an essential strategy in the search for the new, the novel. Such an approach may be felt as unsettling, particularly for those new to doing research and those well schooled into the prevailing views of right and wrong ways of doing research. Being derailed once or many times can feel frustrating, confusing. It can feel like being incompetent and one yearns for someone to say, 'Do it this way'. Yet, each derailment is an opportunity to 'test' alternative ways of doing, thinking and seeing. To do this requires a rereading and a rethinking that takes one into the debates about the nature of knowledge at one level and debates about society, being human and human purposes at another. These themes will be explored throughout several chapters, particularly from Chapter 4 onwards. Derailment often means coming at a text or scene from an unexpected angle. Sometimes the passage of time is enough to generate a rereading. As a simple example, Kuhn's book reveals something of the culture of the time of its writing. Today, to write of 'man' as the general term for agency is to be insensitive to the demands of women to eradicate the gender bias that unconsciously or consciously drives society. Our contemporary sensitivities have derailed his text, allowing us to 'see' something that Kuhn and the readers of his day 'missed'. This is not an irrelevant aside to the notion of 'project'. In order to map the world about, a project demands increasing sensitization to the perspectives of others, their experiences, their interests, their vulnerabilities and thus to one's own as yet unconscious biases. Each 'new' perspective can act as a derailment of one's own, or of dominant views.

Paradigms are thus not just ways of seeing that leave all else unchanged. There are material consequences. For example, Virilio (1996) has described key world events in terms of the impact that inventions have had on communications and the redistribution of power. For him 'power is always the power of controlling a territory by messengers, the means of transport and of transmission' (my translation). Thus the first generals who used horse messengers were able to make decisions faster than those who employed soldiers as runners. Similarly those who used wireless had an advantage over those who did not. Today, it is the impact of the internet that is presenting new challenges to prevailing power orders. Rather than point-to-point communications (that is, a message being carried from point A to point B), information is now broadcast over a network (that is point A to all points at once). Analysing this in simple terms, there is the general who constructs a 'project of war' or battle plan according to some understanding of how wars are won or lost. The plan is conceived strategically, perhaps at the level of ideas read or listened to about the philosophies of war constructed by past strategists. However, these ideas have to be put into practice. First there is the training of the troops. They must learn how to fight, how to obey, how to make decisions if necessary. That is, there is a set of organizational, professional, cultural and social practices they must be able to carry out if they are to be considered competent and if they want a chance of survival. Then there are the materials of war: weapons, modes of transport and communications. These three interrelated dimensions of the war project – ideas, practices and material resources – suggest what is called by Bhaskar (1975) and Sayer (1993) a realist philosophy and methodology for the development of projects. A similar structure underlies the approach adopted in this book. It interweaves philosophy, practices and material realities in exploring events and people's experiences.

The project is both a personal and a social endeavour that has consequences in the material world. Harris (1968) has described how the sciences of the social and the physical interwove and informed each other in surprising ways. For example, contemporary economic views presume that the reason why competition and survival of the fittest is considered fundamental to the market place is because it is consistent with the fundamental Darwinian 'finding' that species evolve through a process of competition where only the fittest survive. Harris, however, shows how the views of the economist Adam Smith influenced Darwin and that it was the sociologist Spencer who made use of the term 'survival of the fittest'. Thus evolutionary theory drew first on economics

paradigm

project

methods

Figure 1.1 From paradigm to methods

rather than economics drawing on the 'natural' observations of the scientist. Such critiques have led many to explore 'knowledge' not as a natural fact to be found through the application of the 'correct' methods but as a social construction rhetorically framed (see Chapter 10).

This in turn has led others to view all knowledge as arbitrary, limited to specific circumstances and interests. With the emergence of the global communications technologies which place the world's cultures into dialogue and contestation, knowledge, beliefs, ways of life can all be considered as lifestyle choices to be adopted or thrown away according to whim and desire. It is in the matrices of global communications that all prior 'world views' or paradigms, secure in their dominance of particular geographically defined territories, find their 'space' and their 'worlds' eroding into the infinite plasticity of cyberspace. Whether as a research student or as a member of staff wishing to commence a research career, or as an academic new to supervising research students, it is in locating one's 'self', one's 'ground', one's 'horizon' in relation to the great debates, the great events of a given period of time that the 'project' may be found. Without such a sense, even embryonically glimpsed, all study and use of methods will result in little more than the play of puppets dangling from their strings, blown by cross-currents. Figure 1.1, a crude sketch of the relationship between paradigms and methods to be adopted by the scientist, focuses on what is at stake:

Although the arrows indicate that all flow from the choice of the paradigm, such a choice is not a simple matter. All is problematic. Indeed, the governing paradigm is rarely clear and distinct but lies unconsciously. The statistical research paradigm may seem to offer a clear and distinct process for discovery. However, what are the assumptions upon which it is based? Do these bias the ways in which the scientist perceives the world? These are questions that are explored from Chapter 2 onwards. The project then is not a simple matter of choosing a subject and then applying methods. The researcher must interrogate its foundations, its paradigmatic assumptions if claims are to be made about the objects discovered, and the world explored in the course of the project. Furthermore, whatever methods are taught as appropriate to a given discipline they bear some relation to a project through which they are organized. Are methods simply neutral or do they in some way rely on paradigmatic assumptions that skew what is collected as data? The project in turn bears some relationship to a paradigm which provides a framework of social, theoretical, cultural meanings and purposes to the project. The arrows of the diagram suggest that methods do not determine a project; nor does a project determine a paradigm. However, the relations are more complex. It is a play of rationales, that is, the exploration of the alternative rationales by which people justify, celebrate or protect their lives. In exploring these kinds of relationships, the project emerges as a process of thinking by writing. Each chapter that follows is a return to the 'same thing', a return that deconstructs what previously had been assumed as solid and so renders the 'same', different. Their purpose is to explore the project as a continuous act of questioning, doubting, exploring. It is a process that has to leave the textbooks behind and subject all recipes to deconstruction and reframing to meet new purposes and novel circumstances.

Finding bearings

Entering a new city, it helps having a map or a local person as a guide. Doing research means forever having to find ways of getting your bearings. To some extent reading about project design, reports of completed projects, talking with experienced researchers and drawing on relevant theories are all helpful in familiarizing the researcher with key issues, theories and processes. As, in a strange city, spotting a key landmark helps to orientate the person who had been lost, so models or images of project practice may help to orientate the researcher. Coming for the first time to the scene, all seems of potential significance, as if each trivial aspect whispers 'look at me!' Amidst this clamour for attention, the strategic landmarks, always available to the researcher are: the *'I'-as-researcher* who *directs attention to* the world composed of various *objects-of-attention*. The relationships between these dimensions can be the focus for initial exploration. The I-as-researcher is in a position rather like Vonnegut's aliens who, in being able to communicate telepathically, are open to all thoughts at once! In order to focus they chose to speak aloud, employing language because

> they found out they could get so much more *done* with language. Language made them so much more *active*. Mental telepathy, with everybody constantly telling everybody everything, produced a sort of generalised indifference to *all* information. But language, with its slow, narrow meanings, made it possible to think about one thing at a time – to start thinking in terms of *projects*.
> (Vonnegut 1965: 202–3)

The project is about differentiation and choosing to focus. Getting things done with language demands framing categories, organizing relationships between them, expressing a point of view. Like Vonnegut's aliens the researcher has to slow things down, write one thing at a time in a research diary that acts as a focus for thinking about what is being seen and experienced. It is the basis for thinking about the project and the ways in which it is framed by the purposes of the researcher. The researcher's values, interests, desires, needs determine what is relevant to the research; the approaches and methods by which to gain access to the worlds of others and collect data; and the literature of debate that places the project in relation to the scholarship and theorization of others. Every individual will construct their own plan for doing this – and break it – in their own way. Unlike a city map, the research plan is more like playing in order to generate possibilities than a strict set of directions to be followed. This playing has a variety of qualities. It can be the 'playing' of a child, for fun, a game of 'what if'. Or it can be the playing of an instrument to see what sounds it makes and how these can be formed into 'music'. Or it can be the playing of a bridge in the wind, increasing the swaying until the point of breakage is reached. Each form of playing provides a new perspective, provides new information on the structures and processes being observed. The researcher can look at the 'globe', a continent, a country, a region, a town, a street . . . The choice of focus from distant to close up determines what is to be covered.

The look of researcher and subjects

Beginning a thesis one can feel 'lost' and overawed at the immensity of a task that demands getting to grips with whole traditions of thought and practice developed over tens if not hundreds and thousands of years. How can it all be covered? Are there a few simple devices and activities that can provide a good starting point? The answer is: 'Yes; well maybe; or at least, in part'. All projects begin in a kind of stuttering. Confident-sounding 'yesses' and 'noes' slide into maybes, ifs and buts. However, there are starting points at once common to all that are also unique: the inquisitive 'look' of the researcher together with the return 'look' of the subjects studied.

What distinguishes social sciences from the physical sciences is that the physicist deals with objects whereas the sociologist deals with subjects who have purposes, who choose or act whimsically, even go against their 'better instincts' and who return the 'look' of the researcher with their own, making judgements, forming opinions, and taking decisions. Although some in the social sciences have tried to act as if subjects were objects, qualitative research focuses on people and meanings.

As the researcher is a subject within a world of subjects, what then is more natural than to begin with such questions as:

- What do I want to do?
- What do I want to find out?

- What do others expect of me regarding the project?
- How do I know that what I have researched will be 'true' in relation to the experiences and judgements of others?
- When I've got 'data' of the lives of others, what will I want to do with them?
- Why am I doing this?
- Why should anyone care?

By interrogating the world appearing to consciousness, the 'look' of the researcher meets the 'look' of others. Like the sweep of a radar the positions of others, objects and their relationships are marked out. The nature of the questions posed guides the 'coverage' of the world about and the way it is mapped in order to locate self in relation to others and objects. Hence it is important to search for guiding questions. However, these do not necessarily arise all at once at the beginning. The search for questions continues throughout the life of the project. Projects tend to be written up as if they are answers to key questions, gaps in knowledge, or issues that have not been noticed before. For example, Meng (1999), in his doctoral study of pupils' views, writes:

> One cannot just connect pupils' views and experience with curric-
> ulum without taking into account the context, it is necessary, too,
> to understand educational policy and teacher culture in Malaysia.
> This complex picture has been researched by three former Malaysian
> doctoral students at (the) Centre for Applied Research in Education
> (CARE), University of East Anglia (Nagendralingan Ratnavadivel,
> 1995; Hannah Pillay, 1995 and Lim, 1997). However, due to the
> focus of their studies, they did not talk to pupils extensively about
> curriculum. This study hopes to close the 'gap' in understanding
> pupil culture, thereby extending the knowledge generated by these
> three doctoral students. The reader will hear me talking to pupils
> and exploring their values and beliefs. But there are methodological
> implications to such an exercise especially as an adult seeking views
> and co-operation from pupils. It is for this reason that this thesis
> begins with the revelation of my values and beliefs as the researcher
> and author.
>
> (Meng 1999: 4)

Already a strategy is emerging here, both methodological and rhetorical. Although the role of rhetorical play in constructing a 'world' of
'truth' and writing up a thesis will be taken up more directly in Chapters
7 and 10, it is worth pointing to the complex pulling together of prior
research 'knowledge', the identification of a 'gap' to be covered, and the
role of text in re-presenting 'hearing' the author 'talking' to pupils as
well as the 'revelation' of the writer's own values and beliefs. Rhetorically

the text produces the appearance of a truth being told (Baudrillard 1990). To accomplish this, there is a kind of complicity in drawing the reader into the sphere of vicariously 'hearing' conversations between the author and others, and reading the personal values and beliefs of the author. The text is a kind of 'revealed truth' (Chapter 6), a truth only the witness can authorize (Schostak 1999a). It is a witness who can claim the expertise to organize, for example, the everyday talk of 'pupils' into technical or theoretic explanatory models of schooling (see Chapter 9 on expert action). There is thus an intimate relationship between the 'self' as witness and the project that describes, or, indeed, evokes the world to be described. The subject and the project are two sides of the same coin determining the 'world' to be seen and how it is to be represented.

There is also a sense in which it is not, a sense in which the project extends beyond the 'self' as individual and even leaves the self altogether to voyage through the multiple readings others will make of it, both others who are known and those who are not yet known or never known, just as I have done with the extract from Meng's thesis. The project plays with the life of the subject as the subject plays with the project. The subject is as much a product of the project as the project is a product of the subject. This strange tension is the source of the creativity of project work. To cultivate it is the aim. The task is to 'map' the 'self/project' as a mutually defining structure and process.

Self/project

The world, as a project, is created in acts of subjects looking towards each other, mapping their desires into the lives of each other, glimpsing themselves in each other's regard:

> Properly speaking, a man has as *many social selves as there are individuals who recognise him* and carry an image of him in their mind. To wound any one of these images of his, is to wound him. But as the individuals who carry the images fall naturally into classes, we may practically say that he has as many different social selves as there are distinct groups of persons about whose opinion he cares.
>
> (James 1890: 294, original emphasis)

This is an early statement of a key dimension of the pragmatist project to create a new approach to social inquiry. Should we believe it? Unpacking James's views demands a look at the debates that formed them. This will be an important step in deconstructing and gaining a critical grasp on the views of those who have drawn on him and have been influential in the development of the qualitative project as it evolved into symbolic interactionism, phenomenology, ethnomethodology and

their various contemporary hybrids. In order to discover one's own contribution and not to be drawn into positions that counter one's own
sense of freedom and value it is important to explore the debates and
ferret out the assumptions upon which they are built. Why? The position one adopts as to the 'nature' of the self influences the kind of
project that can be undertaken. For example, symbolic interactionism
can be employed to underpin two distinct, even opposing, directions:
the self as active agent who may, for example, act from a machiavellian,
anarchistic, or sadian position; or the self as a tranquillized and oversocialized being whose projects are determined by others, 'institutions'
or 'society' (Wrong 1961). Broadly, the symbolic interactionist perspective considers that the behaviour of others cannot be understood through
observation alone. One has to explore their symbolic functions in terms
of their vocabularies of purposes, motives, intentions. Therefore the individual as 'self' is understandable only in the context of the social,
meaningful, or symbolic organizations of experience. To what extent is
the individual unique?

> I do not question that the individual is a differentiated centre of
> psychical life, having a world of his own into which no other indi-
> vidual can fully enter; living in a stream of thought in which there
> is nothing quite like that in any other stream, neither his 'I', nor his
> 'you', nor his 'we', nor even any material object; all, probably, as
> they exist for him, have something unique about them. But this
> uniqueness is no more apparent and verifiable than the fact – not at
> all inconsistent with it – that he is in the fullest sense a member of
> the whole, appearing such not only to scientific observation but also
> to his own untrained consciousness.
>
> (Cooley 1956: 8–9)

What does being a member of the 'whole' signify? This is a question
that can take us off into several different debates about how subjects,
'society' and knowledge are 'produced' and related to each other. Cooley's
own frameworks of thinking grew out of the pragmatic philosophies of
such key thinkers as James, Mead and Dewey. Like any text, the ideas
expressed by any given writer are taken into the multiple contexts of
those who read them and are reinterpreted for the reader's own purposes. Thus when Cooley writes of the 'whole' he is evoking an entire
tradition of thinking, whether one that he is aware of, or one he could
know nothing about because it developed later, or because it is a result
of the particular background reading of a given reader. So, what did
Cooley mean by whole? For Cooley, it is like the wholeness created by
an orchestra composed of individual players. Each have their role, play
their parts, but the whole is somehow greater than the parts. This whole
is in some way self-evident, for Cooley, both for the individual as scientist,

and the individual as 'untrained consciousness'. This separation between I-as-scientist and I-as-untrained consciousness – or better, division within subjectivity itself – is useful to note. It will take on greater significance in later discussions.

The term 'whole' becomes highly problematic if Cooley's sense of its self-evidence is questioned. Does it mean that the individual is part of the whole like a cog is a part of the clock? This implies many things. It implies that the individual is a functional element of the whole. It implies a purposefulness, a teleology, just as the purpose of the clock is to measure the passing of time. It implies a strong structure that holds everything together. It implies mechanisms that bring about a sense of order. Indeed, all these elements can be found in the various sociological, political, economic and indeed psychological theories of the first half of the twentieth century. These debates can be drawn out of the works of people like Lévi-Strauss (1969) who employed a structuralist method to explore world cultures, or Piaget (1970) who applied structuralist ideas to the study of child cognitive development.

The importance of structure as a guiding metaphor for methodology is that is focuses on relationships between elements rather than the elements themselves. This means that any given individual (person or object, symbolic or real) is studied only for its role in relation to the whole structure. Individuality thus is effaced in such a system of analysis. Instead there are categories of individuals, like Father, that stands in a relationship to another category like Mother, or Son, or Daughter. These categories and their relationships are at once biological and cultural. There are others that are solely cultural, and yet others that are logical. Methodologically the point to address is that of the search for patterns, for regularities of relationship between the general or fundamental categories employed by the people or individuals being studied. Take for example the concept of 'wife':

> among the Karimojong [this] would be described by the conjunction of all the contrasts between adult women and children, all the contrasts between unmarried and married adult women, all the contrasts between married women and widows. Thus 'wife' among the Karimojong means a person without the right to own cattle but with the right to use a garden and a milk cow, without the right to participate in religion and politics, without the right to take lovers, but with the right to have a baby's father support it, with the right to live with the husband she married rather than one of her husband's heirs (as a widow must), and so on.
>
> (Stinchcombe 1982: 73)

By making contrasts between categories employed within a group and across cultures, structuralists claimed 'structure is conceived as a set of possible states' (Piaget 1970: 38). That is, structuralists looked for all the possible cultural solutions to a given relationship between, say, the members of a 'family'. Thus structuralism provided one way of mapping society as a whole by categorizing the basic roles and elements of a society and identifying the key relationships between them. The focus was on 'systems', on universalization, formalization. In this approach the individual was lost in the emphasis upon categories and their possible relationships.

The approaches of Mead, Thomas, Szananieki, Whyte and Cooley among others contributed alternatives to the development of a sociological perspective that focused attention on the individual and group, that is the micro level of interpersonal interactions rather than the macro level of social systems. Thus when Cooley refers to the whole, he refers to this macro level as he believes it is experienced by any individual. His problem, in a sense, was the opposite of the structuralist approach. Rather than accounting for the individual, he has to account for 'society', for social 'wholes', for 'systems'. Effectively, for Cooley, the individual is a sign that points to the whole, like smoke indicates fire, or like 'sail' meaning 'ship', as in the statement 'I see three sails'. This kind of relationship, in rhetoric, is called metonymy. However, does the individual actually experience his or her self metonymically, that is, as a part-object finding 'true' significance only in the whole, the 'we', rather than the 'I'? If so, it could be argued that agency resides more in the 'we' that signifies society as a whole, rather than the 'I'. Indeed, it could be said that the uniqueness of which Cooley speaks is effaced in a desire to be included in the 'we', that is to be the same as everyone else, that is, indistinguishable from the other members of a mass. Sartre (1976) described the effect on individuals of becoming a member of a mass as serialization. That is, the individual experiences his or her self as just one of a series. Rather than finding identity and comfort in being a member of the 'we', one finds alienation and loneliness in the crowd (cf. Riesman 1969). The sense of I, then, is overwhelmed by the sense of being no more than a member of the crowd, the 'we'. There are as already suggested many ways of mapping and interpreting the relationship between individual, the group and society as a 'whole'. Exploring the relationship is fundamental to contemporary approaches to social research.

Mead (1934) explored the relationship between the individual and the social in terms of the 'I' and the 'me'. The 'I' is the fleeting source of creativity, the dimension of being unique, the source of individuality. However the 'I' is subjected to the criteria of the social represented by the 'me', the product of the reflection of the self in the eyes of significant others. Hence, the 'me' is that aspect that is framed in terms of the whole, that is, of society. Mead's framework provided a departure point for the development of several approaches in qualitative research, as well as being compatible with other developments stemming from phenomenology and existentialism. However, the emphasis placed by many approaches on the 'me', the 'social self' rather than the 'I', led Wrong (1961) to argue against the oversocialized view of the individual by the sociologists of the day. The 'I' is replaced by the 'me'. The 'me' is metonymically merely a part of the whole series of social 'me's reflected in the social mirrors of others describing who I am, what I should be, who I'm like. The substitution of 'me' for 'I' is metaphoric in that the 'I' becomes repressed, or overlayed by the endlessly mirrored series of social 'me's reflected back to me about myself by members of society. The 'I' is effaced, its uniqueness sacrificed for an identity defined not by difference but by a mirrored similarity. These two ways of interpreting the relation may well be a subjective 'choice' for organizing one's experience in the world.

For Cooley, it allows a particular methodological approach to the study of individuals and society:

Persons and society must be studied primarily in imagination. It is true, *prima facie*, that the best way of observing things is that which is most direct; and I do not see how we can hold that we know persons directly except as imaginative ideas in the mind.

(Cooley 1902: 86)

In this particular social project, social reality and persons become a shimmering passage of images on a mirroring surface, a series of 'me's conceptually organized, placed under headings, formed into recognizable identities. These imaginative ideas, as Cooley calls them, are not arbitrary. They are drawn from the evidence of being with others, initially one's family, friends, neighbours, later perhaps from the media, teachers and others who are significant in the life of the individual. This imaginative grasp of a world, or the process of the imaginative construction of a world, has been well described by Anderson (1983) who conceives of a nation as 'an imagined political community': 'It is imagined because the members of even the smallest nation will never know most of their fellow-members, meet them, or even hear of them, yet in the minds of each lives the image of their communion' (Anderson 1983: 15).

To explore a world is to engage with the particular processes through which it is imagined. Imagination is central to methodology. Its importance will be discussed in relation to the imaginary order of subjectivity in Chapter 2 and to discussions of phenomenological forms of generalization in Chapters 3 and 7. In order to explore the imaginary terrain, the researcher selects a particular focus from, say, a satellite view to a street level view. Each such focus will define what is meant by a 'part' in relation to the 'whole'. The earth is a part of the solar system, as a paving stone is a part of the street. Demands for coverage of the whole will thus depend on the strategic position adopted by the researchers in studying a given social process or circumstance. Coverage of the imaginary order involves describing the events and material structures and processes of the environment, as well as the symbolic and meaning dimensions of life through which, first, 'members' of a group or community conceive of their membership and make demands on others based on their assumptions concerning mutual membership or 'outsiderness'; and second, how members deal with issues of uniqueness and individuality. Rather than mechanical cause and effect, the imaginary order takes its life from motives, desires, purposes.

Exploring purposes

A qualitative research project explores the ways through which a 'self' and its 'world' are constituted and coordinated through an imaginative grasp in relation to experiences of 'Reality'. What 'ties' them together are the intricate web of purposes, motives, interests, needs, demands, feelings and so on structured by the language we use to express ourselves to others and by which we orient our behaviour with theirs and they with us in a world of material structures. Mills (1940) provided a useful starting point in mapping this web. He wanted to 'outline an analytic model for the explanation of motives which is based on a sociological theory of language and a sociological psychology'. Thus:

> The generic situation in which imputation of motives arise involves, first, the *social* conduct. Or the (stated) programmes of languaged creatures, i.e., programmes and actions oriented with reference to the actions and talk of others; second, the avowal and imputation of motives is concomitant with the speech form known as the 'question'. Situations back of questions typically involve *alternative* or *unexpected* programmes or actions which phases analytically denote 'crises'. The question is distinguished in that it usually elicits another *verbal* action, not a motor response. The question is an element in *conversation*. Conversation may be concerned with the factual features of a situation as they are seen or believed to be or it may seek to integrate and promote a set of diverse social actions with reference to the situation and its normative pattern of expectations. It is in this latter assent or dissent phase of conversation that persuasive and dissuasive speech and vocabulary arise. For men live in immediate acts of experience and their attentions are directed

outside themselves until acts are in some way frustrated. It is then that awareness of self and motive occur. The 'question' is a lingual index of such conditions. The avowal and imputation of motives are features of such conversations as arise in 'question' situations.

Motives are imputed or avowed as answers to questions interrupting acts of programmes.

(Mills 1940, original emphasis)

The project is like a conversation framed by the questions the researcher directs to the self, the other and the materiality of existence. If social life is a complex of programmes of action where self is oriented to other, then the project proceeds by unpacking this complex by seeking to uncover and describe:

1 The motives and purposes of the researcher, for example:
(i)   Self-knowledge;
(ii) Improving x, y, z;
(iii) Persuasion of decision makers;
2 Finding the Truth in order to, for example:
(i)   make radical changes;
(ii) preserve what remains as 'good', 'useful', 'needed', and so on;
3 The motives and purposes of 'subjects' as members of the 'world out there', for example:
(i)   as in the points made in 1 and 2 above, plus:
(ii) justifying of self to you-as-other among others and, in particular, you as researcher;
(iii) managing the impressions of their 'self' to manipulate you and others whether or not you are openly in a research role;
(iv) avoiding becoming aware of the consequences of their beliefs and actions.

Asking questions, self-reflectively, in conversation, or in the research interview, the response comes in the form of either an evasion (whether intended or unintended) or an account that ostensibly covers the motives, the reasons, the rationale for the situation:

An account is a linguistic device employed whenever an action is subjected to valuative inquiry. Such devices are a crucial element in the social order since they prevent conflicts from arising by verbally bridging the gap between action and expectation. Moreover, accounts are 'situated' according to the statuses of the interactants, and are standardised within cultures so that certain accounts are terminologically stabilised and routinely expected when activity falls outside the domain of expectations.

(Scott and Lyman 1968: 46)

'What is going on here?' is a key question to ask of any situation. Asking it assumes there is *an* 'answer'. Whether or not respondents claim to have *the* answer or not, what results is an account of what they think they 'know', or what they claim to believe, or the reasons why they do not know, or do not care about knowing, believing and so on. During accounts, respondents may ramble, change the subject, and attempt to please the researcher by providing 'answers' they think are 'wanted' by the researcher. In any case, the account does more than try to explain, convince or deceive someone about a situation; it is also a negotiation of identities as between the questioner and the answerer and can 'cover up' as much as uncover (see in particular the discussion of 'stealth architectures' in Chapter 4). Interviewing, observing and the gathering of documentary evidence are the key methods employed to collect the accounts by which worlds are continually negotiated into being. This play between purposes and ideas in the negotiation of accounts not only structures social behaviour, it shapes the architecture of our material existence:

> It is instructive to consider at closer range the ideas of Mumford, exemplar of the garden city idea in the USA, who was the most influential urban and architecture critic in the country for a period of several decades. Mumford's garden city was intended to combine the enduring values of the village with the diversity of the city. Influenced by Chicago sociologist Charles Cooley's theory of primary groups and secondary associations, Mumford wanted to divide his garden city into six unzoned, cellular wards. The wards would serve as primary groups, the town of 32,000 as a space for secondary associations.
>
> (Lash 1999: 23)

What we have in this passage is a close association between ideas and values on the one hand and social practices and the built material structures of a given group or society on the other. This complex of ideas, personal, social and material arrangement can only be unpacked, if at all, by asking a series of 'why' questions which together map out the problem structure to be explored for motives, purposes, intentions, reasons. This problem structure I find usefully conceptualized as in Figure 1.2.

It is an analysis drawn from a reading of Sayer (1993) and Bhaskar (1975, 1993) that provides a means of systematically exploring the circumstances of a situation, an institution or some more complex organization or social process by studying three interacting dimensions, or foci:

1 *ideas*, the level of symbolic structuring, the play of purpose, law and fantasy in the creation of virtual orderings of the world about;
2 *enactment*, the level of taking action, the legacies of rituals, the schooling of behaviour, the institutionalization of procedures and social

Conceptual/abstract

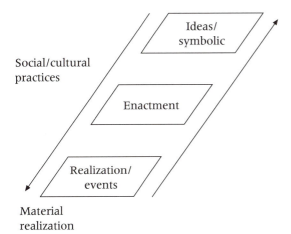

Social/cultural
practices

Material
realization

Figure 1.2   Realist framework

mechanisms that organize the 'right' (lawful) and 'expert' or 'competent' ways of doing things in order to implement or stage ideas in practice; and
3 *real-ization*, the level of making real, of manipulation of the material to produce desired outcomes.

The arrows indicate that there is no particular order implied in the schema, that each are mutually interdependent, that the process of change and action can start at any of the 'levels'. This analytic framework can be applied at the global levels or close up, focusing on the classroom, the street corner, the home. The framework is reminiscent of the Marxist approach to analysing social systems in terms of an ideological superstructure (functioning at the level of ideas, values or symbolic order) and the material basis for the means of economic production. The differences between the realist framework as I want to develop it and the Marxist approach is in that Marxism is essentially a totalizing approach. That is to say, it proclaims a single 'right' explanation with all others being the result of 'false consciousness'. The realist framework as I employ it is essentially agnostic as to the 'truth' of a given ideological framework, or symbolic structure. Indeed, it does not seek to globalize a particular view of the world, rather to provide the means to explore and act at local levels in relationship to other local frameworks and globalizing structures. At this stage, this simple schema provides a means of beginning to conceive of the project within an organizing framework that 'covers' a given 'case'.

Seeking the case

What do I mean by 'case'? I am using the term very generally, indeed as loosely as I can get away with. The 'case' is a useful term only as a framing device for qualitative research. In my view, case studies are misunderstood if they are seen as self-contained spheres. They are also misunderstood if they are drawn into the discourse of statistical theory which demands that samples are categorized into homogeneous groups. Equally, social action and institutional structures and processes are distorted and misunderstood if they are subjected to crude techniques of abstraction for purposes of statistical analysis, or, indeed, the relentless abstraction involved in some versions of grounded theory (cf. Strauss and Corbin 1998). As pointed out by Ragin (1992: 217), the term 'case' is used in a multiplicity of unhelpful ways, expressing 'data categories, theoretical categories, historically specific categories, substantive categories, and so on'. Rather than using the term case, he advocates the term 'casing' to 'bring operational closure to some problematic relationship between ideas and evidence, between theory and data' (Ragin 1992: 218). Operational closure, of course, has the effect of tidying up a complex field of interactions in such a way that the complex becomes manipulable under a given heading. In my view, a case study cannot be some synthetic unity of all the diverse elements to be found within it, if it tidies and thus distorts the realities of the subjects under study.

Typically, the boundaries of a case are imposed in some artificial way – for example, drawing an imaginary circumference around a school, a town, a clinical area, an individual student or any other focus of research whether a person, place, or object. This is a procedure copied, consciously or unconsciously, from statistical practice and transposed into an area of study which is alien to the procedure. It is impossible to so purify 'towns' or seal them from 'contaminating influences' that they can be like the purified samples of chemicals or other substances required for the 'cases' of laboratory experiments. Yet, social statisticians still try to abstract the case 'variables' for comparison and control in the way that Schutz (1976) and Cohen (1944) among others (e.g. Stenhouse 1975, Simons 1981) have pointed out. The case is a convenient way of labelling a complex, a conglomeration, but dealing with a complex is not the same as dealing with a singularity. With a singularity, boundaries are clear and distinct; with complexes they are 'fuzzy' (Kosko 1993; and see Chapter 4), confused, permeable at best.

Mistaking case studies for singularities, or single instances, has often led to the criticism that cases do not provide a basis for generalization and that they are too 'subjective'. In response, many qualitative researchers have advocated multi-site case studies, that is, using several sites in order to compare and contrast the different sites. The methodological naïveté in this is in mistaking a case for an item in a sample, that is, a single instance drawn from some large population of identical (or at least 'similar') such instances. Proclaiming a 'science of the singular' (Simons 1981) implies rightly or wrongly that the case is a 'singular' entity just as a pebble on the beach is a single instance. In my view, a case emerges only in the interaction of the symbolic, the practical and the material and thus the laws of its construction are in the recognition of relationships, dimensions, facts, continuities and discontinuities. A case throws a spotlight giving the illusion that the area picked out is 'singular'. Rather, the case, as a label of convenience for a complex, is a multilayered symbolic network that need not display any internal unity or consistency. Labelling it acts to produce the illusion of unity, typicality and order within everyday affairs. To study a complex is to study the possibilities for structuring, the possibilities for interaction, for social meanings, for restructuring. Where labelling is necessary to generate modernist frameworks of analytic categories (see Chapter 4) that seek to cover the whole, the totality, for postmodernist approaches labels are a focus for deconstruction and acts of labelling create seductive surfaces that work only for local purposes and are constructed in specific historical circumstances (cf. Lyotard 1984; Baudrillard 1990; and Chapter 5).

If the case is produced from the repertoire of codes through which individuals make sense of their lives, by which interactions are managed, and conflicts, social breakdowns and wars are understood and 'sides' taken, then for a researcher to produce a case study is to claim no less than to understand how the world works as a complex rather than as a singularity. Bhaskar (1993), for example, employs the term 'whole' or 'totality' only to refer to the complex 'something' that is the focus of our studies. It carries no sense of unity. If this is so, the question of whether a case study is capable of generalization is therefore to misunderstand the purpose of, and the nature of, a case study. Case studies make no sense at all unless the *processes through which generalization becomes possible in the social world* are the focus of study. The social itself is constructed through the ways in which people *make* generalization a social fact that then has material as well as social consequences. This theme will be taken up again in Chapters 3 and 7 in relation to triangulation and typification as processes of generalization. The case only appears after a series of explorations of the ways in which such generalizations are made by the actors involved; it does not precede those explorations. The project at the same time begins to take shape, to find its orientations through a series of such explorations and in so doing produces the case as the outcome of the project work.

The project gaze

The project, as it forms mentally, is always close to hand, distant and within my grasp yet out of control: in short, paradoxical. Getting one's bearings in this paradox assumes a very pragmatic stance as soon as one is confronted with having to say something to someone about the research. 'So what is your project about?' is often a frightening question. Making the first set of 'good enough' statements is then a welcome relief. A pragmatic beginning, while tactically useful for getting past the first moments of embarrassment when explaining the project, can also be self-deluding. The project being described below has a deeper existential quality that does not simply seek to remain with the superficial categories of social or even scientific taken-for-grantedness:

> I am not a 'living creature' nor even a 'man', nor again even 'a consciousness' endowed with all the characteristics which zoology, a social anatomy or inductive psychology recognise in these various products of the natural or historical process – I am the absolute source, my existence does not stem from my antecedents, from my physical and social environment; instead it moves out towards them and sustains them, for I alone bring into being for myself (and therefore into being in the only sense that the word can have for me) the tradition which I elect to carry on, or the horizon whose distance from me would be abolished – since that distance is not one of its properties – if I were not there to scan it with my gaze.
>
> (Merleau-Ponti 1962: viii–ix)

The existential quality of the 'horizon' of my experience meets its other in dialogue. My world comes into being through a process of self-election, that is, I elect (consciously or unconsciously) rather than select. It implies a political, ethical, symbolic framework, enveloping self in relation to others as the world about takes shape through the engagements and multiplicities of judgements, decisions and actions undertaken. How this self-election takes place is complex, problematic and may not be entirely understood by the individual. It is a self-election emerging through dialogue, resistances, repressions, coercions, conflicts, negotiations, compromises, seductions . . .

It is this world of multiple self-elected worlds that the qualitative research project studies or engages with when it is a programme of applied research. Consequently, when I enter the world of those I have chosen to study it is my gaze in dialogue with theirs that begins to shape the project in conjunction with the literature that I read for inspiration and guidance. How do I enter? To get my bearings in unfamiliar surroundings with strangers can be facilitated if there is a guide, someone who will introduce me to this new scene. Hanging around, becoming a familiar sight to those around may bring the occasion for 'chit chat', for chance encounters that open doors.

To prepare for entry, I need to identify the dramatis personae that compose this world:

> If we can get to know these people intimately and understand the relations between little guy and little guy, big shot and little guy, big shot and big shot, then we know how Cornerville society is organised. On the basis of that knowledge it becomes possible to explain people's loyalties and the significance of political and racket activities.
>
> (Foote Whyte 1943: xx)

So, to engage with street corner society an informant, a gatekeeper has to be found who can pave the way for meeting others without arousing suspicion and hostility. The task is to construct or learn the rhetorics of entrance which consists of passing the tacit tests of entry, not disturbing the polite passage of relationships through which everyday life is constructed.

My field notebooks are typically filled with a 'stream of consciousness' kind of writing where I struggle to gain some bearings upon an impending visit to carry out observations and interviews. Like Vonnegut's telepathic aliens (see Introduction), the task is to render the mass of impressions, feelings, ideas into a linguistic or other symbolic framework (e.g. drawings) in order to generate a sense of what the project could become:

> Late evening and thoughts turn, as thoughts tend to do, towards what may happen on fieldwork tomorrow. Little scenarios based on memories that occasionally go back years as I imagine first encounters. Some image of a senior person appears as I begin a dialogue about 'what is this research about?' 'What do you intend to do?' 'Who will be involved?' 'How much of my staff's time will it take up?' The kinds of questions that shortly before I came to Canada, some Principals and Directors of Nursing asked us as we negotiated access. Then there's the one who wants to know about research methodology 'But if you don't do a survey/quantify how will you know it's objective?'
>
> I know most of that I'll take as it comes, if it comes. Perhaps Ivor has already been through it all with them. Perhaps, they're research weary already. But that's how it begins: little 'simulations' or snatches of possible dialogue flit through the mind. So then I know I'm getting ready, the research attitude/persona/identity is framing up, getting ready to make an entrance and 'do the business'.
>
> (Diary 8 October 1991)

I found this as I looked through my notes of a small project I carried out during a study leave in Canada. As I reread them, I realized that these little scenarios are commonly played out in my mind, not always written down, before I enter the field. My questions and imagery is built up from past experiences of doing research. But how different is all this from the first-time researcher who does not have such experience to draw upon? A matter of degree, I think. Indeed, without all that clutter there is perhaps a freshness, a daringness that the experienced researcher might dismiss and thus miss a great adventure. What the first timer might experience is the fear of failure, of not 'doing it right'. However, in my view a project is built upon failures. Failures are to be sought out like gold. Through failures one is 'taught' by the experts, that is, the members of the world under study, what is 'right'. Failure shows what is at stake for the members of a given community as they seek to school, to show you the errors of your ways and punish you 'in your best interests'. This may be difficult for a student or a first-time researcher to accept – fear of failure is what gives the schooling system its power, all the way to doctoral level. However, apparent failures can be handled as a contribution to 'knowledge', to 'understanding'. Through failure the gaze of the researcher is subjected to the return look of those being researched, and judged. Indeed, the ethnomethodological approach of Garfinkel (1967) was to cause trouble in order to create the circumstances for members of a given group to make manifest the hidden, tacit or unspoken rules of social behaviour. As soon as the familiar ways of behaving are broken, the familar becomes manifest as people cry out 'You should not have done that because . . .', because perhaps it is not polite, or breaks a religious taboo, or makes you and others look stupid. Each such 'error' reveals something about the taken-for-granted rules of 'politeness', 'religious behaviour' or 'stupidity' and so on. Knowing about such approaches as Garfinkel's and the experiences and theories of past research is an important way of sensitizing oneself to what is at stake in doing research. There is no substitute for reading 'the literature'.

The gaze of the literature

Exploration of the literature of debate to generate a descriptive basis for analysis is essential. But how much? Reading everything is rarely a good use of time. In most areas of study a lifetime would be insufficient to scratch the surface. What is required is some strategic purpose to sift out the irrelevant and allow the review of literature to grow according to the developing needs of the project. Referring back to the problem structure – ideas, enactment, realization – described above, a literature review will focus on the ideas or conceptual frameworks that inform practice and the formation and allocation of resources and may be divided as follows:

1 Broad focus.
2 Philosophical underpinnings relating to discipline-based perspective (e.g. sociology, psychology etc.).
3 Discipline-based debates and issues affecting the study (e.g. theories of 'self', 'agency', 'action', 'social change', 'policy implementation' etc.).
4 Methodological literature (e.g. theories of knowledge, validity, objectivity, approaches to analysis, critique, project frameworks such as case study, evaluation, action research, ethnography etc.).
5 Ethical issues relating to conduct of research.
6 Political issues relating to conduct of research.
7 Social and cultural issues relating to conduct of research.
8 Specific focus.
9 Content area (e.g. youth culture, teaching mathematical concepts to 13-year-old boys, etc.).
10 Ethical issues relating to the life circumstances of those being researched.
11 Political issues relating to the life circumstances of those being researched.
12 Social and cultural issues relating to the life circumstances of those being researched.

Although crude, this framework provides an outline plan to develop the literature resource necessary for ideas development and the later 'writing up' of the research whether as thesis, book or paper.

Let us take the broad focus strategy first. The more the researcher has a grip of the key foundational debates the more trenchant are the criticisms and arguments that can be deployed. Typically, this level of debate sets the writer apart from those who only have a superficial grasp. The strategy, however, is not to attempt to read everything. Rather, read deeply, let it be focused around your central interests, and be guided by the critiques that can be levelled against your chosen approach. No one can follow the path of another. The task is to find one's own questions, see how other writers have tried to answer these and then formulate one's own responses. My questions seem always to be of the kind:

1 Is there a 'self'? If so, how can it be described?
2 Why is there injustice and how can it be eradicated?
3 What do others think and why?
4 Why do people do what they do?

I've pursued these questions in education, sociology, philosophy, politics and ethics. When I look at a classroom I want to know what the circumstances of the classroom and what is being 'taught' are doing to the sense of self, the experience, the quality of life of the individuals involved, and what effects it has on their own life plans and actions. I ask whether it is ethical and what alternative political arrangements might be considered. How can I find out? What approaches to methodology will help me and why? What steps may I take to assure myself and others that I have a good argument to make, that the data that I collect is convincing, or plausible or trustworthy? Do I need to focus on processes and thus be close to the subjects of my study? What have ethnographers who have done similar kinds of study done in order to develop their research?

The strategy for the specific focus begins to refine these broad questions. If I interview, or observe, or collect documentation, in what ways can it be said to represent the field of study? This brings me more closely towards the books on doing research. What do they say about how to do interviews and so on? The review of the literature then can be targeted to advance one's thinking in terms of particular issues relating to the chosen methods. What now of the very specific focus of the research, say young people's experiences of being young, growing up and finding a sexual identity? Are there other published research studies on this theme? What did they argue and, in arguing, who did they argue against, and who did they draw on for support for their arguments?

The review of the literature strategy at each level is thus not so much directed towards reading everything there is to read, but towards finding one's own perspective, establishing the key lines of debate in relation to it, and separating out the distinct arguments that can be made and the merits for and against each.

Creating the broad plan

At some point curiosity-driven reading, thinking, observing and interviewing has to be framed into a more specific plan of research. Why? Some reasons have to do with gaining funding, others have more to do with convincing peers or research supervisors that a particular project is worth doing; or to focus one's own mind. Whatever the reason, the plan has a rhetorical purpose: to convince a reader (whether grant-awarding body, supervisor, examiners, other researchers, policy makers or readers in general) that the research being undertaken should be taken seriously as a contribution to 'knowledge', 'theory', or 'policy'. More specifically, the plan defines what is to be done, when and how in terms of: schedules of interviews, observations, data processing interview (transcription, field note writing, document collection) analyses, literature review, project management, reporting and writing up. In addition, there are the necessary resources: e.g. notebooks, computer, tape recorder and so on. Although without this framework in mind when I began my own doctoral research, the key element of 'coverage' became important at every moment in the field. Those interviewed and observed were always concerned that I 'see' *their* point of view and not just those of the powerful, or the most vocal or, indeed, the most 'exotic' (that is, those whose lifestyles were considered to distort the 'reality' experienced by those who thought themselves 'normal').

Getting coverage of a field of study refers to the ever-present anxiety of whether something important has been left out. I recall one of the staff members of a school I was studying saying, 'Even if we disagree with you, at least we all know you've been everywhere and seen everything.' It referred to the way in which I would go to classrooms, be in the playground, the staffroom, the corridors, the head teacher's room, and all the other key 'spaces' of the school. Of course, it was an overstatement. Geertz (1988) has debunked the authority of the anthropologist as author who says, 'Believe me, I was there.' The students would certainly have a different opinion and so would their parents. One cannot be everywhere. One can, however, be in a sufficient number of 'spaces' with a sufficient range of people to justify the claim that a rich grasp of the 'case', the 'context', the 'place', the 'field', had been obtained in order then to make claims about 'validity', 'objectivity' and 'generalization' (issues to be discussed in the following chapters). How then does one construct a plan for coverage in such a way that it is persuasive, plausible, rational, even convincing? And in creating such a plan, how does one avoid it being accused of superficiality, of overlooking the complexity of social interaction and personal experience and decision making?

There is no single way of doing this. Each project has to be tailored to the specific circumstances of the case, its breadth or depth of focus or situation. It will depend, for example, upon such practical questions as:

1 What time period will the project cover? One year, two years . . . ?
2 How far away is the particular site or sites?
3 Can one person do it all? Can a team of a given size do it all?
4 How many people have to be seen and interviewed? How easy will it be to schedule all the visits to the sites?
5 How much money will be needed by me or a given organization to pay for travel, subsistence, secretarial support, telephone calls, paper, postage and so on?

Thus the key practical question is, What can I do with the resources available to me in a given time period? Project design and resource budgeting are, to my mind, intimately entwined. Making sense in resource terms is a useful first step to undertake. It is particularly important on a student grant or loan. There are always ways of reducing costs.

For example, many of my overseas students doing fieldwork in their home country may seek to reduce the cost of fieldwork by arranging interviews, observations to coincide with any visits home to see family and friends. Many part-time home students seek to do fieldwork in their own place of work thus combining work with research. Full-time home-based students may seek to do fieldwork in places near to the university or their home or near friends, thus incurring little or no costs for travel and subsistence by combining visits to family and friends with research. I, for example, during my doctoral studies did my fieldwork as a full-time student on a grant that paid modest travel expenses. I stayed at the house of a friend during visits at no cost. I developed my research strategy by 'playing it by ear'. Since that time I have been involved with many projects and can draw upon previous models to develop research plans. Take, for example, the budget of the following project that did in fact receive funding:

	Year 1 £	Year 2 £	Year 3 £	Totals £
Research staff costs and salaries				
Directors				
Person 1	500	500	2000	
Person 2	3000	3000	1000	10000
Research advisers				
Person 3				free
Person 4				free
The senior team				
Team costs	7000	2000	1000	
Consultancy		8000		18000
Sub-total				**28000**
Research associate				
Salary	19113	20650	11012	
Pension	3546	3830	2043	
National Insurance	1456	1575	845	
Sub-total				**64070**
Administration				
Secretary				
Salary (0.5)	5891	6249	3315	

Pension (0.5)	716	759	403	
National Insurance (0.5)	473	501	265	
				18572
Office costs	750	500	250	1500
Travel and subsistence	5000	5000	2230	12230
Sub-total				**32302**
Overheads				
(on Research associate salary only) 40% of £64070				**25628**
Total				**150000**

This budget had been designed to meet the practical needs of the project. It was a large national project covering about 30 universities and a similar number of other public organizations. It thus needed a team that looked large enough to cover the total number of institutions; senior enough to do this in a fast, efficient and cost-effective manner; and appropriately staffed to cover the range of everyday activities that needed to take place. It needed therefore a group of experienced professional researchers able to go individually to different institutions and talk with equally senior people as well as to act in teams to do fast coverage of a large organization. Hence for a period of four to five days six or seven people could be dispatched to a given organization to interview and observe key people and activities as well as collect key documentation. Over a period of four days such a team would effectively do 20–30 days, equivalent work. As is the case in projects organized in such a manner, a thousand interviews and thousands of hours of observation can be regularly recorded. The whole object of the budget was to demonstrate value for money and where that money would be used to carry out the vital tasks of the project. The senior team could demonstrate that there were enough staff to cover the range of sites necessary to the project. While the senior research team were part-time and could be drafted in for very specific tasks, continuity was handled in two ways. There was the full-time research associate, sufficiently experienced to provide continuity and thus able to form long-term in-depth relationships with organizations and individuals. Second, there were the project directors who would provide the overall grasp and vision for the project.

Look now at the project timetable. It will be seen that the budget mirrors the senior team's involvement. The senior team is used mainly in Phases 1 and 2. Their function is to generate 'coverage' across the organizations. It is in Phase 3 that the in-depth studies occur, guided by the issues generated in the coverage phases.

Research Timetable

Phase 1

Stage 1 (5 months: April 1997 – August 1997)

• Negotiate access • Establish principles of practice • Carry out telephone and questionnaire survey • Study findings of related studies • Senior research team carry out 1-day 'survey' visits in fullest possible range of sites • Senior team identify characteristics of 'successful' assessment practice • Findings checked with (clinical) support team • Sites for Phase 1: Stage 2 selected, taking account of criteria identified through survey, plus criteria of geographical location, level of course, part of the register represented and HEI/practice location history/culture

Stage 2 (9 months: September 1997 – May 1998)

• Senior research team make 3-day intensive ethnography[2] visits to selected HE and partner primary, secondary and community sites (identified in Stage 1) • Observation and interview to identify 'operational definitions' of assessment practice, structures and processes in the full range of clinical environments • Collection of data on resources, staffing, clinical specialisms, support structures, HE culture(s) and clinical practice culture(s) • Identification of other variables • Writing of Interim Report (March/April 1998) • Steering group meets (January 1998)

Phase 2

Stage 1 (8 months: June 1998 – February 1999)

• Core research team carry out further intensive fieldwork to study sites selected in Phase 1: Stage 2, focusing on the one hand through branches, specialisms and levels and on the other through 'issues' • SRA, midwife consultant and co-directors explore issues of validity and reliability • Issues discussed with senior research team and support team • Case studies constructed • Ex-students visited in their places of work (August–October 1998) • Steering group meets (November 1998)

Stage 2 (2 months: March 1999 – April 1999)

• Further detailed analysis of data to flesh out case studies

Phase 3

Stage (4 months: May 1999 – August 1999)

Findings from the in-depth case studies checked with the fullest possible range of institutions, courses and practice areas through regional feedback meetings • Separate case studies written up in booklet form for presentation to and discussion with (a) other healthcare professional groups and (b) senior professionals in non-healthcare professions (education, social work, and police) after the evaluation is finished • Steering group meets (June 1999) • Further cohort of ex-students visited in their place of work (July-August 1999)

Final phase

Stage (2 months: September 1999 – October 1999)

Final report written and delivered.

The broad strategy is that of 'progressive focusing': from wide lens to close-up (Glaser and Strauss 1967) or more exactly 'progressive–regressive' focusing, that is a series of movements from wide lens to close-up to wide lens (Sartre 1964). Thus, at the end of the process moving from broad focus to in-depth studies, there is a rechecking that the understandings developed through the in-depth phase have relevance across the full range of institutions. This form of generalization by relevance is typically of a logical rather than a statistical form. It may involve an analysis of structural relationships, boundaries, processes, variations in cultural practices. These issues will be developed in Chapters 3 and 4. For the moment I want to concentrate on the general shape of the plan, without delving into details of implementation.

This was a complex project. Often, when constructing a plan for a thesis, the student's first thoughts will rival the complexity of a project that would tax the energy and resources of a large and experienced team. The task is to scale it to be appropriate to the resources available. Even if there is no funded budget, there still need to be resources that must be marshalled to carry out the project:

1 Time available – where should limited time be focused?
2 Collaborators – is anyone willing to help? Fellow students/colleagues/ friends.

3 Tools – computer, software, tape recorder.
4 Travel expenses.

If no one else, one must convince oneself that the fieldwork stage of the project is actually viable. As part of the process of being convinced it is important to work out how each phase of the project can be accomplished and at what personal cost if no external funding is available.

The research timetable described above followed a considerable discussion in the full proposal relating to the key issues that the funders wanted to be the focus of the research. Research students may not be in such a position. More likely they will have to generate their own focus and try to convince either a funder or a supervisor that it is worth doing. Nevertheless, the research student wanting to do empirical work will need to consider most if not all of the following:

Project Stage 1 (How much time? Resources needed?)

1 Background – strategic thinking
  (1) Read literature
      (a) Substantive: the relevant discipline(s), the content focus
      (b) Methodological: discussions of issues relating to producing
          knowledge: validity, truth, generalization, objectivity and so on
2 Generate potential aims, objectives, purposes or agendas to guide study

Project Stage 2 (How much time? Resources needed?)

1 Phase 1: Fieldwork set up time and tasks (How much time? Resources needed?)
  (a) Who needs to be contacted and persuaded to participate? Who are the key gatekeepers? Does it involve 'hanging around' in order to meet 'accidentally'?
  (b) How easy are they to reach? Will it be formal or informal? Can it be done by phone, letter, e-mail, or does it have to be face-to-face?
  (c) What information do participants need? Brief note? Full rationale? Will they want to know what benefits and costs will be involved for them personally and for their organization? This is the 'what's in it for them?' question. Or does it have to be done covertly? If so, what is the cover story?
  (d) Ethics
      (i) Are there ethical committees to convince? When do they meet? What are their demands?
      (ii) What are your own values, beliefs, ethical issues?
      (iii) How overt should the research be?
2 Phase 2: Organize first round of fieldwork for coverage of issues (How much time? Resources needed?)
  (a) Observation schedules: places, people, times
  (b) Documentation collection – range, from where, who?

(c) Interview schedules (these may be 'formal', 'informal', 'up front' or 'covert'): who, where, how long?
3 Phase 3: Analyse first-round data (How much time? Resources needed?)
   (a) Key issues
   (b) Emergent theory
   (c) How does it relate to literature?
   (d) What's missing?
   (e) What needs to be found out next?
   (f) Reformulate potential aims, purposes of project, define new directions or refine the original ones
   (g) Select:
      (i) Comparison groups – do the emergent theories and issues generalize to other similar groups in other similar/contrasting areas?
      (ii) Contrast groups – do the emergent theories and issues generalize to other contrasting groups in other similar/contrasting areas?

Project Stage 3 (How much time? Resources needed?)

1 Phase 1: Focus in-depth
   (a) Renegotiate access and agreements on ethics
   (b) Organize fieldwork schedules
2 Phase 2: Analyse in-depth studies, formulate theories, models, representations
3 Phase 3: Check for generalizability or coverage
4 Reformulate overall 'project'

Project Stage 4: Write up (How much time? Resources needed?)

All of this, of course, may seem too neat, too closed, too suffocating. It looks like a recipe. No one recipe is good for all. Nevertheless, it can be used, in small doses, as a reference point in order to maintain bearings in increasingly complex and confused territories. It will have to be revised according to changing circumstances, an issue that will be taken up in the next chapter. Of more importance than keeping to the plan is keeping an account of one's journey, reflecting critically on the experience and finding a way to represent it in the final process of 'writing up'. This is where the pragmatics give way to the lonely yet exhilarating reflections on 'life', 'purpose', 'meaning', 'self' and 'otherness'. The following chapters will explore aspects of this journey.

2

Subjects: choices and consequences

Subjects can be thought about in many ways, whether as subjects of study like mathematics or geography, or as subjects of a king, god or other ruler, or, indeed, as the subject as 'Self', the sovereign centre of the individual as agent, as initiator of action. In each case, subjects are not obviously given but lured into the light, perhaps like moths to die under the glare of too much clarity. In the intimate distance between subjectivity and language there is a continual tension between the conception of a subject as somehow prior to language and the subject as being a product of language. Endlessly becoming a subject with and against language is a lifetime's project. Who am I? is the cliché question most associated with adolescent angst. However, cliché or not, identity is framed and reframed at every uttering of self into existence. Perhaps philosophy is perpetual adolescence frantically asking:

- What do I need?
- What do I care about?
- Why do I care?
- What can I believe in?
- What can I know without doubt?
- How did it all begin?
- How do I deal with others?

In such questions the 'I' chooses its project as a quest for meaning, knowledge and existence in a world of others and Otherness. Each project generates its own basis for producing claims to 'knowledge' of the world as a body as 'subjects' that can be known, studied, utilized to manipulate the material and cultural worlds of people.

Subject and project

Pursuing a project, the subject as 'I' distances itself from the world-as-subject to be 'known about', 'desired', 'manipulated'. Through its projects does the 'I' map or create its world? Mapping suggests a reality 'out there' that can be described faithfully. It suggests also the need for consciousness to be a passive receiver adding nothing and taking away nothing from the sensory flow. Engaging creatively with the world, the self initiates personal, social and cultural projects, shaping the world. Passive mapping and active projection dynamically interact in the production of social worlds. To explore the concept of 'project', several images come to mind. The first is when a light is projected in a darkened room and certain objects light up as others are cast into shadow. Another is when a film is projected onto a screen and the world outside fades away as people are caught up in the film story. A third, rather like the second but for a different purpose, is where a speaker uses a slide or data projector to guide the audience through a talk intended to describe, inform or persuade. Each case illustrates structural comparisons and contrasts. First, there is a subjective splitting between what is picked out and what fades into obscurity. Where the torchlight is shone in a darkened room, the light reveals the 'truth' or 'reality' of what is there, but where the film or slide is projected the white of the screen is rendered absent by the images projected onto it. The light and the surface then are the material vehicles carrying, yet effaced by, the images projected. The 'truth' or 'reality' of the images take the place of the 'reality' of the flat screen. The audience is drawn into the fantasy rendition of the film or the subject matter of the slide presentation. The audience 'sees' what is not actually present except in its virtual representation. The capturing of attention by the screen images provides a way of thinking about conscious reality as a flow of images composing realities 'out there' for the individual. This flow composes the 'imaginary order' of subjective experience.

The interaction between the imaginary, the material realities which convey it and the ways of thinking about and experiencing these realities produces a world of experience for the individual to reflect on, critique or take for granted. The individual's stance towards the 'realities' of personal and social life defines the choices available, together with the consequences of adopting one rather than another.

> *Tony*: I reckon if I didn't go into trouble an' I was still at 'ome I'd be a right ponce, right. No tattoos, nothin'. That's like when I first had my tattoos done . . .'cos everyone else had 'em done. They say, 'go on an' 'ave them done. You'll be one of the boys then.
>
> (Schostak 1986: 86)

Tony was 16, violent and into drugs and theft. He believed that if he had not been sent to a residential detention centre, he could have taken an entirely different course, ending up as a 'right ponce' (that is, 'normal'). As one 'reality' closed, the other opened.

Such realities, however, are not Reality. Employing a Kantian distinction, the phenomena that appear to consciousness do not reveal the essential nature of the thing itself, only its impact on consciousness. There is a play between presence and absence. In the appearance the surface is present, but the 'in-itself' is absent. Tony was conscious of presenting a surface. It was scarred, hard. Inside he knew different and only gave glimpses of what it might be. Whatever Reality is, appearances are deceptive.

Codes and categories organize our interpretations of conscious experiences. Crudely, a word acts like a spotlight; it picks out an object – say a cup – from a crowd of sensory stimuli. Language therefore acts to make the object 'present' and enables us to order the perceptual confusion. In fact, a conversation can take place about cups without any physical cup being present. Language is thus a way of talking about the absence of things as well as talking about things when they are absent. This play of absence and presence is brought about by rules and categories that predate and transcend any currently living individual. The order of language is in this sense imposed upon the in-itself Reality of the individual. As such, language, while it may be experienced as intimate and natural, is also radically Other. It carries an authority that subjects the individual, evoking within the individual feelings, thoughts, ideas, images, thus making present the absent. In this way realities are created in the minds of people, glued together, as it were, by language.

In structuring subjectivity and transcending the individual, language is the matrix, the map, enabling individuals and groups to explore each other's worlds. However, meaning is never entirely public and words are never entirely unambiguous. The word is laden with multiple meanings, some public and beyond my control, some private and still beyond my control, at least in part. The public meanings are discoverable in a dictionary. The private are eccentric, discoverable only by asking, or by psychoanalysis. A private meaning may arise as a given word is associated with key events in one's life. Some of these meanings may be fondly remembered, others forgotten, lying dormant only to be triggered by another event. This splits subjectivity in many ways: at a private and public level, at a conscious (the imaginary) and unconscious (the Dream, the Other) level, and at a Real (in itself, unknowable, unnameable) and 'real' (knowable and nameable for others) level.

The project, like the torch light, or indeed the beam of the film or slide projector, is directed towards something on behalf of someone, the subject or self. In phenomenology this 'directedness' is called intentionality.

In everyday speech intentionality means more than just a particular direction or orientation. It is permeated by 'wilfulness', 'wanting', 'purpose', 'desire'. In each sense the project has an intentional structure: it is a project of a *subject*, directed towards *something* to produce some effect or event according to will, desire, whim. At its most general, an individual's desire to develop a career, to live happily, or to live as a good person helping others is a project just as much as is the more narrowly defined research project of the doctoral thesis or funded research. The project, then, of the researcher is no different from any individual's day-to-day projects. If there is a difference, it is in the attitude framing its undertaking. For phenomenologists, this difference in attitude is crucial to understanding social worlds.

Phenomenology, subject and others

Following in the steps of Descartes, phenomenology (MacDonald 2000) employs a special attitude where belief either for or against the reality, the truth, the rightness of anything said to constitute a 'world' is suspended (Schutz and Luckmann 1973; Schutz 1976). This 'bracketing' as it is often called produced two distinct attitudes to the world: first, a philosophical attitude where nothing could be taken for granted, all was reduced to being mere phenomena; and second, as a kind of reflection of the first, the world of everyday life where all is underpinned by an attitude of taken-for-grantedness until some problem interrupts the tranquil acceptance of the world as it is. A project by problematizing or questioning the world is like a stone thrown into a pond, interrupting the tranquillity, creating ripples that manifest patterns of action and reaction and distinguish the usual from the unusual, thus demonstrating what is essential to the normal range of behaviours of the pond waters and what is not. Bracketing interrupts the taken-for-granted flow, revealing what is or is not essential to consciousness and its objects. It provides a way of mapping the subject, the act of consciousness and the object that appears to consciousness. One criticism is that it privileges the subject – the 'I' that thinks, that brackets, that is the ego-pole of consciousness – rather than unconscious processes. Another is that it abstracts life from its existential dimension.

Existentially, the 'I' as Ortega y Gasset (1957: 46) described it is characterized by mortality and by the fact that no one can actually stand in another's shoes. This is a distance that neither empathy nor sympathy can close. From psychoanalysis, phenomenology is criticized for its emphasis upon rationality and the conscious. In Lacan's (1977a) view the life of the individual is accompanied by an irremediable sense of loss, the loss of being whole (continuous with reality, Freud's oceanic sense of oneness with the universe, or the Mother). The viewpoint of an individual cut from such oneness is utterly unique, radically other to the experiences of others. In this case, what is the relation between subjects in the world? How does or should the subject deal with others? How do people who are radically incomparable to each other enter into social relations? For example, Coathup (1997) was a part-time doctoral student who, as a teacher, wanted to create the conditions for children aged 6 to 7 to be mutually responsible and caring rather than being coercive, manipulative and selfish. She illustrated her concerns with the transcript of four girls who were often in conflict, usually about clothes:

Natasha: My mum is going to get me a skirt.
Kathy: So is my mum.
Christine: I got a new skirt last week.
Tina: I don't want a skirt. I'm getting some waffle tongs to do my hair.
Natasha: I've got those.
Tina: You only said that because I've got them.
Natasha: I have.
Tina: Kathy, you come to mine and I'll do your hair.
Kathy: My mum said I can't do my hair.
Tina: Tell you're mum you're not doing it.
Natasha: Her mum'll see.
Tina: I wasn't talking to you *(Tina again looks at Kathy)* Tell your mum you are coming round. I'll tell my mum to phone her up.
Kathy: My mum won't let me.
Tina: I'll tell my mum.
Natasha: Can I come?
Tina: No . . . my mum doesn't like you and my mum has told the teachers about you and they know what you are like and you'll be in for it.

(Coathup 1997: 203)

Coathup's project of trying to create the conditions in which children could learn to trust, help each other by 'talking out their problems' and grow with each other creatively and happily seemed to have failed. She no longer knew what to do and this depressed her. As indicated in the previous chapter, project plans are subject to change, entailing a sense of 'failure' which can either depress and lead to giving up, or can be transformed into a turning point, taking the project and personal understanding in new directions. This transformation occurred for Coathup when she realized that 'not knowing' was not a problem but a phase in data collection:

If I was to truly understand the children, to begin to truly understand other human beings, then I needed to understand that, I had to be able to be comfortable within a state of 'not knowing' and that knowing more would come if I had the patience to trust in my own organism and my abilities to listen, observe and be openly receptive to children. It was not useful to interpret their 'manipulations' of talking out or their need to make talking out their own, construct it in a way that made sense to them, as some kind of personal attack upon me by the children.

(Coathup 1997: 208)

Coathup's project was like the stone in the pond; it caused a few ripples but soon went back to its former state. At first this seemed depressing until she realized there were no quick solutions, there was only further careful listening, observation, the provision of feedback on what was happening and a kind of letting go in order to allow people to learn in their own interactions with others, like the researcher learning in interaction with the field of observation and interaction. Coathup was exploring both the ethical and educational basis of social interaction. In such interactions, self and other are face to face. What are the methodological implications of this face-to-faceness?

1 People are not things or objects to be manipulated indifferently.
2 The values, beliefs and 'knowings', intentions, imagination, feelings, judgements and so on of others have to be taken into account.
3 A given intended situation has to be set into relation with a range of possible interpretations that others may have of it.
4 The tactics and strategies of others have to be taken into account.
5 No individual is identical to another.

The list is not exhaustive, nor is it meant to be. It is suggestive of ways of thinking about face-to-faceness as a focus for methodological reflection. The fruitfulness of the approach for breaking through the sterile ideal types, faceless roles, and categorizations of approaches that ignore the existential dimensions of living can be seen for example in the various works of Levinas who founded his ethics on a phenomenology of face (1979, 1998), or in feminist works such as Haug and colleagues (1987, 1992) who took a group approach to deconstructing taken-for-granted categories of femininity. However, it is with Levinas that the methodological significance of face emerges. Face signifies the vulnerable sense of depth, unfathomableness, that is the existential 'I' behind the eyes rather than the social surface of the face, composed of its named features of eyes, nose, mouth and so on. Face, then, is not the anatomical construction with names for every part seen in an anatomical diagram. It is again the difference between the 'initself' that essentially cannot be known, cannot be named as such, and the phenomena that appear to consciousness as a surface that can be mapped and named. The mapping and the naming is productive of 'subjects', of 'disciplines' that can be known and hence taught as a part of school or university courses.

There are two kinds of subjectivity here: the subjectivity of the known, named, shared and thus drawn into intersubjective domains; and the subjectivity which cannot as such be shared, that is unnameable, essentially unknowable, yet intimately 'mine', vulnerable. One can recognize in others this dimension, but one cannot know it. Schooling could be said to cover over this essential vulnerability and aloneness through its emphasis on knowing, forming identities, shaping behaviour, beliefs and values. Methodologies founded on this kind of schooling have the effect of contributing to the covering up of that which cannot be known. I reserve the term education for those methodologies that challenge the effects of schooling. Where schooling reinforces the strength and power of a framework or discipline of study and applied research, education exposes its fragility, its temporality, its limitations, and prepares the ground for change, for the generation of difference. The radical task of education (the drawing out of experiences, sensitivities, caring, love, creativity and so on) is to draw subjectivity beyond its aloneness and into the realm of others who like me are unique, alone and desire. Education, as a project, is not about training, nor about transmitting some prior code of belief and sensibility. It is found, in my view, where the 'possible emerges within the grasp of the imagination, to be consciously or unconsciously varied, played with' (Schostak 1989: 211). In the play between the possible and the material, self confronts the other face-to-face in its radical difference. For example, in playing a game of chess, as many moves as possible are imagined, both one's own and one's opponent's. However, depending on the moves already made, only a few next moves will be judged realizable, and of these one will try to choose the one that will give the best material advantage in terms of winning the game.

Like the rules, board layout and pieces in a chess game, social organization creates the conditions for categorization in order to coordinate actions, beliefs and values. Similar to Cooley's metaphor of the orchestra, each individual plays his or her part to create a sense of the 'whole', the 'game'. In this 'whole', one pupil is the 'same' as another because they are placed into the same social category for all practical purposes. Through language the individual is drawn into intersubjective domains where others define the gender, the status, the role, the culture of the individual and render him or her as 'subject' to laws, expectations, duties. The individual is drawn into a game of 'same' and 'difference': you are like this, not that; these others are like me, but *they* are not; this is the way 'we' do things, 'they' do it differently. It is as if there is a social intrigue, a scheming by which individuals come to recognize themselves as being like others and thus in a given social category having particular social relations with other categories. In this sense the existential uniqueness, the initselfness, is replaced by a social category to enable meeting to take place between individuals who say they 'know' who the other is: face is replaced by mask. It can be said, then, that an individual social existence as mask, as role, is the project of the Other. If this is so, then subjective experience is a product of the desires of others in an inter-subjective domain ruled by the trans-subjective categories of the Other. Here the Other can be regarded as the categories, the grammars, the lexicons, the norms of language, culture and social organization. In this trans-subjective framework the subject finds his or her position as pupil, child, boy, girl, good, bad, loved, hated.

There is at this point a methodological choice to be made. First one can regard subjective existence to be fully determined by the Other and so study social behaviour and forms of organization in terms of observable facts (Durkheim 1964), observable behaviours (e.g. Skinner 1953), as empirical structures that can be logically analysed (e.g. Parsons 1949; Lévi-Strauss 1969; Marx 1970; Piaget 1970). Second, one can seek strategies to engage the private dimensions of subjectivity with the public frameworks for communication and so try to understand the meanings accorded by social actors to their behaviours (e.g. Mead 1934; Weber 1949; Schutz 1976) whether these are conscious or unconscious (Freud 1933). Furthermore, one may attempt to explore the relationships between intersubjective demands and subjective experiences and desires in terms of strategic interaction where one individual tries to fool, gain advantage over, or conquer another (Scott and Lyman 1968; Goffman 1970). Here the strategies of self in relation to other resemble those advocated by Machiavelli ([c.1515] 1976), or take on a game-like structure. Or again, other approaches can be adopted where, for example, education, as a form of applied research, subverts the public mask to reveal the private, vulnerable face and draw self into ethical relations with others to allocate resources for creative possibilities. There are therefore many ways of framing the relationship between the subject, the intersubjective and the trans-subjective. Each has implications for the methodological approaches adopted whether focusing attention on macro systems or micro-level interactions; or focusing only on overt measurable behaviour and 'objective facts'; or exploring by asking informants about possible understandings, meanings, motives, in terms of the existential uniqueness of the individual in relation to the social; or describing social life in terms of struggle, competition and the games of strategy, deception and seduction that people adopt.

In the relationship between the subjective, the intersubjective and the trans-subjective there are then two kinds of intentional structuring framing a project: those that point to the ground of an individual's unique viewpoint, a Truth that is unspeakable since others have no point of reference by which to hear it (see Chapter 6); and others that point (or fan out from this existential ground) to other viewpoints that are either mediated by or placed into dialogue through language as Other. Both mediation and dialogue are also existential choices. Being mediated means falling passively into the nets of language and there being reduced to categories that take the place of the individual; to enter dialogue is to engage with otherness on the ground of difference, refusing to be finally placed in any category. Thus, in the field of subjectivity, there are choices that self and other must make and that can only be made either through contest (either to the death in the Hegelian sense, or total submission to the Master by becoming a slave) or in dialogue.

Coathup, in her thesis, struggled with the manipulative designs of both staff and pupils (herself included) in order to formulate an alternative approach to living together. She wanted to create the conditions to move from the Machiavellianism of people trying to outdo each other to that of trying to help each other. To accomplish this required a close and detailed attention to the patterns of everyday life, the ways people talked to each other in order to get what they want, resolve their problems, and have fun. As they persevered with 'talking out', that is, revealing their hurts, their wants, their ideas, their feelings, it started to become a part of their day-to-day classroom experience. Her narratives and dialogues illustrated key developments:

> Jo and Joshua, who are both 6 years old, are discussing a painting/ collage they are working on. There is a major disagreement about the choice of materials. I sent them on the carpet to talk out after a tussle over some tissue paper.
>
> *Jo*: I thought I'd explained to you that I wanted to put tissue on that fish . . . green . . .
> *Joshua*: Well, I don't . . . I said we'll paint it . . .
> *Jo*: Well, I said we'd put tissue on which will be much better . . .
> *Joshua*: Well, when you . . . you put paint on my jumper . . .
> *Jo*: Well, I had to put paint on your hand to stop you doing the tissue . . .
> *Joshua*: It's on my jumper . . .
> *Jo*: Yes, but it meant to go on your hand . . .
> *Joshua*: You are really naughty, you are one of the naughtiest people . . .
> *Jo*: Well, I am . . . but it's harder for me to be good than other people . . .
> *Joshua*: Well, what about my jumper? . . .

Jo: I'll wash it off . . .
Joshua: Well, what about the fish . . .
Jo: Well, we'll paint it and we'll put tissue on half . . .
Joshua: OK.

(Coathup 1997: 240)

By 'talking out', Jo and Joshua could clarify their intentions, reasons
for actions, and judgements, and reach a mutually agreeable solution.
Talking out was the name given to entering into dialogue with each
other, not just telling and expecting obedience. Learning to take into
account the subjectivity of the other proceeds in small, even apparently
trivial ways. This is as true of young children as it is for adults like
Coathup learning to make innovations in her classroom whether as a
teacher or a researcher.

Through dialogue an inner sense of subjectivity that resists solipsism
(that is where the self stands in isolation, bounded only by the self as
author or reference point of all) is constructed. Without falling into the
dialogue of the deaf, Jo and Joshua presented their own 'explanations'
and wants, finally recognized the differences and incorporated them into
a solution. Dialogue acts not as a focus for compromise nor for overcoming the resistance of the other but rather as a dynamic process of interpretation and expression to explore and accept difference. It is through
resistance that the Real emerges in the life of the subject – as resistance
to interpretation, resistance to coverage, resistance to plumbing its depths.
By resistance the subject discovers the multiple 'realities', 'knowledges',
'beliefs' and 'values' of everyday life where people proclaim 'It is your
duty to . . .', or 'Thou shalt not . . .', or 'That's not like you . . .'. Experiencing resistance the subject discovers his or her own 'subjectivity', his
or her own 'identity for others', sense of knowing, personal knowledges
and experiences of self. The methodological implications of these
resistances will be explored later in the chapter as a way of 'mapping
voices' and again in Chapter 3 where during such resistances the 'objectivity', the non-arbitrariness, the 'hardness' of the world and of the
subjective dimension of knowing is discovered. Indeed, resistance and
meaning in life are intimately and fatally related as poignantly illustrated
by Frankl (1963) in his accounts of life in a concentration camp. Those
who lost their faith in the meaning of life lost the power to resist, and
died.

In everyday life, although the choices are not so dramatic, what is still
at stake is the meaning of an individual's life, their sense of autonomy,
their ability to decide and act. It was expressed by Tony (Schostak 1986:
86–7) when he 'chose' to stay as his present identity rather than the one
he could have been, even though he did not expect to live for long
due to his love of street fighting. It was a love that sent him to jail

for attempted manslaughter and led the sentencing judge to liken him to the Hitler youth. He had fatefully storied his life. Focusing on such stories, the researcher analyses how such choices are frozen, creating the appearance of inevitablity, or generates the possibilities for alternative endings (Schostak 1991). Through the acknowledgement of difference, dialogue, contest and repression become strategic choices. Dialogue may involve contest but is not finally reducible to it since to win is to end dialogue and replace it with monologue: the voice of the victor, the voice of certainty and 'Truth' (see Chapter 6). Should research be framed as monologic or dialogic? That is, is there a single or many 'truths'?

Monologic research adopts a standpoint that is both excluded from critique and is the privileged position from which to critique all other positions. For positivistic science Reason becomes that privileged position. Similarly, culturally, socially and professionally privileged positions can be constructed from a given Principle, or set of values or convictions. As an illustration, a medical mentor writes:

> As my leadership role owed little to externally given authority, effective leadership of the mentor project was more likely to be grounded in my own personal, inner authority, the ability to act constructively on an inner belief. Furthermore, working from this position was more likely to be acceptable in a profession ambivalent about leadership and power, for in my perception general practitioners are uncomfortable with the notion of authority, although they have so much of it in their working role, and even less comfortable with the concept of power, so that, for example, in continuing education, more neutral titles like 'facilitator' are preferred to ones which imply authority. Perhaps, like people the world over, the thought of powerful leadership is linked to the shadow side of power, and recalls experiences of being led by those, driven by the pursuit of personal power, determine to maintain total control over members of their working team, operating highly authoritarian structures which either serve to stifle the creative energy of their team, or ensure that anything good which comes from their team is directly attributed to them, and used to advance their own power.
>
> (Freeman 1998: 164)

This 'inner belief' provides a ground of conviction, an immovable point strategically important to the writer. Because of it she can find her bearings in reference to external views on 'leadership', 'authority', 'power'. Then the game plan can be conceived and tactics developed and assessed. Here Freeman looked for tactically useful terms such as 'facilitator' around which a body of knowledge and a focus for expertise can be developed. Thus by understanding the problem structure as it emerges in relation to her own intentions, it can be manipulated at the level of ideas (looking for comfortable terms), the level of enactment (identifying roles, and appropriate structures to shape action), the level of realization (looking at material resources appropriate to bringing the project into effect). The organization of the thesis thus relies upon the acceptance of the key convictions. Undermine the central convictions and the whole edifice upon which the thesis is built crumbles. Take another example:

> After testing had been carried out it was agreed that James should return to his previous school and he would receive (w)hat he needed for extensive difficulties. It was recommended that his educational needs could be met in the following way:-
>
> 1 James would receive 1:1 intensive work in basic litera[c]y skills and classroom support in small groups.
> 2 Spelling should be tackled through a multi-sensory programme in order to circumvent the problems of short-term memory; words should be presented by visual, auditory and symbolic means. Games and computer assisted programmes would be appropriate.
> 3 Reading should be developed through the use of phonics and suitable reading schemes.
> 4 Creative writing could be developed through the use of phonics and suitable reading schemes.
> 5 Creative writing could be tackled through recording a story onto tape and then transcribing this onto paper.
> 6 The integration of reading, writing and spelling tasks should be considered in the areas of themes and topic work which could harness his creative interests.
> 7 Private tuition should continue, as well as parental back-up with the school.
> 8 The remedial services should be involved in the planning and support of these interventions.
>
> Intervention of this nature demands a tremendous amount of time with progress often occurring at a very slow rate.
>
> (Hedges 1996: 25–6)

Here the convictions being explored are those implicit in 'the system': the procedures and 'tools' of the profession. These are the product of a system that at the level of ideas *'knows'* what children need, *'knows'* their values, interests, skills and limitations and, indeed, *'knows'* the influence of their home backgrounds on learning and behaviour. The child in this example has been subjected at the level of practices and material tools to a battery of tests following the procedure of constructing a Statement of Special Educational Needs. The Statement then sets outs formally and legally the course of action. The project, then, is to modify the child's behaviour to fit what the system 'knows' is required 'in their best interests'. Those subscribing to such approaches know where they are going and essentially become technicians servicing the system's demands. For them, there is no place for a dialogue of alternatives. The project either accepts such a monological reality or deconstructs it in order to present the alternatives. Those researchers who accept the monological voice are typically technicist in orientation, seeking to implement policies and the prevailing views more efficiently (e.g. Reynolds 1996). The technicist reduces the individual to being a product, or an element to fit neatly into a system. The educationist facilitates alternatives as the basis for freedom, creativity and democratic relations with others.

The problem is to try to 'loosen' the technicist's grip on what is 'known' (see Chapter 9). Implicit in what is 'known' are major methodological, ethical, political and philosophical issues. In deconstructing through the challenge of dialogue the nature of the project, it may well be that one is also deconstructing the teacher's own personal sense of self, identity and being in the world. None of these are to be tackled lightly. Indeed, a supervisor may well fall also into the position of 'knowing' what is in the best interests of the student and thus what ensues is a contest with either a victor or a draw, rather than a dialogue.

Mapping voices

Dialogic research opens viewpoints to challenge, resistance and critique from each other which in turn may facilitate the appreciation of difference, the potential for cross-fertilization, fusion, transformation and creative production of new viewpoints. It means that unlike the monological strategy, there are no privileged positions, no viewpoint being able to assume a fundamental Principle to impose on others. Dialogic research is like adopting multiple vision, accepting the plurality of possible viewpoints, seeking to engage these viewpoints in dialogue, identifying the resistances each have towards the other. Dialogue then becomes a methodological Principle rather than a substantive Principle. That is to say, it takes no position for or against the truth, reality, rightness or existence of subjective or objective phenomena as being the basic 'substantial facts' of a given world view. Not to do so would be to move from dialogue towards commitment and advocacy of a given perspective, or world. There is no divine or any other supreme mediator of dialogue. Dialogue is an existential position where the subject stands out (*ex-sistere* – to stand out) or stands apart from the background beliefs, knowledge, commitments and so on of a given world view, reaches towards and opens the 'self' out towards 'otherness'. In such a position there can never be closure, finality nor unity. Monologic research on the other hand brings closure and commitment to a single perspective, seeks wholeness, completeness, eternity and finality. The relationship between dialogue, commitment and action will be further explored in Chapter 9. Adopting a dialogic approach in the development of a project means identifying and exploring the range of voices in a given context who have an interest in the intervention that a given applied research project represents in their lives. Initially, this involves the related strategy of going and seeing, being with and learning from the other about their world. William Foote Whyte's (1943) study of street corner society is a famous illustration. The entire focus was upon going and seeing, upon doing field research. As its name suggests this was a study of street life. He described something of his methodology as follows:

> I was on an exploration into unknown territory. Worse than unknown, indeed, because the then existing literature on slum districts was highly misleading. It would have been impossible to map out at the beginning the sort of study I eventually found myself doing.
>
> This is not an argument against initial planning of research. If his study grows out of a body of soundly executed research, then the student can and should plan much more rigorously than I did. But, even so, I suspect that he will miss important data unless he is flexible enough to modify his plans as he goes along. The apparent 'tangent' often turns out to be the main line of future research.
>
> Street Corner Society is about particular people and situations and events. I wanted to write about Cornerville. I found that I could not write about Cornerville in general without discarding most of the data I had upon individuals and groups. It was a long time before I realised that I could explain Cornerville better through telling the stories of those individuals and groups than I could in any other way.
>
> Instead of studying the general characteristics of classes of people, I was looking at Doc, Chick, Tony Cataldo, George Ravello, and others. Instead of getting a cross-sectional picture of the community at a particular point in time, I was dealing with a time sequence of interpersonal events.
>
> Although I could not cover all Cornerville, I was building up the structure and functioning of the community through intensive examination of some of its parts – in action. I was relating the parts together through observing events between groups and between group leaders and the members of the larger institutional structures (of politics and the rackets). I was seeking to build a sociology based upon observed interpersonal events.
>
> (Foote Whyte 1943: 357–8)

Whyte was looking to construct a particular kind of knowledge. In developing the rationale for his approach, he set his strategy in contrast with the alternative sociological approaches of his time:

[through social work statistics etc.] . . . Cornerville people appear as social work clients, as defendants in criminal cases, or as undifferentiated members of 'the masses'. There is one thing wrong with such a picture: no human beings are in it. Those who are concerned with Cornerville seek through a general survey to answer questions that require the most intimate knowledge of local life. The only way to gain such knowledge is to live in Cornerville and participate in the activities of the people.

(Foot Whyte 1943: xv–xvi)

Knowledge is constructed according to the particular attitude adopted and methods employed. Exploring the subjective positions that can be adopted in relation to points of resistance in a dialogue, whether it is a debate defined as 'the literature' or the multiple 'discourses of members' of a given community, is essential to drawing out what is at stake for the subject, the project and the members of that community.

Locating oneself as researcher immediately disturbs a taken-for-granted security of 'knowing who I am in relation to others'. Suddenly, 'I' as well as 'others' are in question:

1 'Who are you?' They ask expecting a reply that grounds 'me' as a researcher who casts a questioning eye around.
2 'What do you want of us?' They look out from, or duck behind, their public masks unsure of the gaze from this 'I' who repeats, 'I just want to observe your practice, don't mind me, I'm harmless, I'm not spying on you, trust me.'
3 'Who do you think we are?' They shift about uneasily, trying to glimpse a reflection of themselves in the way the researcher speaks to them, looks at them, acts towards them.
4 'What do you know about us that you tell to others?'

As the questions multiply the simple sense of 'I', its unity in the face of the world about, fragments, crumbles, becomes hazy, increasingly out of focus until . . . Until a sense of bearings is established there is nowhere to go, no 'I' to travel in company with 'others'. Rather than a single 'I' recognized by others in the same way as I recognize myself, there are as many subject positions for 'I' to be placed into as people who define who 'I' am. As I approach a pupil, do they define me as a teacher, a psychiatrist, a snoop, a mate? Each of these is a 'subject position' that 'I' have to negotiate in relation to my project that I hope to carry out as I study others. Simply, this may be schematized as in Figure 2.1.

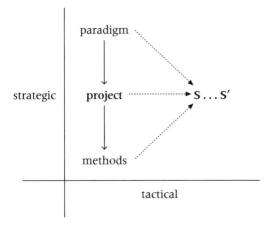

Figure 2.1 Project and dialogue

In my dialogue with others-as-subjects I have a sense of the paradigm that shapes or frames my gaze, I have a sense of the project purpose that carries me into dialogue with the members of a given community and I have an understanding of the methods appropriate to my purpose. Each are aligned in a single strategic purpose: to enable me to gain entrance into their world in a way that I can defend ethically, epistemologically, methodologically. Tactically, step by step, I deploy subjective roles, interviews, observations and the collection of documentation and other artefacts that take me closer to what I want. Strategically, any sense of a unifying 'I' is fragmented by the many subject positions (S . . . S') that becoming a project researcher generates in the eyes of others. Tactically, the subject positions can be analysed in order to see what is at stake by adopting or failing to adopt a given position. What is at stake for the researcher in this continual negotiation and renegotiation of social identities in the field is access to the collection of data together with its 'quality' and 'validity'. As a first illustration, Gaad (1998) spells this out in her doctoral thesis:

> my role was changeable, not only when I switched from the Egyptian side to the English side and vice-versa, which was only to be expected, but changes also arose while working within one case itself. For example, over the period of the field work in Egypt and during my work on Rasha, the Egyptian case, I was constructed and trusted as a *colleague* by Rasha's class teacher . . . when I was asked to 'keep a secret' about the management of the school, and when she was discussing her teaching methods when teaching children who are known as 'with mental handicap'.

In the case of Rasha's mother and on some occasions with both parents, I was clearly constructed as a *messenger* who came from out of the blue to a desperate family to take notice of everything that went wrong in their lives and maybe was expected to help to 'cure' their chosen daughter from the evil condition which they had never had before in the family . . . I was asked on several occasions not only to act as a *mediator* between the family and the school, but also to get more involved and question and investigate the management decisions regarding financial details . . .

Meanwhile, we find a different treatment or construction from the headteacher and his deputies, who treated me as some kind of a *reporter* who was coming after him and his team to investigate his policy and handling of the management of the only special school of its kind in the county . . .

At the private institution for special education, it seemed that I was regarded as an *outsider* – or maybe an intruder – who chose to research special education on the poorly funded and limited skilled special school, instead of taking the opportunity to research the luxury, five star, and certainly more advanced private education where the annual fees then were more than what an entire average working class family earned in several years . . .

(Gaad 1999)

As she explored her research the ways in which she was constructed multiplied, seemingly without end. Far from being a distraction, or a problem to 'remove' from the case studies that she was developing, this framework of subject positions began to clarify what was at stake for the voices or 'dramatis personae' of each case study (see Chapter 10). It enabled her to project a framework that helped her see the key elements, structures and processes of the emergent cases. As an author of a project, she was inscribing the role she wanted to take. In a sense, each member of the key dramatis personae negotiated the way in which her role in their lives was to be 'read'. Between the writing and the reading of her role in their lives and in her work as a doctoral student a negotiated understanding could be reached for the various public performances of her role on the various stages that mattered to her.

Staging connections

Language both 'positions' and stages a 'self-as-subject' in relation to an 'other' as 'thing' or as 'person' or as 'text'. For example:

Well, uh, this is the third school I've taught in so, at least I can probably make comparisons uh, my general feeling about the school is that, there is an awful lot about it which is good uh . . . uh . . . the general philosophy of the school I subscribe to, and that's why I'm happy here, uh because I think it goes as far as human institutions can do to pursuing a philosophy uh in a very general sense, the comprehensive principle whereby uh there is an attempt to get the best out of individual youngsters.

(Transcript, 11 February 1981)

This was collected during my own doctoral research when I asked teachers my usual initial question, 'How would you describe the school?' There is a lot packed into this small extract. It acts like a little map situating the speaker in relation to key features of the world seen from a particular subjective vantage point. One task is to list some key features of the map:

- schools, in particular three that have been experienced;
- congruence of the philosophy of the school with personal philosophy;
- being happy in the school;
- the comprehensive principle;
- human institutions;
- getting the best out of youngsters;
- youngsters.

They all connect to an 'I' as an organizing principle generating a sense of biographical unity, or individuality, or of being an agent within a realm of other possible actors. Whether or not this 'unity' is but a mere subjective fantasy or hallucination covering over the self, alienated in an impersonal cultural organization, it provides a departure point for the creative thinking essential to theory building. The departure point is at two levels. Strategically, the literature can be searched to connect key issues and categories in the extract to, for example, the political and educational debates on comprehensivization. Thus, to get much further requires some exploration of the 'literature'. One glance at even a modest university library will soon indicate that there is here a vast mountain to be climbed. Often this seems too daunting a task and the temptation is to bury oneself in interviewing and observation schedules. However, at the strategic level, reading the literature to design appropriate tactics of data collection and analysis is essential. Referring again to the brief extract above, is there enough there to begin the process of building the project at the strategic level? And does this provide insights to guide data collection and analysis?

I think it does. Indeed, a typical strategy to adopt is that of the part that points towards the 'whole'. This 'whole' can be described as a structure with constituent parts; or as a process with 'phases'; or, indeed, as an agglomeration that, although constructed accidentally, takes on a specific significance as defining a given context for action. Applying this to the extract above we can further propose:

- The comprehensivization philosophy is part of a greater social justice project.
- The process of getting the best out of youngsters is a professional project related to teachers.
- Human institutions, albeit imperfect, can be employed to implement or embody a project.

It could be claimed that these crude first formulations are first order projects, that is they are drawn from the perspective of the interviewee and thus constitute something of the overriding project to which this individual subscribes. They define what for this individual is the project of the society or group that maps out his or her bearings. At a tactical level, the researcher can interview and observe each other member of the key dramatis personae as defined or implied in the above interviewee's accounts. Each such interview provides other accounts from different perspectives on ostensibly the 'same' set of events, concerning the 'same' set of dramatis personae. Often this process is called triangulation (see Chapters 3 and 7 for further insights into the process). A strategy of comparison and contrast can then be employed in order to see what remains the 'same' across a range of viewpoints and what 'differs'. This aids the creation of the categories that members of a given situation or group employ and suggests the extent to which those categories 'generalize' or are 'shared' across a range of dramatis personae.

The researcher regards these first order projects as data to be organized, analysed, interpreted and employed as the basis of theory building. This theory building can be regarded as a second order activity to indicate that this is a project about the projects of others, from the point of view of a researcher who in the role of being a researcher is not a member of the dramatis personae of the everyday life of those being studied. The researcher will call upon a range of other information and knowledge in order to generate some second order, or theoretical statements. For example, being in loco parentis, that is, in the place of the parent, the teacher is a substitute for the parent. This 'substitution' is structurally important because the personal feelings, beliefs and experiences of the individual are effaced by the legal or professional role performed. Similarly, the individual projects of the teacher are 'substituted for' by the greater social projects of the Other, whether these are 'comprehensivization' and social justice, or capitalism and exploitation. Structurally, the individual lives a metaphorical life, the self being substituted by (or fused with or repressed by) the role imposed by the symbolic order. Being a teacher also recalls the part–whole relationship described in Chapter 1. The role of teacher is part of a system of roles, institutions, professional practices and knowledge.

The system as context, then, is structurally implicated and fundamental in any explanatory model of a given teacher's actions, beliefs
and values. More specifically, being this particular teacher, in this particular school, with these particular people, with these particular objects,
tools, buildings, creates a sense of uniqueness. Each object or event can
become an index of this unique context: the smell of chalk, the scrape of
a chair. Change any one and the context changes. Methodologically,
then, there are three routes for exploring how subjective experience can
be impacted on and ordered, each analogous to a rhetorical figure: metaphorically (through a substitution that effaces or fuses with the original);
metonymically and synechochally (through part–whole relations); and
by asyndeton, that is listing rapidly a series of contingent associations
(as, for example, the objects to be found grouped on the teacher's desk
– an exercise book and a pen and a ruler and so on – together these
create the sense of particularity, of this-ness).

Analyses of the contextual and metaphoric frameworks to subjectivity
can be made according to a range of different theoretical perspectives.
Take, for example, Sharp and Green who in a study of progressive
education in a primary school largely based their work in the Marxist
'notion that the problem of how a society understands itself in the forms
of social consciousness which are operative in the society and which
permeate the consciousness of individual social actors, needs to be dis-
tinguished from how the society exists objectively' (Marx and Engels
[1932] 1964). For them, the phenomenologist's methodology of describing the 'surface structure of consciousness, as the phenomenologist seems
to advocate, may mask the extent to which such consciousness may
conceal and distort the underlying structure of relationships (Lukács
1971; Godelier 1972)' (Sharp and Green 1975: 22–3). This is because
actors may not necessarily be aware of the underlying structures regu-
lating the action of individuals.

Research has to provide its theoretical and methodological rationale.
Sharp and Green did so in relation to the 'great debates' that have taken
place concerning the nature of social life and how to study it. The reader
then has a means for generating critiques, exploring Marxist and
phenomenological approaches to see whether their criticisms and judgements are appropriate. Their data analyses can be evaluated according to
their methodological aims. The values, beliefs and practices undertaken
by the researcher contribute to the trust, acceptance and credibility of
the researcher and hence the research. Thus the researcher is the critical 'instrument' through which the project takes place. In short, the
researcher makes manifest the relationships between the Real, the
symbolic systems that map it out and the imagery through which
consciousness perceives the world as a 'reality' that can talked about,
touched and manipulated.

Splitting the subject: symbolic, imaginary and Real

Mead's (1934) distinction between the 'I' and the 'me' splits subjectivity: the 'I' is the creative, spontaneous, impulsive centre of action – the Real as distinct from the social or symbolic, or imaginary; the 'me' is constructed out of the responses of others to the spontaneous acts of the 'I'. Acting like a mirror, the descriptions and responses of others to the self, particularly the images held up by significant others like mother, uncle, teacher and so on, define the self. This play of images defines an 'imaginary' domain for the individual, a domain of surfaces, masks, camouflage, make-up. The 'me', although experienced as intimate, as mine, is also a construction from the outside. It is radically 'other' to the 'I'. Yet the intimacy of the 'I' does not render it clear. It is rather like the eye that looks for itself and cannot see itself except through the mediation of some other acting as a mirror. Being face to face is in a sense being reflection to reflection. Adopting this framework for analysing subjectivity has important consequences for the collection, interpretation and use of data. Rather than a simple categorization of 'self' and 'other', Figure 2.2 shows the complexity of the relationships between 'I', 'me', Other and SELF and OTHER when they meet in some attempt to converse.

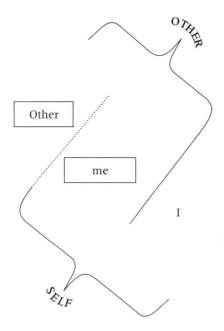

Figure 2.2 Self and Other

The self is radically split or fissured. The 'I' has no direct line towards the other being always mediated by the 'me'. In this sense the 'I' is always alienated by being represented by the 'me' in any social circumstance. The 'I' is reduced to the words employed in the public domain, categorized and expressed through the agency of lexicons and codes not of the 'I's' making. Take the demand: 'I want food.' This demand may be occasioned by a felt sense of hunger which at its origins is a biological need. However, to get the food that is wanted the need has to be mediated by language and pass through the mechanisms and material realities of the radically Other. This is an abstract way of saying that to get what you want you have to depend on words to convey the message and upon the existence of a vast structure that includes the material realities of organisms as well as the cultural realities of farmers, factories, shops, transport systems, markets, laws, systems of exchange and financial structures and processes. Marxist analysis has pointed to the role of the material structures of society and the way in which they are organized in determining the consciousness of individuals. Psychoanalysis has pointed to the role of the unconscious in the lives of people. The relationships between consciousness, the unconscious structures of the mind and the complex ungraspable structures of the world need in some way to be conceptualized.

Now consider:

Child: I want food.
Parent: You always want food when I'm busy.
Child: You never have time for me.

The original demand is now set in the context of the circumstances and judgements of the parent. The busy-ness makes a demand on the parent's time that competes with that of the demands of the child. From the point of view of the child the demands that make the life of the parent busy come from elsewhere, the Other who subjects the parent to the desires of the Other. This desire in Lacan's (1977b) terms comes from the agency of order in the symbolic dimension: the Nom du Père (Name of the Father). In the realm of the imaginary, the demand 'I want food' can be fulfilled by a particular object, say an apple. However, in Lacan's terms desire is never satisfied since no one object can fulfil it. For the child the demand for food is replaced by the statement, 'You never have time for me.' It is a statement that no apple will satisfy. Nor can the parent give sufficient time that will fill the emptiness that must always be there because the parent is always subjected to the desire of the Other.

The Real refers to that level of the flesh, the something that is living, material and not reducible to words. It is the inexpressible sense of I-ness that no mirror can capture. When I try to speak and define myself something is always left out. When others say, 'I know what you're like', or say of something I do, 'That's not like you', I know something is missing. The image, the label splits away from me. Indeed, it leaves me split between my sense of the Realness of myself and the label that stands in the place of this. At the level of the Real a need arises. In order to satisfy this need it has to be mediated by language. It has to be represented by some legitimate demand that I may consciously make of others directly in relation to me who are able to fulfil this demand. At the level of need I may be hungry. At the consciousness level my need must be interpreted in relation to the available opportunities and constraints. I do not need chocolate to satisfy my hunger; any food will do. However, chocolate may in my social group be more socially acceptable than an apple because that is associated with being a health freak. Chocolate may go beyond being demanded at a particular time and become part of a fantasy structure through which my deeper desires are articulated. In order to provide the money that will buy the apples the parent must work and thus time for the child must be sacrificed to the hours of work. The subjective experiences of both parent and child are thus torn in various directions. Their in-itself Reality is overlaid by the ways they must present themselves for each other in social interaction. The child will always be hungry and the parent will never have enough time. The researcher therefore requires a way of thinking through these kinds of complexities. An observation may give one impression that is contradicted by other observations of apparently the 'same' observed event, or during interviews about the 'event'. Judgement as to 'what is the case' in a particular situation, as phenomenologists would say, should be suspended. An event takes its meaning for individuals from the contexts within which it takes place and according to the prior biographical experiences of the individual. It would seem reasonable, therefore, to suspend judgement as to the 'meaning' or 'significance' of a particular event or phenomenon until contexts and biographies have been explored. Even then, what is the status of the judgements made? This will depend on the forms of analysis undertaken, the range of contexts and biographical material explored, the conditions under which the data were collected, the researcher's rationale for the project – all issues to be taken up throughout the book. By maintaining the focus on the 'subject' as individual who, as do other individuals, projects his or her needs, demands and desires onto others and the material world, the researcher can develop a methodological framework to place into dialogue the various modes and moods of subjectivity.

How to do this, involves generating a framework for thinking through the impact of the Symbolic, the Imaginary and the Real (Lacan 1977a) on the subjective life of individuals and groups. Figure 2.3 summarizes the key parallel structures introduced so far.

By the symbolic domain is meant not so much the specific symbols of mathematics or art, but the 'unconscious' dimension by which order

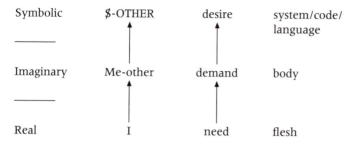

Symbolic	\$-OTHER	desire	system/code/ language
Imaginary	Me-other	demand	body
Real	I	need	flesh

Figure 2.3   The Real, Symbolic and Imaginary

emerges in complex systems. Think of what happens when engaged in speaking with another. There is perhaps a conscious dimension in attending to meanings, but explaining how I know what words to use next, how to arrange them in good English and how I 'understand' the other is another matter. It takes place unconsciously. I just speak. Take the following example from Benhabib:

> From Adam Smith's notion of the 'invisible hand' to Hegel's concept of a 'system of needs,' Durkheim's notion of the organic division of labour, and Parsons' notion of 'generalised media,' modern social theory has emphasised this aspect of modern societies, according to which large domains of social life become functionally dependent upon one another without this being willed, desired, or even known to anyone.
>
> (Benhabib 1986: 127)

The invisible hand of economics is the product of millions of transactions. Regulation emerges. This sense of order emerging, whether as the order underlying language or the 'invisible hand' of the market place is a good illustration of what is meant by the Other as it impacts on the life of the individual. These are perspectives where 'individuals' activities, unknown to them and often unwilled by them, result in law-like regularities, which are intelligible to an observer–thinker' (Benhabib 1986: 31).

Two social projects are framed by these distinctions: first, those of lived experience where the world is intersubjective and identity is socially constructed through the first and second person voices of 'I' and 'you'; and second, those of the observer–thinker, a perspective named the Trans-subjective by Benhabib, or referred to as the Other by Lacan and spoken in the voice of the third person – he/she/it/they/them. Each frames the choices that a subject may make and the consequences that can occur.

The researcher can analyse how individuals relate themselves to others at an intersubjective and Trans-subjective level by detailed attention

to the first, second and third person voices employed during daily communications and research interviews. The intersubjective project is effectively local in scope since it emerges only through face-to-face interactions. It creates both a sense of intimacy, being together and also the
possibility of face-to-face conflict, struggle and resistance. The objective
here resides in the processes of negotiation, dialogue resistance and
conflict that individuals may have with each other. The Trans-subjective
inaugurates the global, and the objective as Law and Power. The
intersubjective and Trans-subjective together constitute the field of play
for the individual by providing the overall Rules (e.g. the law, codes of
politeness, ethical prescriptions, cultural norms and so on) and the face-
to-face means by which these are translated into practice within a particular context (the home, school, work and so on). Each individual
finds their place as a 'subject' within this field of play. In a classroom
there are two key subject positions to 'inhabit': teacher and pupil. Of
each category there are other positions where teachers may be thought
of as being hard, tough, strict and others as soft, easy, weak. Similarly
pupils can be divided into those who study hard, mess about, bully and
so on. Each location in the field of play can either be contested, coveted,
or scorned. Through interviews, observation and the exploration of historical and contemporary documentation this field of play with its subject positions and its contested, coveted and scorned spaces or locations
can be analysed and described.

Imagine the entry to each location in the field of play as a doorway
wide enough only for one person at a time. Suppose only one doorway
leads to a position where all the resources necessary to sustain life are to
be found. This presumably would be a highly coveted space to inhabit. If
only one person can pass through and 'inhabit' the position at a time,
how is the flow of people to be regulated? It could be done through
sheer force. The strongest enters and either controls the flow of resources to others who are positioned outside so that they may live, or
closes the door on them. Perhaps the resources must be processed to
produce tools as well as food. So, the one who controls the flow could
either enslave the others or pay wages of some kind. In this latter case
an economic system arises with a proliferation of other locations in the
field of play being constructed such as: labourer, manager, shopkeeper.
Each individual may have to compete in order to inhabit one of these
'coveted' positions in the field of play if there are fewer positions than
people ready, willing and able to fill them. Of course, some positions
may be more coveted than others; indeed, some may be necessary but
despised because they are dirty. Those who cannot find a way into the
system may engage in violence, theft, or rebellion in order to try and
gain the resources needed. Armies, police and courts of law would be
necessary to ensure that the fundamental order is maintained. Some

may even believe in its naturalness and rightness, while others try to contest it, transform it or overthrow it.

This imaginary scenario began with the 'choice' to adopt a strategy of the survival of the fittest: the strongest won access to the coveted location of control of all resources. Suppose on the other hand another 'choice' was made: to cooperate in the management of resources for the benefit of all. There is considerable evidence to support each side in the debate as to whether competition or cooperation are 'fundamental' in animal and human behaviour. For Darwin as is well known it is competition that is the engine of evolution. Less well known, for Kropotkin (1904) it is cooperation, or mutual aid, that is most characteristic of animal behaviour. What may be considered is that neither are fundamental but that historically both positions have influenced the field of play for human decision making. If the researcher wishes to understand and engage with the development of society then the formation of these coveted, contested or scorned spaces and their consequences for the construction of subjects and intersubjective and Trans-subjective frameworks for the negotiation of identities and the management of social order become a key focus of attention.

The door to the Other as objective field of play

The intersubjective project places voices in dialogue, whereas the Trans-subjective is monologic, speaking only with the voice of the Law. In politics Mouffe (1993) and Benhabib (1986) argue these translate into the social projects of democracy (dialogic) and totalitarianism (monologic). Subjective choices have objective consequences. In games theory Charaud (1997) points to the need that Von Neumann and Morgenstern had to posit the coercive framework of society, which functions like a trans-subjective subject in order to maintain the rules and the ultimate intelligibility of the game. Charraud as a mathematician and psychoanalyst explored games theory in relation to Lacan's theories of subjectivity. In the symbolic all possible games and strategies are potentially present. This structure of possible games and strategies organizes choices and consequences in the real and the imaginary by determining the profit and loss involved in allocating resources to needs, demands, whims and fancies. The real, in this instance, is the reality composed of the rationally imposed rules, regulations and hence legitimate calculations for moves that can be chosen to meet desired aims. The imaginary is structured in the face-to-face demands that the players make upon each other. In two person games and zero-sum games one strategy can usually be shown to be preferable to others. In more complex games, where betrayal, trickery and cheating are all possible moves, the game is actually a meeting, or a crossroads, of two or more games. It is at this point that simple rational calculation breaks down, or at least becomes confused, deceptive, ambiguous and the question 'What game is being played here?' is both critical and potentially irresolvable except as a game of the contest of games. Every game has its consequences. The complexity that results is beyond an individual's grasp to define and calculate all possibilities. The choice is between either the belief that order may be discovered, whether in Reason, Faith, Law, Tradition, or Common sense, or the acceptance of uncertainty. How the other is framed – as Lawfully organized, or uncertain – determines the nature of the 'objective world' and the projects that can be carried out.

3

The Other: its objects and objectivity

Discussions of subjectivity seem to evoke objectivity as its companion term. To speak objectively implies the speaker is not subjectively colouring their words with feelings, prejudices, values. There is an aura of neutrality. Indeed, objectivity is saturated with the authority of science and professionality, connoting a specialized way of doing things to arrive at the 'facts', a picture of 'reality' and of 'truth'. Or, the objective can simply be the focus of attention, or of consciousness of the 'something' that is 'outside' the 'self'. In this latter sense it is the Other for the Subject. The Other can be conceived of as consisting of all the objects of consciousness that exist, or are experienced as being outside, or independent of, the 'self' and its sense of subjectivity. A critical appreciation of the modes of 'objectivity' provides a means of mapping, analysing, evaluating or critiquing social phenomena.

Many competing perspectives and methodologies exist for doing this. What is data for some may not be accepted as data by others. To have the power to proclaim what is 'known', 'real', 'true' is to have the Midas touch. Wherever Midas looks the world turns first to data, then, with the fabulous touch, it turns to nuggets of knowledge. The construction of 'expertise' is a valuable commodity in a market economy. Beyond market concerns, however, is there, as in the quantitative sciences, an 'accepted practice' for doing qualitative research by which the researcher may securely, confidently deal with assuring validity, objectivity, generalization at both the strategic and tactical levels of the project?

Strategically, there is the 'vision', the way of 'seeing' or 'grasping' a world. Tactically, there are the methods employed to achieve some strategic vision, or goal. Qualitative research has spawned a number of strategic-level approaches that at once suggest perspectives (ways of seeing, viewpoints) and methodologies (ways of producing 'knowledge'). Is a case study a perspective (whether framed as the singular instance, or as the multifarious complex) or a methodology (the approach to describing structures and processes rather than sampling from the many)? What about an ethnography? Is it a methodology, or a way of indicating that the researcher goes and observes, even lives with, the people being studied for very long periods of time? Or does it simply refer to a much shorter 'going and seeing and being with them'? Think now of doing an evaluation of some policy innovation being implemented in a given profession. How does the collection of data differ in an evaluation from carrying out a case study or doing an ethnography? Then there is Action Research that seeks to bring about changes through reflection on practice (Elliott 1991). Is it only the active engagement by the researcher/ professional that makes it apparently different from a case study or an ethnography or some other kind of qualitative research? Each of these through the marketing of expertise generates courses of study in various methodology programmes. In addition, various new 'isms' are from time to time formulated by the knowledge entrepreneurs. Approaches become 'Goffman-esque' in adopting the dramaturgical model, or Lacanian, or Schutzian or Foucauldian. There is no problem in this – apart from the various reinventions of the wheel that arise. It is a legitimate and, indeed, often highly creative way of developing a career as well as facilitating and deepening insights into ourselves and our worlds.

Is there then an accepted way of 'doing qualitative research'? Probably not. However, a lot of what researchers do (tactically to achieve their objectives) – of whatever persuasion from Marxist to postmodernist (at a strategic level of philosophy or perspective) – look remarkably similar even if the results may be startlingly different. Research has a pragmatic 'doing' side that raises a number of problems for the 'doers'. Each in their different ways, they must attend to these problems if they are to enter a community of voices who agree to give each other some speaking and listening time. Each has to convince or at least have a rationale that causes debate about how the key problems are being handled. This is as true whether it is in a thesis open to assessment by examiners or a publication seeking a wider stage. Debate thus provides another dimension to 'objectivity', that is, openness to public debate, interpretations, challenges, and judgements. The thesis takes its sense, its value by taking up a position in relation to others and Otherness.

What are the key problems in creating the conditions for dialogue in a thesis, report or publication? Some relate to the *production of data* and the *ways in which it is collected*. Others focus on *analysis* and the *production of 'findings'*, 'what is known' as valid and generalizable, what can be explained and what can be understood. For others the concern is about the *ethics* of 'doing things to people and the planet', of transforming them into objects, subjecting them to the whims and powers of those who watch, weigh and manipulate. At each step in the research, a map of the problems and opportunities emerges. For example, when an individual enters the field as a *researcher*, a range of problems and opportunities appear:

> ... since I am an insider researcher I am likely to stumble across interesting data at any time during my normal duties. Unlike an external researcher who enters the field for a given period of time and then exits, every moment of my own professional life is likely to generate data. To suddenly announce, in the canteen, or in the middle of a post-mortem, that I am assuming the hat of a researcher and recording proceedings would be ludicrously impractical. Worse, if at an operational scene, someone present objected, they could have no assurance that I would not record the matters regardless of their objection, other than acceptance of my personal integrity. If they did not accept this assurance, then the continuance of the scene examination could be jeopardised with all the associated implications.
>
> (Anonymised: MA draft 1999)

The researcher draws some key distinctions – insider/outsider, researcher/subject-as-data, trustworthy/not trustworthy – that specify the particular problem and opportunity structure being faced. A series of speculative if-thens sketch the field of play. Making the first move is never just routine. It cuts the field in one way rather than another, limiting the next move, and thus creates the conditions for all the following steps.

More generally, creating a map is rather like taking pictures from different vantage points. From a spaceship one sees the earth and its relation to the sun and planets. From an aeroplane the scope is reduced to seeing a town, its relation to the villages surrounding it and the interconnections of roads and paths. The closer one gets the more detailed are the features. Depending upon the researcher purposes, data collection can be limited to either the long range or 'macro' views or closer up 'micro' views, or a combination that studies the complex relationships between the 'micro' and 'macro' or 'global' and 'local'. Next, a choice emerges about how to represent what is seen. Should one employ the language of the people being studied, using concepts recognizable in their own conversations; or should one use a more specialized language, appropriate to, for example, sociological or psychological discourse? The choice will depend as much on audience as it does on the nature of the subject matter. Often, only a specialized vocabulary will do. Mathematics and physics, for example, would be impossible to develop without the specialized nature of their terminology. The choices can be represented as in Figure 3.1.

The study may be constructed in any of the quadrants of the diagram or across the quandrants. It may move along the axis from global to

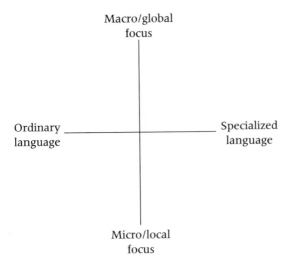

Figure 3.1   Focus and discourse

close up studying the impact of the global on the local and vice versa. From a global position some researchers choose theoretical perspectives that enable them to 'see' and study what seem to be the big (or macro) structures of a given society; from the local position they may choose theoretical perspectives that enable them to focus in on the detailed interactions of individuals (or micro level). At this point the polar terms global and local provide a crude but useful way of discriminating. In debates about contemporary society and the impact of increasingly powerful information technologies and networks, the terms global and local have taken on what many see as new significance (explored in later chapters). Whatever focus is chosen, the researcher may represent the conversations of those being studied in the vocabulary they actually use, or may seek to abstract from these categories hidden structures, or make connections that provide explanations for what previously seemed inexplicable. Each choice presents a slice of the totality[3] and begins to define the problem and opportunity structure faced by the researcher.

Strategic cuts

One cannot begin without making a cut. Every time I say 'I'm looking at this, not that' I use language to pare away the inessential. When I ask others to look there too, to see *this*, not *that*, I am manipulating their awareness of the world, focusing it to conform with my seeing and speaking. They too can join this contest of attention on the 'real', the 'objective', the valuable' the 'desirable', or indeed, the 'disgusting', the trivial, the mad, the bad. They can say 'But you're looking at the wrong thing, if you just look at this, not that, you'll see how good and just the world truly is.' Every look is decisive for the individual, the community, the world. Seeing is believing: 'I saw it with my own eyes. Honest. It's true.' The multiple ways of seeing create the multiple worlds that can be mapped through the tools of language that strategically manipulate meanings using sarcasm, irony, punning, metaphor, metonym and so on. Each cut defines a context, an aura that marks out the field of observation: I am looking in this way, not that; it is this focus that I mean, not that; everything that falls into this spotlight of my attention forms the context I am talking about, the rest is excluded. As I talk a context into existence by the verbal cuts I make, shaping attention in this way, not that, the context is indeed a context, (with-text), a field of study composed of the texts that I produce in talking about it. Each such cut is strategic, stripping away the unwanted:

Focusing was influenced and guided by motivation, the role and orientation of the researcher such as in selecting what to leave out, what to mention briefly, and what to focus on. For example, I believe that as a professional educator who taught children with Down's syndrome in England, I found it hard to ignore the effect and influence of this role on selecting certain interviews or parts of interviews with teachers, which touched matters and issues that I used to be interested in as a teacher (and am still interested in), for example, the relationship between parents and schools and also the issue of labelling children with Down's syndrome. I also strongly believe that my role as a mother of two young children influenced, in one way or another, the selection of which parts of parental interviews to expand more and which to mention briefly. Again, being a native Egyptian, with a reasonable knowledge about the Egyptian cultural values and contexts, probably influenced the focusing and the selection of the Egyptian data which was to be presented as a part of this thesis.

(Gaad 1998: 17)

Strategically, Gaad wanted to explore and render as explicitly as possible the issues and problems at stake in each decision to focus in one direction rather than another. Indeed, she questioned herself as a reliable or trustworthy reporter and translator of cultural experiences. To develop understandings and insights, she read books on translation theory, experimented with ways of making translations, employed her experiences in the two countries to highlight differences and systematically mapped out the groups of individuals whose views she should draw upon:

In order to achieve the aims of the research . . . which involved
stating what is similar, what is different, and what could be learnt
from each other, I started by drawing a circular diagram for each
case containing the child's name in the middle. Then I drew a bigger
circle around this one with a greater diameter which symbolised the
child within the network of concepts relevant to her life. This circle
included the majority of contexts the child could be involved with,
such as cultural, moral, traditional, etc.

(Gaad 1998: 51)

Her first attempts resulted in complex diagrams representing the many
possible contexts of an individual's life. However, she soon decided that,
as well as the global picture, she needed 'a little diagram' focusing on
what she believed were three key levels:

• The child as a part of her family. The family level included both
  parents, members of the immediate family (i.e. brothers or sis-
  ters), and relatives if available or involved.
• The second level was the educational environment level. This
  started off with the non-educationist members of staff like care-
  takers, secretarial staff, health visitors, school psychologists etc.
  Then this level passes through the support team . . . then comes
  the teacher . . . finally reaching the top of the school academic
  ladder and finishing with the management team . . .
• The third level was the national policy level for education, which
  starts with Local Educational Authorities. I needed to interview
  some officials who were involved (whether directly or indirectly)
  in decision-making . . .

(Gaad 1998: 51)

From this a design emerged that would help ensure coverage of all the
major participants in the life of each child. Comparing and contrasting
the emergent structures in each case focuses attention on key factors
decisive in the education of each child.

To delve further, three strategic dimensions can be employed to ensure
coverage:

1 *A level of ideas, or conceptual structures and processes.* Individuals can
  be interviewed and documents scrutinized for their philosophical,
  conceptual and value frameworks. Questions focused on: what are
  the educational values that teachers, parents and officials have?
  What are their philosophies of teaching and learning? What are their
  visions for the future? This begins to fill out the conceptual maps
  by which individuals account for their actions, describe their worlds
  and define what is problematic, what is possible and what is not
  possible.

2 *A level of practices, mechanisms or procedures* whereby ideas are realized in terms of action. From interviews, documentation and observation the formal and informal procedures or 'ways of doing things' employed to bring about events were related to the formal and informal beliefs and ideas held by the individual actors. Questions include: how do you go about teaching 'x'? Can you tell me the process that was involved in developing this particular curriculum? Can you describe what happens in a typical day? What do you have to do to get 'x'? The maps that arise are, on the one hand, in terms of the relationships between individuals, groups, organizations, systems. On the other, they describe the institutional mechanisms (timetables, committee structures) and procedures (routines, approved sequences of events to be followed in order to make things happen) and other more general social practices (rituals, codes of conduct).

3 *A level of organizational and material structures, resources and tools* which serve to manipulate the real world. Without the appropriate material tools of course nothing can be expected to happen. Without appropriately qualified and experienced staff, without decently equipped classrooms, and without the real time being available, all the best ideas and thought-out forms of action will collapse. Questions include: what are the numbers, experience and qualifications of staff? How much do you have to spend on x, y, z? Do you have x, y, z? What do you need in order to . . . ? What develop are organizational and system maps that include the material architectural structures and tools as well as the symbolic architectures of power and responsibility through which line management operates.

Reflecting upon this realist structure (Sayer 1993), questions can be formulated relevant to the problem and opportunity structure related to each 'level' which may provide a map as in Figure 3.2.

In this 'architecture' there are four levels. Starting from the top, suppose through interviews four distinct discourses were identified. Each discourse conceptually structures experience, activities and the use of resources to produce desired outcomes. Suppose Discourse 1 is related to the 'official' view of what is intended. It is what is described in policy documentation and articulated by management in their public statements and conversations with the media, or with auditing agencies. Thus the intention is that Discourse 1 is enacted by Practices 1 using Resources 1 to produce Outcome 1. However, in reality it may be that a set of short cuts must be employed because people are not sufficiently trained to operate in the official manner (Practices 1) so they are restricted to the less expert Practices 3. Indeed, this is also necessitated because instead of the ideal equipment (Resources 1) there is only the old-fashioned equipment (Resources 3) available for use. Opportunities

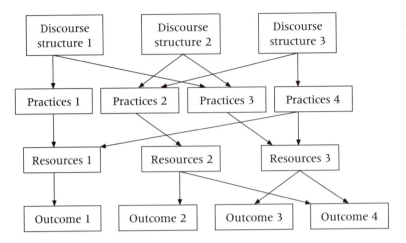

Figure 3.2   Discourse architecture

are lost because of the ineffectiveness of the practices and the out-of-date resources. Other routes may be followed depending on the discourses, practices and resources employed.

By listening to the members of a given social context, say a workplace, suppose you discover that as well as the official discourse, 'Discourse structure 1' there are counter-discourses as represented in 'Discourse structure 2 and 'Discourse structure 3'. Take, for example, Discourse structure 2. Careful analysis of interviews reveals that under this view there are two alternative practices that can be undertaken in order to achieve a desired outcome. Say that Practice 2 is perfectly safe to employ but Practice 3 is dangerous. Now it may be the case that the values, beliefs and knowledge articulated in Discourse structure 2 reveal that the danger involved in Practice 3 is not understood or, indeed, openly scorned. Furthermore, it is believed that the Outcomes 2, 3, and 4 are all preferable to Outcome 1. Under such circumstances, members of the group who share Discourse structure 2 will, if they believe Outcome 3 is the best of all, and if there is no other countervailing reason, attempt to employ Practice 3. In order to make effective change in working practices, therefore, it is essential first to map the complexity of the social processes and structures underpinning practice. In this way the conceptual errors, the missing and inappropriate mechanisms and cultural practices as well as the resources that are lacking, misallocated or inadequate can be identified and courses of action designed to rectify them (see Chapters 8 and 9 for a detailed discussion of the issues involved in designing courses of action). Establishing this architecture requires building it from the 'ground up', that is, from listening to what people see as opportunities or problems, collecting their textual productions and watching them at work in their world.

As a more concrete example, for a small-scale project I carried out during a study leave with a friend, at that time a professor in a Canadian university (Schostak 1992), I was to map the current curriculum of a local school. From interviews I explored the conceptual structures of teachers as they described 'the curriculum'. Different individuals and different departments had their own ways of describing, accounting for and putting the curriculum into practice. In their own words, they defined problems, opportunities, the mechanisms, procedures and cultural practices they employed and the resources to which they had access. To develop my tactics for coverage of people, places, organizational structures, processes, resources and issues I began as follows:

The first steps towards a mental map were made the night before in my lodgings. This was based upon a set of notes and memories derived from a conversation with Ivor about a week before. It was a kind of checklist of data to get: interviews, documents, observations, places/locations in the school. There were also orienting questions:

- nature of curriculum on offer; how it was developed;
- processes underlying delivery of curriculum: administration;
- organizational mechanisms for delivery, monitoring, quality assurance;
- who has responsibility for what;
- how decisions are made;
- educational beliefs/purposes;
- student/school profile – socio-economic;
- choices/options available for students;
- role for staff development in curriculum development?
- study of the breadth of curriculum available, the way it's developed, administered, delivered in practice, monitored and its impact on students.

(Fieldnotes 9 October 1991)

In a sense, this crude framework with its final statement about the scope of the study provided my entrance ticket into the school. In various forms I replayed the statement and asked the questions. With this I was able not only to orient myself but also the people I met: 'Well, it's a brief study set up by [name], you may have heard about . . . No? Well, he's a prof at [name] and is doing an historical study of the school. There's someone else who's doing the history bit, and my brief is to get a contemporary picture. Of course, I can't cover the whole school in all its complexity in this short time, but I can at least get something of what it means to a range of teachers and a few students . . . Do you mind if I tape record? Of course, I'll anonymise whatever I write for publication . . .'.

The recordings, the notes and the memories mesh with reflections, research discourses and texts of all kinds. The product, in some way, is this text which represents a peculiar kind of journey, a journey that points to other possible journeys, other ways of narrating experiences common to a number of raconteurs who together write themselves into the history of the school.

(Schostak 1992)

Maps of problems and opportunities evolve during time. Each return to the field, each relistening to a tape recording or rereading of notes and documentation generates new insights. It finishes only when the thesis or book is complete. But that is only one kind of ending; others are deferred as personal learning continues, and debates ensue from the readings of examiners or reviewers of the research.

Getting in deeper

The social arrangements that compose a world either serve to further interests in various ways, or frustrate them. This can be explored by analysing people's vocabularies for examples of motive, interest, care, desire. Getting in deeper, that is, deeper than the publicly promoted image in order to get at what may be hidden or impossible to record by quantitative methods, requires spending time with the community under study. How much time? That depends on the nature of the project. Take for example the project outline in Chapter 1. There a key part of Phase 1 strategy was three-day intensive ethnographies.[4] Three days does not sound much. However, consider three days multiplied by five members of staff. This can result in the equivalent of 15 days' worth of interviews and observations. Now multiply that by the number of visits made, say 20, resulting in 300 days' equivalent data collection. This was a strategy aiming towards 'coverage' of a range of contexts. It was effective in achieving its purpose of collecting data across different institutions and categories of staff and students in those institutions. It was not so effective in analysing in depth, that is, focusing on the processes of day-to-day experience. For that a different kind of strategy was required involving more time to be spent getting to know individuals and their activities. Again, how much time? There is no recipe answer to this. Trying to get close to an individual or group may be frustrated by their hostility, insecurities, indifference or other reasons. The quality of the time spent with them may be so poor that no matter how long is spent little is learnt apart from their strategies to fend you off. This, of course, can produce an interesting, but different, project from the intended project of getting to know their lives from their point of view. If, however, a breakthrough is made and people begin to allow the researcher to be with them in increasingly intimate, sensitive and friendly ways then the time necessary to get to know the 'world' of the individual group or community depends on the range of people, contexts, activities and situations to be seen, heard, 'lived with' and described. Much of this will depend on the purposes of the researcher: whether exploring the working life of the individual as a health worker, rather than their family life as, say, a parent. Selection will cut the range of relevant contexts to be explored as well as individuals or groups to be interviewed and observed and thereby reduce the time commitments necessary. Once contexts and key actors relevant to the study have been identified then the time necessary depends on the extent to which the researcher can get actors to provide accounts of their experiences in the different contexts. This means getting access to the 'stories' they tell themselves and others about their lives and the world about. These may be glimpsed through anecdotes that people draw on to justify, amuse, describe, illustrate. Or they may be more considered biographical (e.g. Goodson and Walker 1991) or autobiographical accounts (e.g. Linde 1993). Such material could include very personal accounts related to an individual's experience, whether dreams as in psychoanalytic studies, interviews intended to draw out material, or recordings of a range of interactions in working and personal life. Although there are a variety of approaches that seek to 'get close' to those being studied, they are often loosely brought under the heading of 'ethnography'.

Before the rise of 'scientific' ethnography there were the accounts made by travellers, missionaries and explorers who came back from distant lands bringing tales of the exotic lives of those they met. The anthropologist Malinowski (1922) sought a basis for his studies in scientific methodology. In the introduction to his seminal book he made the case for 'giving a candid account' of how he collected his data. From this the classical anthropological approach to doing ethnographies was born. He described his first encounters, how he as a novice had to build trust, attempt to communicate through 'pidgin English' and so try to glean something of the culture of the people. He argued there was a difference between 'a sporadic plunging into the company of natives, and being really in contact with them' (p.7). In the field, the ethnographer then has

the duty before him of drawing up all the rules and regularities of tribal life; all that is permanent and fixed; of giving an anatomy of their culture, of depicting the constitution of their society. But these things, though crystallised and set, are nowhere *formulated*. There is no written or explicitly expressed code of laws, and their whole tribal tradition, the whole structure of their society, are embodied in the most elusive of all materials; the human being. But not even in human mind or memory are these laws to be found directly formulated. The natives obey the forces and commands of the tribal code, but they do not comprehend them; exactly as they obey their instincts and their impulses, but could not lay down a single law of psychology. The regularities in native institutions are an automatic result of the interaction of the mental forces of tradition, and the material conditions of environment. Exactly as a humble member of any modern institution, whether it be in the state, or the church, or the army, is *of* it and *in* it, but has no vision of the resulting integral action of the whole, still less could furnish any account of its organisation, so it would be futile to attempt questioning a native in abstract, sociological terms.

(Malinowski 1922: 11–12)

So how should the 'scientific' ethnographer proceed? He provides three approaches:

1 *The organisation of the tribe, and the anatomy of its culture* must be recorded in firm clear outline. The method of *concrete, statistical documentation* is the means through which such an outline has to be given.
2 Within this frame, the *imponderabilia of actual life*, and the *type of behaviour* have to be filled in. They have to be collected through minute, detailed observations, in the form of some sort of ethnographic diary, made possible by close contact with native life.
3 A collection of ethnographic statements, characteristic narratives, typical utterances, items of folk-lore and magical formulae has to be given as a *corpus inscriptionum*, as documents of native mentality.

(Malinowski 1922: 24, original emphasis)

This framework then leads, according to Malinowski, to the 'final goal' which is

to grasp the native's point of view, his relation to life, to realise *his* vision of *his* world. We have to study man, and we must study what concerns him most intimately, that is, the hold which life has on him. In each culture, the values are slightly different; people aspire after different aims, follow different impulses, yearn after a different form of happiness. In each culture, we find different institutions in which man pursues his life interest, different customs by which he satisfies his aspirations, different codes of law and morality which reward his virtues or punish his defections. To study the institutions, customs, and codes or to study the behaviour and mentality without the subjective desire of feeling by what these people live, of realising the substance of their happiness – is, in my opinion, to miss the greatest reward which we can hope to obtain from the study of man.

This is a clear statement of Malinowski's project which sets into relation the subjective and the objective fields of multiple subjects, multiple viewpoints, and multiple contexts. Its very language locates it within a particular time context that can be critiqued from later historical vantage points. Indeed, for example, Fontana (1994) provides a useful overview of critiques from other theoretical perspectives and the developments that have taken place, or have the potential of taking place, under the impact of feminism, post-structuralism and postmodernism. Importantly, as well as methodologies for doing ethnography being developed by anthropologists, there was also a sociological route influenced by the broadly symbolic interactionist approaches of the Chicago school (Park 1916; Thomas and Znaniecki 1927; Mead 1934) and, later, Blumer (1969), focusing upon the meanings of behaviours from the viewpoint of the actors. Data collection included participant observation, that is, like the Malinowski approach, getting close to the lives of individuals by carrying out observations while participating in their everyday lives. Like Malinowski, there was a concern that fieldwork should be framed within a scientific project. Thus:

Approaches to scientizing interactionist fieldwork included analytic induction (Lindesmith 1947) and grounded theory (Glaser and Strauss 1967). Detailed instructions on the 'appropriate' ways to conduct research and what constituted 'valid' data were included in these methods in an attempt to render sociological ethnographic methods more rigorous.

(Fontana 1994: 205)

During the latter decades of the twentieth century, this scientizing approach to doing ethnography has come under attack by those who critiqued the so-called authority of the ethnographer, that claims merely to describe the lives of others 'naturalistically' (see also Hammersley 1984; Geertz 1988; and Chapters 4 and 5, this volume). Fontana (1994) discusses ethnographic approaches that emphasize the accounts made by insiders rather than researchers, and upon the dialogue that can emerge between researcher and insider as a means of exploring different conceptions of 'what happened' and the 'world'.

In general, getting in deep involves finding out how the actors 'see' themselves and others as 'characters' closely involved in the 'action', or being remote from the action, important, unimportant and so on. Ask one individual who the key actors are and you may get a quite different list from that of another person, almost as if all are acting in different 'plays' on different stages, in different worlds. Yet they may all be in close proximity in the same physical location apparently in the same 'organization'. How different individuals handle their own problems, their feelings, their anxieties and present a face to others is of both strategic and tactical importance for the maintenance of order in their lives and establishing a sense of being in control. It is in the field of play that exists between people all engaged in the same arena of transactions, the same framework for contestations, and for matching resources with opportunities, needs and problems that existential dilemmas arise, taking the research deeper into the kinds of judgements they make and the reasons for the decisions and actions they take.

The following is an illustration from a small-scale six-month study of the experience of junior doctors. For them, it was frequently life on the edge (Schostak and Schostak 2000):

I: You've encountered unhappy outcomes already?

T: Yes, the first day on Obstetric ward, I had a stillbirth, thirty-nine week, and had to examine the dead baby . . .

The trainee is asked to talk about this a little further. She says 'the midwives were quite kind' and 'they get quite upset about stillbirths themselves', as, indeed, 'everybody gets upset as well'. This kind of information allows the researcher to begin the process of sketching the key characters, events and relationships in the trainee's working life. With each question focusing on the event, the enveloping structures, the routines, the emotional tenor, and the professional demands are mapped out.

She has worked in Paediatrics before and therefore seen babies die, but this was her first experience of 'the trauma' of delivering a dead baby.

I: Were you there for the delivery?

T: No, I wasn't. I was while she was in labour but I wasn't there when the baby came out because I was busy somewhere else. But I had to examine the baby afterwards, and I mean look at it, and do all the paperwork and everything.

I: And did you talk to 'Mum' afterwards?

T: Um, very briefly, but I think she got main, got the main counselling from the Consultant, and, and the midwife.

During the interview the interviewer can notice and attend to any vague phrases, or gaps in description in order draw out the details. An example is 'busy elsewhere'. What was the nature of this busy-ness, what were the reasons she had to be 'elsewhere'. Is being 'elsewhere' a lapse of professional care? Each step, each reply, has implications, some bureaucratic, others deeply personal, others strangely impersonal, even political in terms of maintaining a professional role.

T: I think there is, there is the problem that as a doctor you have to, um, to kind of keep up some kind of respect and, um, professionality, um, and I think if, if they perceive you as the weeping um . . .

I: The weeping woman?

T: No, not even that, but if they, they, I think that what's awkward is if they lose their, they have to rely on you as well, and they have to kind of be, well, what, what can I say, they, I think there's a balance of, um, express, being honest and open and expressing your, your feelings appropriately, not appropriately, expressing your feelings, and, um, keep on going. It's er, it's so difficult to express. Generally what I can say, is that I haven't felt in this job that I had to keep an artificial professionality or keeping up whatever. Er, I felt I could express, and especially with the midwives, talking, we did, we have talked about how sad it is, and how it feels and everything.

As first analysed in Chapter 2, physiological needs are always mediated by the symbolic Order by which everyday life is organized. In this case, the impact of the death on the subject could only be expressed through the prevailing symbolic structure, that is, the norms, values, routines, personas accepted by the community about. For the individual, there is the sense of managing some Real event (trauma, feelings, anxiety) in relation to an objective field of expectations. Getting in deep like this involves the researcher getting to know the personal, the deeply felt. It can be acutely stressful as Cannon (1989) found in her study of patients dying of breast cancer. Getting in deep has ethical and political implications (see Chapters 8 and 9) that need to be explored.

From the most deeply felt, the researcher oscillates back and forth from coverage at the most global and abstract levels, to depth at the local, or individual level. It requires what has been called a method of progressive–regressive focusing (Sartre 1964), a shift from the close up to the broad view and back again. Each refocusing fills in detail, and identifies structures persisting over time and across context, or that are unique to a given context or set of circumstances. At each return checks can be made for 'coverage', for accuracy, validity and indeed generalizability of categories and emergent theories. There are echoes of this strategy in the grounded theory of Glaser and Strauss (1967; and its more recent accounts by, for example, Strauss and Corbin 1998). However, their approaches seem to me to squeeze out the existential connectedness in a relentless progressive focusing towards the abstract.

Now, to what extent is this progressive–regressive method dialogical in nature? To the extent that it merely records what people say in the manner of what Fontana (1994) called the scientizing approach of classical ethnography, there is no dialogue. So, in the illustration above, to what extent is there dialogue between the doctors and other professionals? There was a sharing of feelings. However, this is not dialogue in the sense I mean it if it is just being able to get feelings into the open as a form of 'relief', gaining emotional support and generating a sense of mutual support. This may be valuable in its own right. However, by dialogue I mean the mutual exploration of difference, the attempt to understand (not necessarily agree with) the viewpoints of the other, and the enrichment of one's own viewpoint and potential for acting differently. To explore this in more detail, I turn now to the question of placing viewpoints into relationship with each other through a process called 'triangulation'.

Triangular cuts

Triangulation evokes the image of map reading. By correlating coordinates on a map one can pinpoint a particular location. Ships can navigate through the apparently simple operation of charting their position in terms of latitude and longitude. Triangulation in qualitative research seems to perform several different kinds of function. One is similar to the navigation metaphor. Here, it seems to me, triangulation acts as a process of coordinating the attention of individuals to produce a 'shared reality', that is an objective field where one subject instructs another subject how to 'see', how to reach, or how to organize their actions in relation to the 'object'. This is a function I contrast with my concept of dialogue as a means to explore difference. Another function of triangulation is to provide a means of cross-checking. For example, the statements of one individual can be cross-checked with those of another individual. Or single individuals can cross-check their perceptions of a given object by varying their perspective on it. A particular object from one standpoint may look solid, but by walking around it, say, it can readily be seen that the object was really two- and not three-dimensional. By touching the object, what seemed to be made of rock by sight alone may turn out to be a clever illusion of paint on canvas. This form of triangulation, then, is a way of mapping the objective field of study from a variety of viewpoints and methods in order to gain information that enables judgements about 'truth', 'validity' and the status of the phenomenon in terms of its 'reality'. The objective field of a given group of individuals is thus essentially intersubjective in nature, that is, constructed by the ways subjects coordinate themselves in relation to each other and the objects they claim to 'see', define as 'real' or as 'illusion'. Coordination here does not necessarily imply that in the intersubjective/ objective field each individual shares common meanings about objects, or sees them in the same way or accords a given object the same status.

Indeed, coordination may be coerced, or brought about through seduction, deceit or, even, mistake.

Triangulation is not a magic solution to the problems of assuring validity, truth, generalization and objectivity. However, it does provide a means of exploring what is at stake for individuals when they try to coordinate actions in relation to a material and symbolic world of others. Through this exploration from a variety of viewpoints, validity, truth, generalization and objectivity become issues to be debated as people search for ways of informing their decision making. Thus, according to Silverman (1993: 156–8), triangulation was developed to overcome a number of recognized difficulties in fieldwork such as not being aware of what events had occurred before entering the scene, being misled by informants, overlooking the effect of the researcher's presence in situations, and the socialization of the researcher into the social group to such an extent that they become blind to the tacit understandings underlying the processes they are involved in. For example, by using multiple sources of data collection (documentary analysis, interviewing, direct participation, observation, reflection), it is argued that comparisons and contrasts between these can indicate the generalizability of accounts and theories. Thus statements can be made like, 'This account or theory is "true" of this group, under this context, but not that group or that context', or 'This theory is accurate for all these groups under all these contexts'.

By focusing on the tension between subject positions and how individuals and groups seek to coordinate their own attention and that of others, triangulation can be made more sophisticated through the analysis of intentional networks (Schostak 1985). Drawing on the phenomenological approach to intentionality (see Chapter 2), intentional networks are constructed according to the ways subjects (whether embodied, textual or virtual) are oriented towards each other and the objects of their 'gaze'. A complex multi-dimensioned and multi-contextual intentional network comprises a 'world for all practical purposes' to its members. As a simplistic example, I may interview Bill who may speak lovingly of Ann and hatefully of Tim. Thus I may seek to interview Ann and Tim who may or may not speak of Bill but may speak of others. And so the process grows. The exponential growth of this process can be imagined. Where should one start in order to explore intentional networks? From one point of view, where one starts and where one ends is arbitrary. This is because there is neither beginning, end, nor centre to an intentional network, hence there is no 'right' or 'wrong' place to begin. As always, where one begins is from one's own agendas, interests, motivations and physical location in a given setting. However, what is not arbitrary are the kinds of intentional structures erected to control relationships, actions and the access to, use of, and deployment of objects. The outcome of an exploration and analysis of intentional networks will always be incomplete but there is something like a map emerging of the relation between the glimpsed parts and their wholes. This process is a kind of aligning of the different perspectives that members of an intentional network may adopt one towards another and the objects of their world. By cross-referring viewpoints over time, some bearings in these complex worlds can be achieved, particularly when an intentional network is populated by the multiple possible selves an individual may project across different contexts, over time with different people, through dreams, fantasy, fiction and so on. As such the method of generating intentional networks is consistent with triangulation.

Where Silverman (1993) criticizes triangulation is in employing multiple theories and methods as a way of overcoming partial views. Method triangulation (Denzin 1970) is a form of eclecticism that hopes to overcome the limitations of one theory by 'adding' another. For example, many contend that quantitative and qualitative methods can complement each other and build the bigger picture, forgetting or letting slide the embarrassment of the contradictions raised by the adoption of essentially incompatible assumptions. Many qualitative researchers still appear to bow to the greater power of statistical approaches to define 'real science' in the popular as well as the political mind. The partial, context-bound, case-like studies of the qualitative researcher fail to generalize, they say. What is meant by generalization here? In the quantitative sciences it refers to the statistical procedures that must be followed if the findings drawn from the study of a relatively small number of individuals (whether living creatures or inanimate objects and substances) can be said to be 'true' of the whole class of individuals from which they were drawn. Qualitative research by its very nature cannot conform to statistical requirements, thus the findings of such research, it is argued, is not generalizable. However, it may be recognized that qualitative research 'adds' something to statistical research. This 'something' may be the meanings, the feelings, the sense of the lived that cannot be measured and thus drawn into statistical manipulations. Often this 'something' is characterized as 'depth' in contrast to the 'breadth' or the 'coverage' that a quantitative project design supposedly delivers. Thus why not employ quantitative approaches for generalizability across contexts and qualitative approaches to provide the illustrative depth? Why not indeed? Because of the incompatibility of assumptions about how to represent, what to represent and why to represent. Where the statisticians require purification, the qualitative researchers see the raw, the ill-fitting, and refuse to compromise. Where the one sees identity, homogeneity, or likeness, the other sees difference. Where the one works in the medium of the measurable, the univocal, the static, the stable, the other works in the medium of the symbolic, the plurivocal, the fluid, the dynamic. A million still pictures of incremental changes flashed in sequence before the eyes may present the illusion of movement but the experienced flux and meaning of life has still to be captured. If the purpose of research is to understand, explain, express, represent something of the lived then its methods must be open to the full range of ways in which life is lived and expressed.

Generalization cannot be restricted to a single authorized method. There are many different approaches to generalization that research can explore, debate and employ in order to inform judgement, beliefs, opinions, and knowledge. For example, there are processes of generalization in logic and mathematics that are not as such experimental but rather create the conditions for generalization to take place through the adopting of a set of assumptions and conventions as in a game. The rules and conventions of one game of chess are identical for all games of chess, even though each particular game may differ. Thus the overriding structures and conditions that govern play can be described in general terms without having to study individual games. The study of individual games can aid in the exploration of the general consequences of particular strategies. Whenever a particular strategy is adopted then this limits the choices the other player may make in response. The development of strategies and counter-strategies is highly creative but takes place within a system of rules and a framework that is defined by convention (e.g. the board, rules and the initial arrangement of chess pieces). If I make a particular move, I do not necessarily need empirical confirmation as to whether it is 'right' or 'wrong'. The logic of the situation will determine that. A poor player is one who does not sufficiently explore the logic of the situation. That logic is 'general' to the whole framework of action. One does not do a sample of the squares and the pieces on the board in order to study the 'behaviour' of chess pieces; rather one studies the logic of the whole. Games, of course, can be said to be restricted forms of social behaviour. Nevertheless the game metaphor has been studied and applied in politics, economics and a host of other everyday situations such as Berne's *Games People Play* ([1968] 1975).

Rather than games being voluntary, their general 'acceptance' may take place through coercion where by military power a dictator can force millions of people to be moved like chess pieces. The general structures of society established by the dictator through force then frame individual actions. More subtly, the social conventions, laws and insecurities of most individuals in a market-driven society also create the conditions by which individual actions are framed. The logic of such situations is not, however, simply given like the rules of chess. Rather, their logical structures have to be discerned through a study of informal and tacitly held cultural conventions, habitual ways of doing things as well as the more formal frameworks of laws and cultural and religious traditions and belief systems.

Generalization, in a sense, is constructed by, and flows across, an intentional network. Through its multiplicities of viewpoints comparisons and contrasts can be made. What is the 'same for me' and the 'different for me' are identified, so generating the boundaries setting one group off from another as well as establishing the continuities. The emergent categories, boundaries and continuities are thus intersubjectively validated across the network. Since the network is always incompletely known to a given individual, it is imagined as a part of a whole (Anderson 1983). The structural relationships to the whole are experienced by members in the network in ways that are non-arbitrary (that is, that resist any whim, wish or fantasy that they should be otherwise). This approach is based on what Husserl called eidetic variation, that is, the variation of something in imagination until the invariant structures, properties, elements, dimensions of the 'something' are revealed. Take, for example, a triangle. It can have equal sides, or one side longer than another, or two sides longer than another. However, what happens if one of the sides becomes a curve? It will no longer be a triangle but a segment of a circle. Or what happens if a fourth side is added? Again, it will no longer be a triangle but will become something else, a rectangle of some kind. In short, in order to remain the object 'triangle' there are limits to the variation that can be performed without it losing what is essential (that is, invariant in all possible variations on the theme of 'triangle'). What is happening here? I, as conscious subject, am directing my attention towards something, the concept of triangle. At each variation a new facet or meaning content of the triangle is observed whether in imagination or in reality through perception of triangular objects. This process of systematic variation reveals both the limits to change and also the extent to which the object or entity can generalize across circumstances and contexts.

While Husserl hoped to determine the essences (the invariant features or structures) of objects in ways that universalized them, social forms are not open to such universalization. However, Schutz (1976) employed the weaker yet more appropriate concept of typification, where one thing is regarded by a social actor as 'the same as' another thing. The task of the researcher for Schutz was to draw upon these typifications to generate sociological types. Exploring the views of members of an intentional network thus identifies what they regard as the same and what is different. Generalization is thus a social construct of given groups. Qualitative analysis of these 'types' are therefore the 'second order' products of generalization drawing on the 'first order' accounts of social life by actors. Hargreaves *et al.* (1975), drawing on Schutz and Mead, employed this approach in their study of deviance in the classroom. Through interviews and observations, they explored the

names or categories – or constructs, or labels, or types – with which
we make sense of others. The names are evaluative, and they direct
our action. We avoid 'obnoxious' people just as we avoid 'poison-
ous' fruits. To type other people – to name them, categorise them,
label them – is an inherent part of understanding them. In itself, it
is not something one should or could dispense with.

(Hargreaves *et al.* 1975)

The type emerges as the underlying structure that patterns intentional
networks, creating the basis for generalization. It is a work of the symbolic processing of everyday life, rendering life recognizable, relatively
predictable, ordered, accountable through language and other forms of
symbolic expression. Generalization is produced by the way in which we
agree to use language in order to map our world, coordinate our behaviour towards each other and to the objects of the world and to account
for our actions to each other within it. Qualitative generalization therefore does not depend upon reducing the elements of the world to single
instances that can be measured and manipulated and subjected to the
sampling procedures of the quantitative sciences. Rather, qualitative research focuses on the logic of situations, and the ways in which something is constructed as an object in relation to other objects and to
subjects through the webs of language (see Chapter 7). Qualitative
research studies the social construction of objectivity, of subjectivity, of
relationship, of generalizability, of universalizability, of sense and non-
sense as practical accomplishments throughout a range of contexts. Generalization, thus, as some attribute independent of human action and
intention, is a chimera and the politics of generalization will be later
raised as an issue in Chapters 8 and 9.

Generalization, or typification, is the product of identifying 'samenesses'
over time. It is in that sense also dependent on memory, or recording in
some way. A given instance that is recognized to be the same as others
is recognized through comparisons in memory. Its meaning as 'an instance that is the same as all those others in this category' has the
structure of the future past; the instance is what it *will have become* under
the process of generalization. Happening once is nothing. Happening
several times begins to set up a pattern in the mind of the interpreter:
every time Bill comes to visit, it rains! From one point of view this, of
course, is a mere correlation, a juxtaposition of events that have only an
accidental relationship to each other. Bill does not 'cause' the rain. However, in the mind of the interpreter this 'everytime-ness' builds a sense
of generalization, even of cause in some cultures where the role of 'rain
maker' is valued. Although there may be no sense of cause–effect, there
may be the sense of a sign rather like red sky at night signifying the
likelihood of fine weather the following day. The redness does not 'cause'

the fine weather. However, through such a process 'misconceptions' can become 'facts' from which can be built 'laws' that 'explain' how particular events in the world are produced.

Consider the beliefs widely held in the Western world during the Middle Ages of the Earth being flat, or of the Earth being the centre of the universe. At the time there was 'good' evidence to support these beliefs. This evidence was drawn from a variety of philosophical and religious sources and the apparent evidence of the senses: from the ordinary field of vision the world about apart from local hills, valleys, mountains, looks essentially flat, the sun rises and sets and thus circulates the earth, as do the stars. How then does one break through particular ways of seeing that seem so self-evident? Scientific method offered its answer. Its evident success and power in the remodelling of our views of ourselves, reformulating our place in the physical universe and, indeed, reshaping the material world itself, provides just as powerful a lock on our perceptions, judgement, thinking as did the traditional and religious perspectives of the pre-scientific eras. These scientific views have come under critical scrutiny from a variety of perspectives. Through dialogue the implications of alternative world views can be explored, not necessarily to leave one particular view triumphant and all others crushed, but to enhance the process of creative productivity leading to new possibilities for thinking, doing, living together.

What is it that connects one sign to another? Or a particular sign to its object? Is it the sense of a regularity, a law-like behaviour, or the existence of a command that compels a particular relationship? Semiotics, as the study of signs, provides an approach to exploring such relationships in everyday life and will be discussed in more detail in Chapter 5. At this point, it can be said that generalization can be constructed in many different ways depending on the system of beliefs, conduct and ways of 'knowing' of a given individual or group. Thus, generalization is whatever it is *made to be*. It is the 'thou shalt' of a given social and practical order that provides the framework for the 'seeing', the 'emergence', the 'production' of generalizable relationships. In the quantitative sciences (that is, the systematic use of mathematical and statistical theory to produce forms of 'knowing') it is the 'thou shalt' of homogeneity, the control of variables, randomization, sampling procedures and the application of abstract formulae to the purified categories of the recipe or of the ritual performance of the laboratory. In the qualitative sciences (that is, the systematic analysis of meaning structures and processes to produce forms of 'knowing') it is the 'thou shalt' of the symbolic order through which the flux of possible meanings are fixed (whether through coercion, negotiation, convention, play or, indeed, accident) for all practical (and personal) purposes in intersubjective exchanges. Is it possible, however, to conceive of a social state that accepts no 'thou shalt', no sense of 'this causes that'? Lacan (1993), for example, has discussed psychosis in terms of an inability of the individual concerned to 'fix' signs with particular content (or, more specifically, signifiers with particular signifieds – see Chapter 5). Jameson (1984), drawing on Lacan's analysis, has described his views of contemporary changes in society in terms of a schizophrenic breakdown in the relationship between the marks that are supposed to carry particular image or meaning content and that content. This issue will be taken up in Chapter 5 where generalization, cause and effect and objectivity come under attack from writers who have come to be known as 'postmodernist'. In the sense that the qualitative sciences explore meaning and the structures and processes that convey meaning or, indeed, meaninglessness, they have a precedence over the quantitative sciences since the latter must be mediated by (not contained within) the meaning structures that only the qualitative sciences are able to address.

Circular cuts

Intentional networks have been explored in terms of the triangular cuts they support: that is cross-matching multiple viewpoints to see what is the same and what is different within context, across context and over time. However, as already hinted, intentional networks also support a circular strategy that moves from part to whole and back to part again in a cyclic motion – often called a hermeneutic circle. Take the following passage:

> . . . and antenatal clinic was like there were anywhere between four and six people around to see all these women, so, um, if there was a really complicated case you just didn't take it anyway. If it was a case that was interesting you might have taken the case and had a quick chat with the woman and see what it's about, and then discuss it with the Registrar or with the Consultant. So this was actually really quite good. Um, you could choose just seeing somebody who was routine for whatever reason just being there because being very young or a little bit older, but no problems in the sense of a real problem and so by seeing them more often, feeling the tummies, you got an idea of what is normal and what not. So, by doing things, yes, you got experience of. So it progressed and probably, patients you at the beginning you would just briefly talk about, 'These and these findings, to me it looks normal. Is that alright? Can I send her off or shall I organise that?' By the end of the six months you didn't discuss these cases, you did your writing, signed it, and the patient was sent off without being seen by somebody else, or

the case even discussed. Um, so, in that sense, it made, we made progress. Yeah, first, even so-called backwards looking where normal things you discussed, and in the end you knew what was normal, what was expected, and you could send these patients off without anybody asking you any more, 'Are you sure what you are doing there?' It was expected that you knew what you were doing and that was quite alright.

(Schostak and Schostak 2000)

In order for the places, events, roles and interactions described in this passage to exist there have to be structures and processes that are 'greater than' the parts mentioned. So, what is the whole of which this fragment is a part? Many whole–part possibilities occur to the mind. Here are a few:

Whole	Part
Hospital	Particular clinic
General/typical case	Instance of complicated case
Learning process	Instances of learning
Decision process	Instances of decision making

This initial simplified analysis already maps out areas for further data collection in order to be able to describe how the parts relate to the postulated features, elements, dimensions of the whole. How do these parts and wholes relate to each other? How do these parts articulate the whole, and how does the whole make the parts possible? In Figure 3.3, the central axis may construct a downward sense of hierarchy, or a two-way flow of decision making as between the various roles. From each role perspective fans out to encompass the hospital, the ward or particular people like me. Each swirl of the spiral thus describes a 'level', an 'horizon' whose closure and completeness are more imagined than Real.

That tradition in qualitative methodology called hermeneutics is typically imagined as a spiral that moves between individual, say a consultant, and the greater whole of which he or she is a part, the hospital. Consultant, registrar, midwife and junior doctor form an intentional network that spirals through several contextual levels. Only by interviewing and observation can the complex intentional relations between each individual and each level be mapped through which their 'worlds', their experiences, are constructed.

Broadly, hermeneutics refers to an approach towards interpreting the 'meanings' of texts. There are, according to Howard (1982), two directions to go: the Anglo-Saxon or the continental route. First, the Anglo-Saxon:

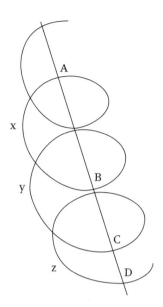

A = consultant   x = hospital
B = registrar   y = ward
C = midwife   z = these patients
D = junior doctor

Figure 3.3   Hermeneutic spiral

... one begins with the acceptance of some bit or expression of knowledge or of some mental attitude as a given for discussion. With this in place as an accepted focus in a universe of discourse one tries to expose the conceptual map that permeates this universe, hoping to reveal the otherwise hidden logical lines of force. This type of analysis may reveal the need for a revision of our naive understanding of the logical network. It may suggest a sub-area where a special kind of logic needs to be developed.

(Howard 1982: 37)

Any transcript will provide the basis for drawing out the logical relationships between members of an intentional network, an organization, a social order. The logical arrangements between key categories, social practices, cultural codes and resources can be mapped and the subject located in the multiple fields of play. In order to make the analyses more detailed and sophisticated than allowed for by the one extract one generates a plan by which to 'cover' the range of sites, categories of individual and sources of information concerning the organization, social order and so on implicit in the increasingly detailed map of logical relationships that emerges as interviews, observations and documentary analyses are undertaken (see Chapter 1). Indeed, individuals in a given social circumstance (classroom, hospital ward), like the hermeneutist, have to 'read' their circumstances, and analyse the conceptual maps and cultural practices employed by others when they engage in social interaction.

Alternatively, I can adopt another tradition within hermeneutics. The inclination of continental philosophy, writes Howard, 'is to raise about some isolated bit of knowledge or mental attitude a genetic question: not "What is the logical pattern of the given?" but "How did this given come about?" or "What are the conditions necessary for its appearance?"' The move is from 'what happens' to 'why does it happen?' This latter question opens questions of causality, the search for the generating conditions of, in particular, the impact of ideas on practice. What then are the conditions under which the mental attitude of the trainee doctor came to be that she could distinguish what was normal from what was not normal? Or, more widely, what are the conditions under which the concept and associated cultural practices of the hospital could come about? To do this, I need to explore the conditions of knowing, behaving towards others, making accounts of situations. My directions are likely to appear more philosophical, more historical, more political, more global. I will want to explore the connections of the ideas of the individual and the group with the ideas in circulation from context to context, from place to place, from historical time to historical time. For example, how is it possible that this particular trainee could undertake the actions she did in this particular hospital and make the particular accounts that she did were it not for the whole edifice of medical education, the health service, the political battles undertaken by generations concerning the nature of the 'good society' and the appropriate way to allocate resources to individuals and groups? And what about the nature of being human, the essential condition faced by all in its existential or psychological 'reality'? How I understand this will be to generate an account that the individual may not have explored yet which will embed the individual in a wider, more complex agglomeration of narratives. The task of generating such an account can either seem daunting and perhaps dispiriting, or seductive and exhilarating. For the poet it may be true that the universe can be seen in a grain of sand; the researcher may indeed draw upon all the arts of the writer at his or her disposal but, no matter how experienced the researcher, the project has to be shaped, boundaries drawn, and the research made manageable. How can this be achieved? My suggestion is:

1 reflect on the original objects, aims and search questions of the project. Have these changed due to ideas read, data collected? Or have they become 'lost', 'confused'? If so, reshape (or get back on course in

relation to) the original objectives, questions, aims. Concentrate data collection efforts on the original, or modified aims etc.

2 keep close to the data and seek those sources of data that most clearly express or challenge emergent ideas, theories, interpretations, analyses relevant to your research objectives, aims, questions etc.

By framing the project in terms of the multiple narratives that shed light on your project aims, questions and objectives, the objective field of subjects in terms of the stories they tell can be mapped. The methodological importance of narrative can be judged in such writers as Danto (1985) who underpins his understanding of all knowledge, whether it occurs in the scientific laboratory or at large in society, as fundamentally narrative. For him:

> To ask for the significance of an event, in the *historical* sense of the term, is to ask a question which can be answered only in the context of a *story*. The identical event will have a different significance in accordance with the story in which it is located or, in other words, in accordance with what different sets of *later* events it may be connected. Stories constitute the natural context in which events acquire historical significance . . .
>
> (Danto 1985: 11)

Now, returning to the data extract, how may the terms 'hospital' and 'clinic' be interpreted in relation to the notion of story or history? It may be unfamiliar to think of a hospital as an event. It looks fixed, given; a place may be where events take place but not an event itself. However, it is an event in the sense that it is the product of many historical actions. The hospital as event is the taking place, or articulation in concrete terms of a vast complex conceptual map (that may or may not be consistent within itself) through which activities are ordered, materials arranged, tools manipulated and armies of people managed. The intentional network, thus, can be conceived of and explored as a framework of stories that interact as histories, biographies, or as fragments of what might have been, wishful dreams that may tragically colour a life and that are daily staged in the material and symbolic architectures that frame them. This intentional network frames the potential for dialogue. Exploring it can show what is at stake for given individuals, groups, institutions, and systems in opening up to dialogue.

How then does one begin this process? It involves:

1 Locating and mapping the key 'subject positions' that can be inhabited by individuals in relation to the positions of otherness that they recognize (you, she, he, it, they, them and so on) and the Other seen as God, Them, Tradition, Law and so on. These can be explored through

the everyday conversations or interview-based accounts, anecdotes, and stories of people.

2 Mapping the intentional networks from the points of view of people who inhabit a particular range of subject positions as evoked through the accounts they provide.

3 That is, formulating what appears to be individuals and groups who share common beliefs, values and ways of conducting themselves and those who appear to differ.

4 Getting in 'deeper' by creating the conditions for a dialogue between individuals about how they differently see and experience their lives and the world about.

This list is not complete, nor is it meant to be. Its elements will be returned to, explored, added to and developed as the book proceeds. Making a beginning always involves a risk, being a 'novice', otherwise how could anything 'new' be discovered? The objective field of the project is progressively delimited, shaped and elucidated by the responses of the people being studied. Thus the first task is to gather accounts through interview and observation of people in action. Through their accounts they describe the members of their world, how each relates to the other and what events tend to bring them together or set them apart. By exploring these accounts researchers can make their own judgements as to what interests them, what is relevant to the original statement of their 'project', what challenges that original statement, and how the project may need to change in order to take advantage of changing interests, or novel circumstances and opportunities. Thus, as researchers engage in a dialogue with the world views of others, their own perspectives and insights change and develop. This dialogue may be internal to the researcher or it may be made available to the people being studied through, for example, conversation or writing. It is through such a process that the researcher can break through the taken-for-granted or authoritative ways of seeing that limit the development of alternatives (see, in particular, Chapters 8, 9 and 10).

Behind the triangle, beyond the horizon

In the discourse of Lacan there is always a third involved in any conversation between two people. Between mother and child there is the Name of the Father. How is this statement to be read? Each is but a position in a triangular relationship. It does not matter which real individual, male or female, actually takes up a given position. The Name of the Father is the authority of the Code, the Law, the Thou Shalt, the taken-for-granted pragmatic and typically tacit social rules through which the predictability and order of social life is maintained. Triangulation as a methodological concept thus takes on another more interesting reading. It is not hard to hear the half sounded 'strangulation' that is implicit in the triangulation of views to generate a 'sameness', an intersubjective consensus concerning the validity, generalizability, lack of bias (or objectivity) of something thus triangulated and bound to a context, a situated practice. How does one get out? Is there a way to get at the back of the triangling of views, to find a fourth? A fifth? An Other?

This play of words points away from the easy closure that may be found in the triangulating embrace. What is not covered up? What escapes the 'thou shalt'? It is an attempt to move beyond the given. But how does one see, think, act, feel *otherwise*? There is, of course, no *one* way of doing this. It is an activity that will keep many more generations of social scientists in happy disputation with each other all their lives. As researchers who want to explore, write and influence their contemporaries we engage therefore in a play of reflections on what we do, and propose interpretations. To engage in this play it is necessary to map out the terrain of debate: Who says what and for what reason? This mapping of the terrain of debate is a way of building up a personalized set of analytic tools that are always in the process of being both constructed and deconstructed. Perhaps at this point we can return to the question of method triangulation, not to endorse it but to reinterpret it. By setting methodologies, philosophies, theories in *debate* with each other it is not to cover or complete a given picture or bit of 'reality' but to understand how our own reasons, purposes, interests, experiences were formed. More importantly, we may discover new ways of being and acting.

4

Handling complexity and uncertainty

Getting close to others means grappling with the complexity of their lives as individuals, as members of groups, as participants in the cultures and social and material structures that frame their lives. It means becoming accustomed to never being able to know all, never being certain about the status of interpretations, 'findings', 'knowledge'. Science, of course, was born through the desire to know and, in particular, to know with certainty. Hence, Descartes wanted to discover the point of certainty upon which to build, just as Kant wanted to discover the limits of reason to determine what can be known and that which should be left outside the range of reason. If Reality is Rational in structure, then reason can cover it like a virtual glove where each point on the glove corresponds exactly to each point in Reality. However, Reality, in the sense I want to use it here, is the object of all thought but cannot be plumbed by thought. It is in this sense Kant's noumenon, the something that cannot be known in-itself. Picking up a rock one can say 'I know what it is.' Really, one only knows how it *appears* to consciousness – its surface appearance. What it is in-itself, its Being, its 'insideness', one can never know. Break it in half, one does not get closer to its insides, its essence-in-itself. What is revealed is only another surface. To talk about atoms is only to talk about a particular way of symbolically representing and theorizing the basic structure of the rock as it appears to consciousness in relation to the chosen framework of reasoning about it. It is not the same as *knowing* its Being, its Reality. The Being of Reality can be criss-crossed with symbolic representations – like a virtual glove – without ever affecting what it is in itself.

Recall the example of the gestalt figure, imaginable as either a duck or a rabbit. Neither way of talking about this image says what it is in-itself. Even to point out and label it as an ambiguous figure only provides another way of talking about it rather than establishing its being. Being cannot be fitted into any category. Representation and the Being of Reality are two distinct orders that never cross from the one into the other; figuratively, the virtual glove never actually becomes the Reality to which it seems to correspond. Similarly, one does not live theoretically, but existentially. By existentially, I mean the sense of being in a situation that another cannot occupy, that is, no one can live for me, no one can enter into my being and experience all that I am experiencing. No theory can capture all that I experience and all that I am. To adopt a way of living that is guided by a theory will inevitably 'leave something out' in terms of my feelings, desires, interests, needs. Furthermore, codes of conduct established by civil laws, traditions of religious commandments, the definitions of what it means to be a 'good person', or 'normal person', place a boundary between my being as a living, thinking, desiring creature and how I ought be or must be according to a given social set of expectations.

Representation replaces the Real by something manageable, and makes of it an object of conversation. The categories through which representations are framed are metaphorically a way of cutting up Being, chopping off the bits that do not fit by creating boundaries. Words creates meaning by marking out boundaries. Take, for example, the words 'flesh' and 'body'. Flesh is differentiated from bone but provides no picture of any particular part of a body. By naming, the power to indicate, focus attention, cut an object out from the confusion of the Real and manipulate it is enhanced. Every such 'cut' or boundary has an impact on the subjective experience of an individual from birth to death. Yet, it is the very processes that cut, that eliminate or reject aspects of the Real that do not 'fit in' to the symbolic frameworks of social life, that 'connect' and indeed enrich and facilitate the development of individuals and their cultural and social relations with others. How then does one handle this incredible complexity and uncertainty that seems inextricably melded with the nature of being an individual within the multiple possible and actual 'worlds' of everyday life? One solution has been to ignore it. The principal rule adopted by many is to simplify in order to control. Thus, for example, by concentrating only on what can be seen and measured all the messy feelings, emotions and 'insideness' of human life can be eliminated from the equations, the models, the procedures by which to explain and control individual and social life. The consequences of adopting such simplifying procedures have often been tragic in personal and social terms. However, if one cannot simplify without engendering tragic consequences and one cannot create theories that cover everything, how then can complexity and uncertainty be handled? It seems like an impasse. Rather than *the* approach, perhaps there are many approaches, each limited and thus provisional, each needing to be set into debate in order to explore differences and consequences. If differences are accepted, then theories do not become frozen but are more like shifting, multi-layered patterns blowing across the transitory 'surfaces' created when people negotiate, contest, reject or agree about what is 'real', 'good', 'sane', 'desired' and what is to be rejected, ignored, or eliminated. For the researcher, the resulting complexity and uncertainty is not to be feared and shunned but is the lure, the field of research that never ceases to amaze. It demands not the recipes of scientistic approaches but an openness to creative exploration.

To grasp what is at stake, Figure 3.4 represents a progressive 'loss' or reduction towards simplicity and mathematical exactitude. Reality is designated by 'X'. The only way of thinking about 'X' is as a complex, dynamic 'something' that is initially undifferentiated by human perception and intelligence. It stands outside language as the Other to language. How can this 'something', this 'X', this Other be mapped, described, represented so individuals can find their way about in relation to it, anticipate events, order their experiences of it, and make sense of their lives?

Myths and religions have provided a multiplicity of ways of pinning down the nature and purpose of 'X'. Powerful categories such as 'nature', 'divine', 'good', 'evil' and so on form the underlying categories ordering this 'X' into something knowable, and workable. All such categories have throughout time been contested. That is, there are no fixed boundaries parcelling up the 'Real' into nice packages and boxes, except for the conceptual boundaries, 'packages' and 'boxes' made by people who continually contest their 'truth'. The 'real' does not force its categories upon us. Rather, we make categories as a way of handling the 'Real'.

In Figure 4.1 the categories x1, x2, x3, x4 are 'placed' on the Real. One could call this the light of reason at work: like a floodlight projected out into the night 'capturing' a passing cloud or a plane in a circle of light. Such concepts help us to see entities that are distinct from other entities. Our perceptions are thus composed by sensation and concept. The one cannot do its work without the other. Our perceptual grasp of 'X' (through the perceptual acts of x1, x2, x3, x4, x5) is thus reduced to 'A', the perceptual grasp (or gestalt, or 'whole') that results from the individual acts of perceiving X. It must be emphasized that 'A' does not equal 'X' but that 'A' is the way in which 'X' is perceived within a given social community. Some of the entities captured perceptually at 'A' can perhaps be adequately described through language, say x2, x3 and x4 (whereas the other escapes linguistic capture, there being no word for them). Thus 'B' does not equal 'A'. How we talk about our perceptions ('A'), although richly complex in itself, can never be a full substitute for the perceptions themselves.[5] Moreover, of the ways in which we can talk about our perceptions perhaps only one, x3, is measurable. Thus, 'C' provides a very restricted way of describing or mapping 'X'. At each

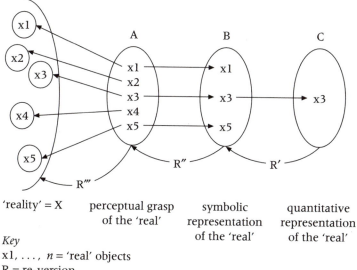

'reality' = X   perceptual grasp   symbolic   quantitative
                of the 'real'   representation   representation

Key   of the 'real'   of the 'real'

x1, . . . , *n* = 'real' objects
R = re-version
A = 'perceptual grasp' of 'X'
B = symbolic representation of 'A'
C = quantitative representation drawn from 'B'

Figure 4.1   Reduction of the real

stage a reduction is taking place. The statistical reduction, in this analysis, is the most severe of all. In what way then can x3 be said to be a
representation of X? Does x3 in some way stand for x1 to x5? Is there
a part–whole, or metonymic, relationship between them? What kind of
operation is it when C maps back onto B, and B onto A and then to X?
The projection back, as if it were a faithful mapping of the X, of B or of
A, is a re-versioning of the symbolic, the perceptual and the real in
mathematical terms.

The model, albeit crude, provides a way of thinking through a number
of methodological issues. It may reasonably be asked:

1 Is representation at 'C' adequate to map 'X'?
2 Is information provided at 'C' appropriate to inform action, since action takes place not at 'C' but in the material real world of 'X'?
3 Is it better to employ a richer symbolic representation even at the cost
of not being able to reduce all to quantitative measures?
4 Is the symbolic framework for representation that emerges a path
towards the X or a distortion (a re-versioning for, say, ulterior purposes) of it which turns attention away from it?
5 Do symbolic forms of representation reveal, replace or construct reality?

Such questions can be extended indefinitely. If we know reality only through the interpretational categories projected upon it, then researchers like Morgan's (1986) accountants who he calls 'reality constructors'

can shape the reality of an organisation by persuading others that the interpretive lens provided by the dollar should be given priority in determining the way that organisation is to be run. This, of course, is not to say that financial considerations are unimportant. The point is that thinking about organisation in financial terms is but one way of thinking about organisation. There are always others, and these are usually forced into the background as financial considerations gain a major hold on the definition of organisational reality.

Similarly, it is important to deconstruct the researcher's 'interpretational lens' through which realities are 'shaped' or 'represented'.

Purification

Constructing categories is critical to the formation of an 'interpretational lens'. The simplest categories, if they can be called that, are those that are either 'conventional' in nature or tautologous, that is simply taken to be what they are by definition – x is defined as a letter of the alphabet because it is defined as a letter of the alphabet. Other kinds of categories can be non-problematically created because each of their members are 'pure', that is, each member is a member only because they share identical characteristics. Every phial of sulphuric acid is the same as every other phial because the sulphuric acid has been purified. This, however, is not the case for human beings. No one human being is an exact replica of another in all their looks, thoughts, deeds, social circumstances and personal history. Yet, it is still possible to say John is like Bill. The difference is between categories that are composed of homogeneous members and those that are relatively heterogeneous yet share enough qualities in common to be placed into the same category for certain purposes. Thus the implication, as Cohen (1944: 134–5) pointed out, is that

In the end, the truth of a generalisation from a sample depends on the homogeneity of the group with respect to which we wish to generalise. A single experiment on a new substance, to test whether it is acid or alkaline, is much more convincing than the result of a questionnaire addressed to millions of army men to measure their intelligence. For the latter is not a simple quality of a uniformly repeatable pattern. In this respect the methods of social statistics are gross compared with refined analysis, so that when our analysis is thoroughgoing, as it generally is in physics, one or two samples are as good as a million. If what we are measuring is really homogeneous, one is sufficient. In the social field, therefore, statistics cannot take the place of analysis . . .

In this relatively early statement of the problem from the point of view of the philosophy of logic the issue is already clearly posed that the elements or 'units' of social analysis are not as readily amenable to the logic appropriate to statistical analysis as are the data of physics. In the exact sciences (essentially those that are mathematical, or amenable to mathematics such as physics, computing, engineering) it may be possible to generate data that can be placed into categories where each member is identical to each other member:

A	B	C	D
aaaa	bbbb	cccc	dddd
aaaa	bbbb	cccc	dddd
aaaa	bbbb	cccc	dddd

However, it is not sensible to translate the power of the methods of the exact sciences into those of the social sciences. Translating the scientific methods of purification literally into the social and political realms has had tragic consequences throughout the twentieth century. Scientific discourse, inappropriately placed within political contexts, has produced world visions that privilege racial purity and genetic superiority. If science ignores politics, ethics and human purposes, it becomes inhuman, terrifying. This is why there must be a primacy of analysis over calculation and manipulation in order to ensure science is always open to critical reflection and dialogue from multiple perspectives and interests.

Judgement and the creation of boundaries

As Schutz (1976) pointed out, atoms do not make decisions or judgements about how or whether to act or not. People, however, create their own laws, risk their lives, and lie. Social facts are not stable in the sense of being capable of being rendered a 'pure' or refined substance like sulphuric acid. Rather than relations of identity (involving a one-to-one matching of features) there are relations of similarity (where a judgement call is made as to whether one member is sufficiently like another to be placed in the same class) and relations based on difference. Essential to the creation of boundaries between 'sameness' and 'difference' is judgement.

Judgement is framed by desire, wish, fantasy. These are culturally organized in terms of ethical, religious, political, economic and aesthetic values.

The concept of polythetic classification for which Needham (1983) drew upon the results of studies not only in his own field of anthropology but also in the areas of botany and zoology seem to approximate the requirements for the study of social forms. Polythetic classification recognizes that not all members of a class have identical features in common with all other members of a class. Rather than a relation of identity what is called on here is a relation of 'similarity' in situations not of certainty but uncertainty. The lines of argument depend upon reasoning framed not by deductive means where truth is guaranteed by the operations of logic but by plausibility where trust is to be earned, not taken for granted.

A polythetic classification or taxonomy has the following form:

1	*2*	*3*	*4*
abcd	efgh	ijkl	mnop
bcde	fghi	jklm	nopq
cdef	ghij	klmn	opqr
defg	hijk	lmno	pqrs

All members of category 1 share at least three qualities in common with at least one other member of the category. However, abcd has only one letter in common with defg. Should they therefore be considered to be sufficiently different to be in different categories? If this is the case, this will lead to problems about placing cdef. Is cdef more like defg than, say, abcd? If that is true, then the problem moves to bcde – should that go to the new category or remain with abcd? There is no real hard and fast solution. It depends on the purpose of the categorization; that is, on the particular intentions of a given person or group and the plausibility of the rationale.

As an example, nurses in the UK are increasingly being asked to take specialized roles. Some specialize in working with children or the elderly, some learn to work in the high-technology environments of intensive care and others are drawn to mental health care or learning disabilities and so on. Are they all the 'same' when placed into the category 'nurse'? Clearly there are real differences between the distinct nursing specialisms. Perhaps it can be argued, as many nurses do, that there is an essential core of values, principles, beliefs, philosophy that is common to the nursing professional no matter the differences in terms of specialist branch of nursing. However, in interviewing nurses considerable variation can be found in what they consider to be essential to nursing. These differences influence their views as to how nurses should be trained, what the core components of that training should be, and how their performance should be assessed. Increasingly also, nurses are taking on the specialized treatments previously the province of the doctor. Where then are the boundaries between nursing and medical care? When do nurses who progressively take on specialist medical functions become neither nurse nor doctor but 'something else'?

The fluidity and fuzziness of boundaries increases the potential to manipulate them for ulterior purposes as, for example, in advertising cigarettes. In the 1950s smoking could be described as cool, fresh tasting, relaxing and be associated with athletic, outdoor activities stressing a healthy lifestyle. The associations are continued through tobacco sponsorship of major sporting events. Through such associations attention can be deflected from physical health dangers to the desired state of the smoker being associated with sporty, or smart, or sophisticated images. However, in effect this 'desired state' does not exist 'out there in the world of everyday relationships' until it is 'copied' by those who buy cigarettes in order to project the desired image and thus create two distinct groups: those who project the desired image, and those who do not. In this sense, there is no 'original' that is being copied, rather, there are only copies: the advert which represents itself as a copy of a particular desired state; and the individuals that 'copy' and so make 'real' the desired image. The advertising image thus projects the possibility of a real thing, the desired state of being, but the 'real thing' comes into being only if people copy the advertising image. Is the world that results, counterfeit? Or, is it a world beyond the counterfeit in that the original had never existed? In the first case, there remains the sense of there being a Real that the representation counterfeits or, in more general terms, simulates. In the second, the Real is entirely irrelevant as a given representation refers not to some Real but to another representation. In this latter case, one can no longer define 'Truth' in relation to some Real thing. What then happens to the concept of truth?

Since Machiavelli politicians have perhaps always known that the mastery of a *simulated* space is at the source of their power, that politics is not a *real* activity, but a simulation model, whose manifest acts are but actualised impressions. It is this blind spot within the palace, cut off from architecture and public life, which in a sense reigns supreme, not by direct determination, but by a sort of internal reversion, by an abrogation of the rules enacted in secret, as in primitive rituals. A hole in reality, an ironic transfiguration, an exact simulacrum hidden at the heart of reality; and on which the latter depends for its functioning. *This is the secret of appearances.*

(Baudrillard 1990: 65–6, original emphasis)

The politics of the real depends on the control of appearance, the manipulation of boundaries and the massaging of judgement. Analysis of how the simulacra, the management of appearance, works in personal and social life is a fundamental aim of qualitative research. It is fundamental in two ways: first, to explore the effects and implications of a given methodology employed to study personal and social life and second, by exploring the impact of representations on subjects in relation to the realities of their lives change, creativity and the realization of alternatives may be educated (drawn out) in order to inform judgement, decision making and action. Although these issues will be taken up in more detail in later chapters when discussing postmodernism, politics, ethics and action, what is at stake can be glimpsed from Baudrillard's (1994: 20) invitation to

organise a fake holdup. Verify that your weapons are harmless, and take the most trustworthy hostage, so that no human life will be in danger (or one lapses into the criminal). Demand a ransom, and make it so that the operation creates as much commotion as possible – in short, remain close to the 'truth,' in order to test the reaction of the apparatus to a perfect simulacrum. You won't be able to do it: the network of artificial signs will become inextricably mixed up with real elements (a policeman will really fire on sight; a client of the bank will faint and die of a heart attack; one will actually pay you the phoney ransom), in short, you will immediately find yourself once again, without wishing it, in the real, one of whose functions is precisely to devour any attempt at simulation, to reduce everything to the real – that is, to the established order itself, well before institutions and justice come into play.

This simple thought experiment, for me, describes well what is at stake in the interrelationship between methodology (e.g. construct an experiment employing the rules of science, formulate a way of representing the 'real' in such a way that people believe it and act as a consequence of it) and the Real (as, for example, the Kantian in-itself) and 'realities' of social organization where others act towards each other on the basis of what they perceive, believe or take for granted to be 'real', 'good', 'proper', 'true' and 'materially solid'. As argued in Chapter 2, whatever counts as real is conveyed by the linguistic or symbolic frameworks available to us as the means by which to represent and communicate about our experiences and 'realities'. For Baudrillard, what is at stake in exploring simulations is that *law and order themselves might be nothing but simulation* (1994: 20, original emphasis). If this is so, then qualitative research as a project is subversive when it reveals the simulated or feigned nature of law and order, and the 'objective field' (see Chapter 3), and revolutionary when it educates (draws out) alternative simulations as a basis for law, order and the objective field. The subversive and revolutionary potential of qualitative research will be discussed further in Chapters 8 and 9. Where might alternatives be drawn from? As suggested in Figure 4.1, a given mode of 'grasping' the Real or form of representation leaves out or represses alternative ways of categorizing and framing the Real through representations. Furthermore, representations can be framed that conceal, disguise or indeed 'invent' realities. Thus, the Real itself can be repressed, ignored, forgotten, just as frameworks of thinking can deceive subjects into believing they are witnessing something Real. Just because something is forgotten or repressed or concealed does not mean to say that it no longer has an effect. Indeed, analysis may be conceived as a way of deconstructing the solidity, the 'brute factness' of appearances by focusing on the flaws, contradictions, disputed boundaries, the 'repressed' and so on. Analysis is the midwife of the return of the repressed. The repressed, concealed, forgotten, are all potential sources for the development of alternatives in conditions of complexity and uncertainty.

Handling complexity and uncertainty means that the researcher does not close down debate in order to simplify but continually raises questions. In my view, complexity and uncertainty can be handled by:

1 placing different viewpoints into dialogue in order to explore differences and limits to categories, maps, structures (see next section of this chapter);
2 resisting closure and thus producing a 'problematics' (a range of issues, questions, problems in relation to the Real) rather than a complete classification of objects or phenomena that together are claimed to constitute the Real and thus the True (see Chapter 6);
3 educating judgement through debates about what is problematic between different viewpoints in order to find courses of action that are ethical and politically (see Chapter 8) effective, and respect the provisionality of 'knowledge' in order to engage in action (see Chapter 9).

Educating judgement involves placing the multiple ways the Real can be framed into dialogue.

Framing the Real

Qualitative research seeks its data from the ways in which realities are framed and potentially reframed. Boundary disputes are a rich source of such data. When, for example, is an unemployed individual perceived as unlucky yet proudly standing up for himself or herself; and when as a benefit scrounger? When is a single parent a responsible caring adult; and when a feckless drain on society? So, which is right? The question could be settled by saying that each result in different 'realities' and that neither reality is 'correct', simply different, if it were not for the effect on the allocation of resources between the different groups in society. Thus the different terms that can be applied mark out politically contested territories and have different implications for the rule of law and order and the allocation of resources. Data from each can be collected and placed in a matrix created from boundary constructions and negotiation in an intersubjective field of action. It is in this intersubjective field that possession battles are pursued through games of positioning. Boundary negotiation between rival groups can be a rich area for data collection, revealing the complexity of what on the surface seemed simple.

What is at stake at a more fundamental level in boundary negotiations is revealed in what may be called 'edge-work'. Internalizing a category, as previously discussed, creates an existentially felt difference, an 'edge' – sharp, jagged, hard, soft – limiting the extensibility of a 'body', of a 'me-ness'. Living on the edge brings the danger of 'falling off', a 'loss of firm ground', a loss of horizon, together with a vertiginous collapse. The loss of one's edge is the loss of bounds, of power. Maintaining the appearance and the felt reality of one's edge is essential, a continuously negotiated process, symbolically constructed.

It is during edge-work that benefits and costs are realized in terms of internalizing the alienating structure of language. A project (benefit) can only be conceived through accepting a loss in the sense of being whole. Every boundary means that something is cut away and becomes a 're-mainder'. It is rather like the industrial waste which in turn becomes pollution that arises as a cost of creating the industrial materials of contemporary life. In order to understand our realities, we need to understand the material through which they are constructed, that is the processes of symbolization that include languages, as well as mathematics, logics, cultural iconographies (whether religious, political, fashion), codes of social behaviour and so on. This may sound ambitious, in fact too ambitious not only for a beginning researcher, but one who is experienced and whose funders want a specific 'result' or set of 'findings'. It is at this point that supervisors and introductory books on doing research proffer their advice to reduce the scope of the enterprise. It sounds as if the researcher will be drawn into endless studies of every dimension of personal, social and cultural processes before being able to collect and analyse data. However, the ambition is not to cover everything – that is impossible – rather it is to avoid what Silverman (2000: 61–3) calls simplistic inductivism, or naïve naturalism, that is, the belief that to study social reality all that is required is to go and observe and write down what you see. The ambition is to disrupt this kind of naïve naturalism by focusing upon the symbolic structures through which one 'sees' the world about, framing it into an 'objective field' which represent the coordinating structures employed by members of a given group.

Symbolic structures are essentially systems of coordination, by which an individual can name points relative to each other, recognize their own location and position themselves, or be positioned by others, in relation to the location of others. This system of recognitions and locations defines an objective field for its members and hence provides the basis for understanding the work of the gaze in promoting and fashioning a project. The matrix of recognitions and locations that unify or bring individuals into relationship with each other creates also a boundary or system of exclusion that separates its members from those on the 'outside'. The effect of the gaze is medusa-like; it freezes the shifting undifferentiated 'whole' into segmented and manageable/manipulable objects. It paves the way for the occurrence of the 'hole': that which escapes, that which is 'outside', that which 'breaks through', 'tears' and interrupts the frozen realm of the gaze. The hole and how to manage it is the cost of the gaze. There is always the energy that must be expended in sustaining the boundaries, keeping out the outsiders, repairing the tears and repressing any doubt as to the reality, truth and goodness of the social order. The benefits of the gaze accrue from 'knowing where you are' in relation to others and the real (as defined by a given gaze, not the Real which is 'beyond' all gazes and can only be experienced as a 'hole' in the fabric of representation). Between the 'whole' and the 'hole' is the edge. Living on the edge is to be human.

The gaze freezes and binds. This is the basis for the imaginary where demands are made by self towards others. Demands are urgent, and entrap individuals into closed dyadic relationships: 'I demand that you . . .'. And where resistance to the demand occurs, the results can be explosive, unless there is some other kind of framework through which the urgency can be diffused into 'patience' with a promise of a later reward for present sacrifice. This alternative structure is what Lacan calls the 'symbolic'. Here the closed dyadic relationship is replaced by a triadic relationship, the symbolic 'Other' that replaces the real 'other' in the relationship. The real other is the biological father, or whoever fills that place. The symbolic other is 'God', 'Law', 'Custom', 'Culture', 'Them'. How does this work? It is rather like the way that money functions in an economic system. It mediates by substituting for the concrete real. It can do this because it in a sense subsumes the 'value' of the real. Rather than eating the apple, one takes the use of the apple as 'stored value' to be 'cashed in' later. Why does it not all collapse? What maintains the system is the power of the Other formulated like the implicit promise of a banknote that it is valid currency, exchangeable for gold or apples or some other desired object or service. And the banking system is in turn sustained by police, military, law courts and all the other agencies of social power. However, promises can be broken and power deployed for alternative purposes as different organizations compete; or when the fantasy of power collapses (Zizek 1992). Whether it is interactions in a bar, special needs provision in a school, employer–employee relationships in a particular country, or the global power of multinational companies, demand, desire and their relationship to the maintenance and collapse of power in a given situation or context can be studied in each 'case'. The global may be seen in the local and vice versa. The relationship between local and global will be further developed in Chapters 8 and 9.

Complex edges, courses and icebergs

During the project, decisions are made as to the courses of reading, observation, interviewing, reflection and analysis that are necessary to the collection of data and its use when writing up. Such a course constitutes a curriculum taking shape as the project evolves. Finding ways to express the complexity of the project involves learning the alternative gazes of others as they interact with one's own to create the complex worlds of everyday life.

Objects are created and behave in different ways according to the apparently structural organization in play that holds a self in a complex, shifting and uncertain relation to its Other. This apparent structure fundamental to the gaze finds its expression through the multiple codes of subjects as they represent their needs, intentions, demands and desires to each other. How may these complexes of text woven into 'realities' that produce the experience of being situated in a given place and time with others be represented? In order to illustrate the framing of a project in relation to others I will draw upon a small study of my own written during a study leave in Canada. In this study, as one way of indicating the meshing of the material, the symbolic and the experiential, I coined two terms – architexture and archetexture (Schostak 1991) – drawing on the imagery of architecture:

> Le Corbusier, in designing his cities, distinguished between the 'way of the donkey' and the 'way of man'. The donkey will detour around any obstacle. The path is winding and rambling. There is no hurry to get anywhere. The way of man, he said, was of straight lines, that is, of direct action. The latter is the world of rational architecture and town planning. It has its complement in the rational bureaucratic design, hierarchical organisational structure with its lines of authority and the delivery of planned curricula in teaching. To make a pun, it is the architextual world of rational discourse, constructed to impose plans and behaviours to accomplish pre-designed outcomes. Counter to this are the resistances made by the reluctant

conscripts, or hired employees of the plan. Alternative to this, is the exploratory ramble where the development of experience, the accidental encounter and the unexpected discovery is the purpose of the journey. To continue the pun, it is the archetextual world of personal, social and cultural experience producing a curriculum which develops through time taking its own unexpected twists. Such a narrative is an architecture of time, place, discourse and event through which is composed an identity in history.

My architectural gaze created a space for thinking about the project, or more precisely for thinking the project into being. There is an interaction between my subjective experience of otherness, the otherness of the people and places studied, and my own modes of thinking, my ways of challenging my own frameworks through reading, playing with metaphors and deconstructing key terms. That is to say, there is an edginess, continually negotiated, deconstructed, reframed, that constitutes my sense of being a researcher engaging in reflection on others, their 'otherness' and their possibilities for action as well as my own possibilities for writing the project as an experiment in learning and in representation.

In the formation of edges by which to negotiate one's existence with others, their worlds, their realities and the Real world, the pun – in this case architexture, archetexture and architecture – becomes more than a rhetorical device. There is the edginess of voices:

The connections between the city and the school are carried in the voices and the experiences of the interviewees. The connection is there as a symbol and as an experience. It is a strength and a problem. It is enshrined as 'History'. History is a kind of journey through time, a progression from one point to another, one stage of development to another, narrated from some present point of reflection. It may be a single grand narrative of Progress (the rational planning architextual view); or, an aggregate of mini-dramas, a coagulation of biographies and of countervailing discourses (the experiential archetextual view). However, it is not either/or, rather a complex of both which creates a reality (perhaps some complex of realities) which is different from either. The history of its telling congeals around organising images, some of which aspire to a dominant view through which a history may be told, a vision of the future promoted and a plan of action for the present rationally constructed; and some tell the story of difficulties, failures, battles. During interviews, when people tell a narrative account of development, changes, or events that have passed by these hang together, not randomly but as an architecture of time, place and event drawn together to compose an identity in history.

This identity in history provides a particular way of thinking about a curriculum. This is a life curriculum – a curriculum vitae – standing in stark contrast to the curricula constructed for formal qualifications or national curricula. The life curriculum is closer to the project that engages with material and social realities in order to achieve the purposes of a particular individual or group. Official or bureaucratic curricula are exhausted of life to the extent that they are experienced as alienated from the needs, interests and desires of those who undertake them at school, college or university. Constructing a research project implicates the researcher in a particular kind of life curriculum, one that generates a curricular challenge to all that the researcher claims to know, and all that others claim to know. Cartesian methodical doubt and phenomenological 'bracketing' have already been described in terms of the challenge they represented to traditional forms of 'knowing'. The curriculum challenge is of the same order but instead of selecting a privileged form of challenge (like phenomenology), it explores the different forms of challenge that alternative perspectives have for a particular framework of thinking, knowing, valuing, and acting. The effect on the identity-in-history of a curriculum challenge is that the boundary between self and otherness transforms from an edge that maintains a boundary to become a hinge that opens doors to new vistas, new ways of seeing, new paths to tread. For the researcher, identity can thus be a rich source of curriculum challenge through which to build a project. It begins by exploring the identities of others as expressed in their everyday action, their conversations, their writings, their interviews.

An identity, its edges composed in time – the 'just in time' negotiations of everyday action – cuts out a course to define a direction, a reason, a purpose to living and working and being. Interviews, for example, can be analysed for key imagery, expressed values, arguments, or rationales that underpin a way of life, a course of action, or a reaction to an event. Each interview, observation, document or artefact used by individuals can set in train a 'course of study' or a 'course of reflection and action', that is, the study of a life curriculum. A life curriculum is essentially a journey cut from the chaos, the messiness, the jumble of people's cultural droppings. It is a journey that has to be grasped over time – always 'just in time' – an explanation is given, an account of a day or a life's work is drawn up – knitting the fragmentary experiences into some kind of multi-dimensional whole or coexisting plurality of wholes guarding attention from the hole into which all accounts will tumble at the end of time. The tiers in which the official curriculum is framed has at its higher levels in the hierarchy a bureaucratic/rational structure, the grip of which is loosened through the processes of interpretation as it passes to the sites of actual implementation, and so tears the binding textures. The gap that emerges between official intention and actual outcome has perhaps the felt shape of a tear, unutterable.

Any sense of a 'master text' as a rational instrument of control and standards setting reaches its limits in actual implementation, as each individual negotiates a space for their own identity and agenda. It is at the site of practice where negotiations take place, for example, between teacher and student that the letter of the text becomes reinscribed with the visions, beliefs, interests, needs and conflicts of communities of diverse people. How then do researchers get at this complex process and then formulate their own projects?

As an illustration, the principal of the school I studied at this time articulated a key vision which framed the texts received from the higher levels for purposes of articulation within the school. The imagery employed by the principal defines his role in relation to the staff and the purposes of the school:

> I always use the term 'keep the ship on course', and I know the *Titanic* and I've read E. J. (inaudible). And this thing lists along. However, part of my role is to make sure that happens and that we all are aware of the downs and ups and the peaks and valleys which happen. And in a school like this they're gonna happen. That's a given. But I've gotta keep the ship on course.
>
> That mission statement[6] which took us quite a while to develop is another part of my role. To make sure that we understand what we're trying to do. There's always an ideal. We're not going to make it, probably. But we're sure as hell going to try. And that is in every classroom. Now the objective is that teachers . . . they had a part in developing it, understand it. But the kids know what it is. [A] lot of things we do as educators, we know. Hell, nobody else knows.

The sense of keeping the ship on course, the potential icebergs, the misdirections, provides an imagery through which relationships between staff, students, community and the wider political and social environment are organized. It is an imagery which raises the limits of its sphere of and scope for rational planning. As such then it already contains the idea of a curriculum challenge to the rational implementation of official school curricula. The iceberg is always potentially there, waiting to punch a hole through the most watertight project. The ship as school, curriculum, identity, project, generates a discourse of direction, striving, and perhaps nobly failing. Fundamentally, from the point of view of the principal, it inaugurates a democratic discourse to make the acts of educators open to public accountability. This in itself is a central contribution to what counts as the curriculum of the school.

The 'mission statement' which hangs on the principal's office wall and 'is in every classroom' is an indicator of a discourse that has been put into place, an effort to make a set of values and principles stick, that is, resisting the slide of meanings, the tendencies to interpret or misinterpret. Keeping the ship on course requires management strategies that promote feedback, constantly engage staff with the central purposes and provide the limiting edges beyond which all fails and falls. It also requires a way of hearing those discourses that are at the margins or even 'over the edge' that are normally out of hearing. For example, the principal considers he gets feedback from teachers but 'probably don't have enough in place to do that with students'. Nevertheless, he does have informal methods for generating feedback as he describes:

> Remember I go back to the visibility thing. Look I'm here awfully early in the morning . . . and it's not, like I don't come to spy on anybody. But when I stand at that mail room down there I can do more in a half an hour from 20 to 8, 20 after 8, talking to every bloody teacher that's in there to find out certain things. And I don't. So, if we have this new initiative in broad-based technology in a certain area, and I just say 'How's it goin'?' and they go '(moaning sound)'. You know it doesn't take me too long. And when I talk to kids, like I know, I know what's on talking to kids, now, if I can talk to the right kids. In that 'Broadcast School' [the name of the broadcast group in the school], . . . We have a new teacher there from CBC [Canadian Broadcasting Company], and I talked to the present students in that programme. So I said . . . 'How's it going over there?' And he said, 'It's like a breath of fresh air.' He says. Well, I mean there's the answer and uh. But if they had wanted to sabotage me, you know, in a way um, I can't, they might do it for a while but not very long.

This can be read as a kind of curriculum statement. It is 'teaching' me as researcher to 'see' the rationales, the ways of thinking that the principal is keen to point out ('Remember I go back to the visibility thing . . .'). The principal has a clear map of the intentional networks composing his school and how he can intersect with these to maximize his felt sense of 'being in touch'. These are frameworks for the researcher to latch onto in order to construct a sense of how the school is articulated from the perspective of the principal. Like the principal, others too have their 'maps' and through their interviews can 'teach' the researcher to 'see' them. Each such map either overlaps or contradicts, or bears no relationship to another. Together they comprise not a unity, nor a totality, but a complex that exists like an iceberg, part seen, part submerged. The project then can develop as an attempt to see increasing numbers of 'sides', 'facets', edges, nodes of this complex and its relation to other complexes such as the school system, political and legal organizations, the media, community groups, gangs, families and so on.

Just as the researcher seeks a way of getting a sense of 'what's going on' in a given location, so the principal has to find ways to gather evaluations of the workings of his school. He does this again through the metaphor of the ship when saying how he places students at the centre of his vision for the school. In fact, students are so central to his vision that he sees himself as their court of last appeal, overriding teachers at times in the interests of the students:

> ...If they (teachers) don't agree with the VP or the parents I'm the next court of appeal. I reverse some of the decisions which they don't like but I think, that's part of my role ... Sometimes I think that we're all out of whack and huh, I said it was simple and easy but I can understand why for some kids the four walled classrooms are not the place to be. It wasn't for me really either. And uh, there are alternative forms of education. Maybe not enough. Maybe because of convenience the other thing, we're too structured in our 76-minute periods, which is too long by the way anyway. I'd go nuts.
>   ...To keep the ship on course, we do these things. But a lot, a lot of kids do very well though, like, like. But of course that's the plum of everything: the kid who's had it rough, rough, rough but somehow works full time and does it. He's got it together. Like those kids make you feel good. Other kids who are good thinkers and smarter than the teacher which is, no problem there, and are enthusiastic and work orientated and, they do it. So that's the good news, you always, there's good feedback usually. Especially at this school because they're so bloody honest. I mean (laughs) they'll tell you one way or the other.

The ship – *Titanic* or not – is going somewhere. There is some notion of a goal, a place to end up. However, it is not a simple matter of making directives so that all are acting in concert. Rather, like the architecture of the school, there are a multiplicity of levels, of scenes of action, most hidden from each other given the sheer impossibility of knowing all that is going on, being everywhere at once. There is no complete access to information – unless it is by stealth. Understanding the opportunities and resources for stealth, as well as the mechanisms and practices through which stealth is realized in everyday life, is essential for the researcher.

Stealth, uncertainty and complexity

The metaphor of the iceberg can be reconceptualized as a stealth structure, part seen, part hidden. A stealth architecture (Schostak 1999a) occurs if there is something to be obtained in a context of contesting and concealing voices. Stealth technology and architecture hides more than it reveals. There is thus a surface which is open for observation but also a bar or barrier to seeing the whole of the stealth architecture. For the architect or designer, the object is to present a misleading surface. One may think of those glass-coated skyscrapers which reflect the buildings opposite and the sky and clouds above, thus at least partially disguising their own shape. Or, more darkly, one may think of the stealth bomber which is supposedly invisible to traditional forms of radar. For the re-searcher or investigative journalist (or, indeed, spy) who wishes to see beyond the surface in order to discover what is hidden, there are two problems: first, how to recognize a stealth object and second, once re-cognized, how to get inside it, discover what is being hidden.

As expected, there are no simple answers to this. I first explored the issues in relation to lying (Schostak 1983), and although at that time I did not use the notion of stealth architectures, I did draw upon Goffman's concepts of strategic interaction and impression management drawn from the worlds of espionage and political duplicity. My research focus was on incidents where teachers or others accused someone of lying. How, I asked myself, does one penetrate the surface of a given 'story', 'explana-tion', or 'rationale' in order to 'see' what 'really' happened, or was the case? This was asked at two levels: first, how do teachers and pupils go about constructing, deconstructing and revealing the 'lie', and second, how does the researcher develop a methodology that distinguishes between the 'lie' or misleading surface representation, and the 'truth', the 'actual case'?

With such questions we make our return to the central issues of philosophy and science in its most general sense, that is, the ways of knowing that inform judgement and action. My phenomenological frame-work at the time permitted me to think in terms of what was certain in relation to what was not certain. The interview transcripts and my ob-servation notes were my data. This textual information provided the surface, composed of signs in relation to each other. From this could be analysed such structural subject positions as accuser/accused, judge/judged, and these could be mapped onto the school-framed subject posi-tions of teacher/pupil, pastoral care teacher/academic subject teacher and so on. Questions regarding who has the power to accuse could be raised as well as the implications of this for the maintenance of social order and control. The phases of breaking into alleged lies and defending against accusers could be mapped and correlated with the power struc-tures of the school and other social organizations such as policing. In claiming to be able to recognize lies, a teacher could claim to 'see through' the surface defences of the individual because 'I know you pretty well by now'. Such claims permit teachers to construct a narrative of motives and actions concerning a child which then justify judgements about how to punish or deal in some way with the child:

Deputy: It sounds to me as if, from the way you're describing it, it wasn't just you two standing there and everybody cleared, there'd be probably half a dozen lads standing there and a couple having a quiet fag in the church doorway and somebody else keeping 'cave' for Mr Jones or another teacher going past. It would be that sort of situation, was it? And people beginning to come into school from the town centre. Is that what was happening, Jacko?

(Schostak 1983: 81)

In trying to get at the 'truth' the deputy head teacher drew on his years of experience at the school which provided insight into the typical events, behaviours and attitudes of the youth in the area. During interviews with some of the accused, some mentioned the teacher's uncanny ability to see through their stories.

Rather than the 'truth' of whether a child did or did not commit a particular act, I was interested in another implicit 'truth'. This 'truth' was to do with the social order itself and its 'meaning' in terms of the individuality, dignity, sense of self-worth and freedom of individuals to trace their own course in the pursuit of their interests and the fulfilment of their needs. This 'truth' was revealed more in the ways that teachers justified their actions towards the pupils:

While one accepts . . . that we should be training free thinkers, . . . we're not ready for it. We couldn't cope with it. Ultimately it becomes a matter of 'You'll do as I say' . . . That's the attitude we adopt right through the system as far as I can see. As I say, it's difficult to visualise how else we do it. That's how society operates I think, isn't it?

(Schostak 1983: 79)

The analysis of incidents of alleged lying thus enabled me to pose a curriculum challenge to schooling and to explore 'beneath' the surface of the textual accounts of 'what happened' to the underlying frameworks of power through which resources and life chances are allocated to individuals and groups. This analysis itself can of course be challenged. Post-structuralist and postmodernist approaches might challenge its apparent emphasis on structures and its drive towards essences (defined as that which is invariant across all possible variations). Psychoanalytically informed approaches might criticize its apparent reliance on consciousness and rationality. These issues will come increasingly to the fore during the second half of this book.

The implications of discussions so far for analysis are that rather than the Cartesian or scientific metaphor of clear, distinct and unambiguous objects, the stealth metaphor is more suited to represent action within

concepts/ideas/
philosophies/
belief systems

practices/mechanisms

resources/tools/
material infrastructure

outcomes

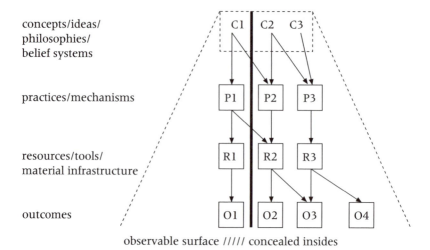

observable surface ///// concealed insides

Figure 4.2   Stealth architecture

the symbolic realms of everyday realities. Its architecture is organized at surface and barred levels, that is to say, levels that are repressed, censored, forbidden or rendered illegal. Hence its conceptual organization is likely to manifest one dimension while occluding other dimensions. Equally its practices and resources are split along the dimensions of what can be made manifest and what are to be covered. Figure 4.2 draws on the realist approach to research described by Sayer (1993) but reformulated to illustrate the stealth architecture.

To illustrate the figure:

As one example of a stealth approach to analysis and to bringing about change the ACE research, Phillips *et al.* (1994) described the use of 'tick boxes' in assessing the learning of student nurses and midwives in clinical practice. The 'tick box' is a mechanism by which assessors can tick off the specified competences that they have seen the student accomplish. Essentially the problem with this approach was that a) different assessors employed different subjective interpretations of the tick box statements which defined the competences; b) not all assessors were able to see the performances of the students; c) not all assessors actually understood the process and deferred to the students' interpretations of what to do. For all these reasons and others the assessment data was inadequate to the purpose. Nevertheless, for all practical purposes the boxes were ticked and the assessments signed by the assessor. Thus on the open or 'surface' side of the diagram one could make the case that the concepts (C1) concerning the assessment of professional education were being put into practice (P1) and by using staff resources as assessors and using tick boxes as the material tool of assessment (R1). The combination of concepts, practices and resources thus led to the outcome (O1) of assessments being made which were then the evidence base contributing to pass or fail. On the hidden side were a host of contrary practices, and contrary conceptions of what constituted 'competence' and indeed what constituted the professional 'vision' of care appropriate to nursing and midwifery. Thus C1 like all conceptual frameworks is ambiguous and leads to alternative interpretations concerning practice (P2). Hence the outcomes (O2 instead of O1) of the whole process were certainly unintended and hence somewhat dubious. Although the illustration is necessarily oversimplified, the use of the model is that it can be applied to highly complex social arrangements to show the extent to which official and unofficial conceptual frameworks are being articulated in practice through the use of appropriate mechanisms and resources or tools or material infrastructures. An institution or, using a more general term, an agency is effective to the extent that it can marshal its stealth architecture to work upon its material environment to produce a range of outcomes that meet its needs and interests. Educational research has as its field of critical action the study of agencies whether these are at individual, institutional, local or global levels.

(Schostak 1999a)

The model of stealth organization provides a way of designing project plans for exploring complexity in terms of its impact on social organization, the self and the formation of spaces where stealth work can take place. For example, in a classic study of Chicago gangs, Thrasher (1927) proposed that gangs formed in the interstices, the 'fissures and breaks in the structure of social organisation' (p. 22). These are places where the rule of law breaks down and is replaced by the rule of the gang. The work of the gang in claiming territories is in the sense described above under cover of the bar, that is, out of the reach of official forms of authority. This sense of being out of control, that is, out of the reach of adults, is pervasive in Thrasher's descriptions of crowded city life with its slums, frontiers and industrial areas. Each side of the bar, there are the different agencies that marshal their stealth architectures to obtain what they want: the control of resources to their own different ends. This model may be employed in the analysis of any social formation whether it is city life, a hospital or a street gang. The individual members of a given group such as a gang or staff of a school, or members of a mass as in a street or a football match, are all able to exploit the circumstances to produce advantages for themselves 'under cover', or 'out of reach'. The ways in which this is done by the many agencies of social and personal life add further dimensions of complexity to the forms of social action. Qualitative research studies the agencies, defined in the broadest of terms, through which personal and social life is organized to allocate resources to address needs, interests and opportunities. It has as its aim the education of alternatives in order to inform judgement, stimulate creativity and explore potential courses of action. This aim will be developed in greater detail in Chapters 8 and 9.

Project design implications

Drawing on the above discussions, there are five dimensions of the analysis of issue and problem structures in concrete contexts, that a project may address in its design which may be summarized as:

1 *structure*, its analysis:
 (a) at abstract level: concepts/ideas/values/symbolic structures
   (i) the professional mandate[7]
   (ii) conceptual frameworks underlying 'assessment', 'competence', 'profession' and so on
   (iii) principles
   (iv) values
   (v) academic, professional and occupational knowledge bases
   (vi) the wider context of cultural symbolic systems[8]
 (b) at concrete level: material structure
   (i) physical architecture and geographical locations (with reference to their implications for communication, control, monitoring, group cohesion and so on)
   (ii) role structures (formal and informal)
   (iii) institutional and inter-institutional mechanisms
   (iv) communications structures
2 *mechanisms* – at both conceptual/abstract level and concrete/material level: formal/informal, intended/unintended
 (a) ways of acting/behaviour
 (b) rules governing ways of acting (verbal and non-verbal); rules of entry and exit
 (c) ways of interpreting and talking about and justifying ways of behaving
3 *procedures* (as institutional, cultural repertoires ordering sequences of action) at both conceptual/abstract level and concrete/material level: formal/informal, intended/unintended
 (a) institutional/cultural/sub-cultural stock of knowledge concerning procedures, or how to act in a given circumstance
 (b) personal enaction

   (i)   the actual repertoire of discursive practices available to an individual from their particular locale in a group or access to appropriate stocks of knowledge, procedurally applied to account for or propose adoption of a particular procedure

  (ii) biography

 (iii) as a site of multiple perspectives, demands, roles whether leading to procedural confusion, ambiguity or to increased opportunity for development, alternative actions and innovation

 (iv) as an agent of action

4 *events*, concrete/material level, includes

  (a) coordination, organization, manipulation and transformation of matter

  (b) the physical documents produced

  (c) implements/machines handled, employed

  (d) the words uttered, written

  (e) the buildings produced and their internal spaces arranged, filled with equipment, and so on

  (f) coordination, organization, manipulation and transformation of social objects

  (g) the concrete practices, utterances, behaviours through which things get done

  (h) the actual interactions, their forms or patterns of accomplishment

  (i) the particular individuals and how they react to and organize themselves in relation to each other

5 *bar*, the impact of the boundary

  (a) on the production of edge work

     (i)   on the 'self'

    (ii) on the dramatis personae

  (b) on the formation of interstices

The five dimensions listed above interact and there is no implication of priority in the order of the list. They can be used to generate general research questions to guide the development of a project at strategic and tactical as well as overt and covert levels. However, like any architecture, the model itself is a construction, a fabrication that hides more than it shows. Its complexity is not enough to map all that can be mapped because all maps fail to penetrate Reality.

5

Sense and nonsense – braving the postmodern, broaching the novel

If the 'modern' is associated with the 'forms of knowledge' required for industrialized society, increasing urbanization, the rise of the 'mass' and the fragmentation of family and community life, the increasing speed of communications and the formation of new principles for the foundation and organization of society rationally (Owen 1997), then Le Corbusier (1927) provides an architectural image of modernism's transformative zeal:

> A great epoch has begun. There exists a new spirit. Industry, over-whelming us like a flood which rolls on towards its destined ends, has furnished us with new tools adapted to this new epoch, animated by a new spirit. Economic law inevitably governs our acts and our thoughts . . . We must create the mass production spirit. The spirit of constructing mass-production houses. The spirit of living in mass-production houses . . .
>
> (Le Corbusier 1927: 12)

Modernism positioned, indeed subjugated, the 'subject' within the mass, governed by discoverable laws, and thus the object of rational principles of engineering. Postmodernism can initially be seen as a reaction to the perceived inadequacies of 'science'. Rosenau (1992: 10) makes six criticisms of science in its modernist forms, in summary:

1 Impatience with the failure to produce the dramatic results promised by modern science's most enthusiastic supporters increased and fostered cynicism.
2 Attention began to focus on the abuse and misuse of modern science. It became clear that in some cases modern science legitimated the preferences of the powerful, justified normative positions that were mere preferences rather than 'scientific facts'.

3 A discrepancy was apparent between the way modern science was supposed to function in theory and how it actually worked.

4 The ill-founded belief that science could solve all problems confronted the obvious incapacity of modern science to remedy the major problems of the twentieth century.

5 Modern science took little notice of the mystical and the metaphysical dimensions of human existence; rather it made such matters appear trivial and unworthy of attention.

6 It had little to say about the normative and the ethical, the purposes to which knowledge, scientific or otherwise, should and would be put.

What then is the postmodern? Owen (1997) traces a number of different uses. First, 'postmodern' used as a 'periodizing concept' appears in the mid-twentieth century. That is, it simply calls the end to one period and announces the beginning of another. But what is different? Best (1994: 34), for example, points to Foucault's conception of the postmodern era as 'new configurations of knowledge', Baudrillard and Kroker's vision of it as 'new forms of media and technology' and Jameson's focus on new forms of culture. For Jencks:

> The Post-Modern Age is a time of choosing. It's an era when no orthodoxy can be adopted without self-consciousness and irony, because all traditions seem to have some validity. This is partly a consequence of what is called the information explosion, the advent of organised knowledge, world communication and cybernetics. It is not only the rich who become collectors, eclectic travellers in time with a superabundance of choice, but almost every urban dweller.
>
> (Jencks 1987: 7)

Does this suggest that postmodernism refers simply to a fashion parade of styles and ways of living? Or is there

> a new, distinct form of social condition, that is to say postmodernity, characterised by a complex (non-mechanical) system which 'appears as a space of chaos and chronic indeterminacy, a territory subjected to rival and contradictory meaning bestowing claims and hence perpetually ambivalent' (Bauman 1992: 193)
>
> (Owen: 15)

For Jencks the contrast is between the making of products, and the manipulation of symbols:

> Whereas a Modern, industrialised society depended on the mass-production of objects in a factory, the Post-Modern society, to exaggerate the contrast, depends on the segmented production of ideas and images in an office.
>
> (Jencks 1987: 44)

According to Jameson (1984), such changes as these give the post-modern its characteristc 'depthlessness'. That is, a given postmodern text, image or other object is not located within a greater whole, or life context. This seems in direct contrast to the previous chapters that explored the relationships between the part and the whole, the 'surface' and the hidden as in the metaphor of the iceberg and the stealth architecture. Using a methodology informed by hermeneutics, they sought to explore the meanings of the fragment (a particular extract, event, sign) in relation to a presumed 'greater' text.

What methodology, if any, is appropriate to the 'new' social conditions? Recalling the earlier discussion of the 'case' as a 'complex' and not a 'singularity', the stealth metaphor can be given a postmodernist twist without the need to assume 'depth'. This twist has to do with seduction, deception and illusion. Indeed, Baudrillard (1990) sees it as characteristic of the postmodern media age where the object of, say, advertising is not to speak of the object being sold, but to create an image for it that seduces consumers. The 'truth' of the object is not what is sought, rather it is the desire of the consumer that is to be aroused. Hence the 'surface' of the object, whether a car, a tube of toothpaste, or a politician seeking re-election, is to be transformed to provide the illusion of satisfying the desire of the consumer or voter. Seduction is thus a form of stealth 'technology' applied to images in order to create illusions. Seduction takes on many forms whether it is about facial make-up, the fashion industry or indeed architecture. In a dialogue between the sociologist, Baudrillard, and the architect, Nouvel, the strategies for creating seductive spaces are explored (Baudrillard and Nouvel 2000). For example, Nouvel draws on what he sees to be happening in cinema, and describes how he likes to play on the depth of field in his architecture and so distort perspective:

> In a building like that of the Cartier foundation, where I willingly mix real image with virtual image, it means that in the same shot I never know whether I'm seeing a virtual image or a real image. If I look at the facade, as it is greater than the building, I don't know if I'm seeing the reflection of the sky or the sky through a transparent surface . . . If then I see a tree through three glass planes,[9] I never know whether I'm seeing a tree before or after the transparent planes, or the reflection of the tree. And when I plant two trees in parallel as if by chance in relation to a glass plane, I can't know if there is a second tree or if it is a real tree.
>
> (Baudrillard and Nouvel 2000. My translation from the original French)

Seduction, of course, could be employed for many different purposes as in the previously discussed stealth and deception contexts, or it could be used as in sensual, perceptual, conceptual play, for enjoyment alone. In creating his architectural projects, Nouvel provides a model of how to go about generating the new.[10] By bringing into creative dialogue sociology, philosophy, and cinematic practice with his own knowledge of architecture and his spatial imagination, possibilities for novel designs occur to him. Similarly, the qualitative researcher can generate creative dialogues through imaginative investigation of apparently quite different domains. Why? In pursuit of the new, the different, the alternative to contemporary ways of seeing.

Afraid of being wrong, a researcher may well shy away from the 'playful', the 'new', the adventurous, the creative, the ambitious, the apparently nonsensical. So often the researcher is warned not to be too ambitious,[11] to build bit by bit upon the foundation of previously accumulated 'knowledge'. However, this assumes a particular view concerning knowledge, that is, that it is progressive, developing linearly, rather than, say, by revolutionary jumps (cf. Kuhn 1970). Moreover, a key criterion for the doctorate typically requires some indication of novelty, the new, as a contribution to knowledge. This can either be the new 'bit' to be placed on the accumulating pile of scientific facts and verities, or the radical toppling of the pile and its replacement by another vision. To be truly novel in this latter sense is rare indeed. It is the stuff of Nobel prizes and histories of 'great thinkers'. If one is to think something new, then the cautious advice is to think it in a small way. However, the example of Nouvel's approach to creativity in his own field offers an alternative strategy. It is to bring the 'new' into being by engaging in imaginative dialogues with the ways of seeing, thinking and doing to be found in the many perspectives people bring to the world in their professional or cultural activities.

If the slow accumulation of knowledge is a way of being faithful to a particular approach to doing science, then discussions of the new as imaginative play shift the project from considerations of faithfulness (that is, faithfully describing and analysing the object of study) to that of seduction (that is, the creation of new spaces for thought, action and enjoyment). These ideas can further be developed by the way in which Tschumi (1999: 33–4) described his rethinking of architecture:

This fresh examination of all the rules inherited from the nineteenth century and a large part of the twentieth led me to seek a new approach, focussing on architecture's peripheries and limits at a time when many had taken refuge in a historicist recentering based on memory, constants, or typologies. It was on the margins that some of us sought a possible renewal of architectural thinking. We occasionally turned towards artistic explorations and the varied polemics of literature, philosophy and cinema. Architecture was no longer an autonomous, isolated discipline but participated in the movement and confrontation of ideas.

What Tschumi and his commentators describe throughout their book is very much the problematic of creating newness, or novelty. When architecture is hypothesized as being 'defined, and therefore dissociated, through three elements, space (the fabrication of physical or material spaces), movement (the movement of bodies in space), and finally, the event or use', he is also describing what I conceive of as the nature of project work. Through the confrontation of ideas and materiality, spaces (relations between ideas on the virtual plane as well as relations between objects on the physical plane) emerge. The movement of bodies (of knowledge, of living beings, of machines) takes place through the spaces constructed. The uses of these spaces, both virtual and physical, are to be found in the events that take place. A space is created in the interaction between the gaze of the researcher and the focus of that gaze: the subjects, objects, spaces, and events of social life. This is a space constructed at the margin that can be inhabited, opened up and discussed. Such margins are productive arenas for the new.

Tschumi (1999: 42) goes on to describe the design intention behind his project to construct a new National Studio for Contemporary Arts at Fresnoy in France. Essentially, the project involved transforming a disused industrial complex, taking its old functions and replacing them by new ones, allowing new spaces to emerge as the new is superimposed on the old. In particular a new highly technological roof was placed above the original roofs of the buildings:

> It's the in-between that really matters, and it takes on an immense presence at Le Fresnoy. Between the structure of the new roof and that of the old tile roof appears an unexpected space, a space that is somewhat residual, since it was never drawn or composed, but resulted from the logic adopted throughout this project. This extraordinary space derived from the concept appears as a 'gift' or 'supplement': a space where anything might happen; a place of experimentation; a place located on the margins. This in-between space quickly became a fundamental condition of the project.

It was almost by accident that I saw this book, when walking around a bookshop, La Hune, in Paris. Its imagery struck me as an architectural metaphor for the kinds of project designs that I had been developing in education and applied social and cultural research. A bookshop, like a library, is a space designed to maintain differences between categories of books. Each shelf is labelled so that no one can get lost. However, reframing the stacks of books as a kind of collage where film, literature, philosophy, architecture and so on create new spaces for interactions of ideas transforms the silence of the tomes into an excited mental play of possibilities:

> Our proposal for a great 'electronic roof' was a technically and architecturally elegant solution, but the implications of the concept were what attracted me. On the one hand, the roof suggested a kind of 'transprogramming' or 'crossprogramming' by which the most diverse and disparate elements could coexist. Modes of construction from different epoch, styles without the least affinity, uses and functions lacking any common point could together become generators of a wholly other modernity – a modernity of absolute heterogeneity. Here we crossed paths with some of today's theoretical concerns. The heterogeneity of Le Fresnoy also recalled something of the contemporary city, making it as much a project of urbanism as of architecture. On the other hand, the great roof evoked the absolute level of concept, what we might call the problematic of the hangar in the history of architecture. The hangar has fascinated architects throughout the second half of the twentieth century, positing a tension between the event inside the box and the box as container of the event.
>
> (Tschumi 1999: 39)

The project becomes the imaginative play of difference within and against forms of conceptual categorization and coverage. Modern science has been fascinated with conceptual coverage just as architects appear to have been fascinated by hangars. This recalls the emergence of stealth organizations outside the limits of coverage by the law. Typically, stealth occurs in the margins, under cover, creating the necessary minimal surfaces by which to cloak activities that the public should not see. What is now being suggested is that this very process can be reframed as a project of invention, creating and reclaiming interstices, margins, the in-betweens as places for transformation. The in-between is a space that emerges in the play between sense and nonsense or the radically different. The demand for novelty in a project can be satisfied by exploring difference, in-betweenness, and non-sense as a condition for the new.

Difference, viewpoint and the discourse of the new

Difference is existential in the sense that 'I' am fundamentally different from 'you' so that, as described in Chapter 2, my horizon is unique. When I die, this horizon vanishes for ever. My project finds its novelty in the uniqueness of this horizon that bounds my experience, my biography. Each project is suffused by this uniqueness of perspective, a uniqueness always mediated (perhaps transgressed) by language and, in

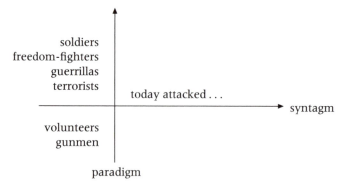

Figure 5.1   Discourse

particular, by the specific forms of talking about the world or 'discourses'. Discourse, as employed here, is a place where 'language systems and social conditions meet' (Hartley 1982: 6). For the researcher, an understanding of discourse provides an approach to the play of viewpoints by means of which world views are constructed, maintained and hence potentially deconstructible as a basis for creativity.

Discourse can be imagined as something like a glue providing the stickiness holding the social circumstances, meanings and signs in place, albeit not too securely. There are discourses for every kind of social activity, whether for academic activity, the discourses of the family, domesticity or of the gang. In order to distinguish discourse from language, language can be crudely imagined in terms of the dictionary of words that composes it (the lexicon) together with the rules (grammar) through which words are selected and combined for use in actual utterances or textual productions. This gives two dimensions: the *paradigmatic* and the *syntagmatic*.

In Figure 5.1, the paradigmatic is shown as a menu of possible choices between words that can be used to fit a slot in a given sentence. The paradigmatic is atemporal, with the 'lists' of words given as it were 'all at once', that is synchronically. The syntagmatic consists of the actual words chosen from the menu. The syntagmatic unfolds or emerges over time, or diachronically as word follows word. Discourse frames the actual choices made in speech or writing to accomplish specific purposes. For example, the discourse of the freedom fighter is quite different from that of the Ruler of the dominant regime. The words chosen to describe the world and the actions undertaken will be selected to express their distinct positions, values and political goals. The freedom fighter may not talk about attacking, so much as liberating. Those defending the dominant regime are more likely to use the term terrorist rather than freedom fighter, and will seek to employ words evocative of heartless destruction.

In more general terms, language is essentially a system of differences at both paradigmatic and syntagmatic levels. The famous example is between 'sheep' and 'mutton'. The difference is critical as can be seen in the example of the terrorist and the freedom fighter. The difference, of course, is no less critical for the animal – as sheep it is free in the field, as mutton it is dead and ready to be eaten. Discourses thus act to determine the place of a subject in relation to an object or other subject, an object in relation to other objects and in relation to the needs, demands and desires of subjects. Similarly, at the level of phonemes, 't' is different from 'd' regardless of the accent employed in their pronunciation. That is to say, the difference is 'pure'. Put another way, a given language introduces systematic differences into the subjective experience of the world in ways that at the public or intersubjective level the individual cannot arbitrarily alter.

Methodologically, language, discourse or, more generally, 'sign systems' have been at the heart of qualitative approaches to the social. For example, Levi-Strauss drew upon the lingusitic theories of de Saussure to justify his structuralist analyses of societies, Lacan reinterpreted Freud's theory of the unconscious as being structured like a language and in architecture Zevi (1994) argued for a re-examination of the language of architecture in order to free it from classicism. In its broadest terms, semiotics is the perspective that explores the relation between language and its objects, that is its referents'. Hence, as Gottdiener (1994) argues, for example, one cannot appreciate contemporary developments, in particular postmodernism, without an understanding of semiotics.

Making signs, finding referents

De Saussure (1966) and Pierce (1931) independently 'explored the problem of knowledge arising from the idea that our modes of understanding the world depend on language, itself understood as an organised system of signs' (Gottdiener 1994: 156–7). Of the two, de Saussure had the earliest influence on the development of semiotics. According to him the sign is composed of two 'sides', the signifier and the signified: the signifier is the material vehicle (the mark on the page, the visual, acoustic or other sensory impression); the signified is the mental content associated with the signifier.

Rather than following de Saussure's diagrammatic representation of the sign, Figure 5.2 will enable links to be made with other developments, particularly in relation to Lacan who explored the impact on subjectivity of the signifying system.

The figure suggests that the signifier and signified, though separated, are fixed together in order to point to, or refer to, some object in the

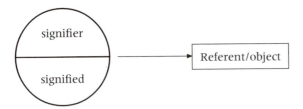

Figure 5.2   The sign

world (referent/object). For de Saussure the signifier and signified were rather like water and oil, never merging, always sliding over the surface of each other. In order to communicate, this eternal sliding would have to stop, become fixed in some way, before it becomes possible to 'mean' or signify some thing. What then is the fixing agent? De Saussure's answer was something he called *la langue*. This 'exists in the minds of socialised residents of society and ... instantly links signifiers with signifieds. Meaning was a simple matching game' (Gottdiener 1994: 166). Methodologically, then, the study of a social group proceeds by analysing their discourses in terms of key social categories. The social categories can then be structurally organized in terms of their structural relationships, typically binary structures. For example, Lévi-Strauss (1970) discussed culture in terms of the 'raw' and the 'cooked'. Cooking in the societies he studied came to signify the transition from a natural state to that of being accepted into society and taking up a specific role within it. Thus, to become cultured is to become unnatural, that is, no longer 'raw' but 'cooked' or transformed by cultural processes into some finished or fully 'cooked' state.

Nevertheless, the question of why a particular signifier 'sticks' to a particular signified cannot just be assumed away by the postulating of a structure, *la langue*, that performs this role automatically. What may perform this role? Garfinkel (1967) constructed experiments to exploit what he called the tacit assumptions that underlay the 'rightness', the 'taken-for-grantedness' of a particular way of seeing the world. He persuaded his students to adopt the attitude of the scientist and so employ scientific discourses within contexts that would normally call for the ordinary everyday discourses of social life. For example:

> The victim waved his hand cheerily.
> *S*: How are you?
> *E*: How am I in regard to what? My health, my finances, my school work, my peace of mind, my ... ?
> *S*: (Red in the face and suddenly out of control.) Look! I was just trying to be polite. Frankly, I don't give a damn how you are.
> (Garfinkel 1967: 44)

Rather than some sort of neutral structure occupying space in the head of an individual, *la langue*, there are tacit understandings, unspoken rules that are kept in place by an emotional charge.

The experiments revealed first, the power of the emotional effect to bind people into the rules of politeness, of taken-for-grantedness and second, the catastrophic space that emerges when the banality of the everyday is challenged. It is when the boundaries collapse that the void can seem to invade the protected realms of the self, the normal. Placed on the edge of nothingness one either withdraws into a shell to deny the threat, explodes in anger to destroy the threat, becomes numb so as not to feel any threat or opens out to the void as an experience. These are different ways of existentially dealing with the fear or exhilaration of nothingness. This nothingness is a catastrophic space for individual and social order, threatening their very existence. What such a space reveals is a loss of referentiality, a loss of bearings.

Methodologically, what does one do now? Like Garfinkel one can explore the limits of referentiality, pushing people over the edge and seeing what happens. It can develop as a way of exploring what I earlier (Chapter 4) described as edge-work. However, edge-work loses methodological significance in relation to Jameson's characterization of postmodernism in terms of a loss of affect and a loss of connection with 'history'. The loss of referentiality, the loss of boundaries, the loss of 'fixity' just described in terms of a catastrophic space for those locked into a given social order now loses its capacity to shock, as individuals experience a loss of affectivity and society loses a sense of a dominating history by which to bind, explain and provide meaning to individual existence.

Loss of referentiality, drift and fading

Central to Jameson's (1984) understanding of postmodernism and of the global order defined as 'late capitalism' is Lacan's conception of schizophrenia as a state where the individual experiences a breakdown in the capacity of signifiers to produce stable meanings (that is, to fix a signifer to a signified). Without there being a 'master signifier' to act as a reference point, a point that glues events into a History, a Social Order, a Meaning, all is experienced as drift. Rather than doing a sociology of drift (Matza 1964) one can explore drift-work as a methodology articulating the experience of the postmodern condition.

The artist Fromanger provides an image through his work of a world that has no central point of focus, no structure organizing individuals into some 'deeper' meaning. There is simply the flux of one thing after another without an ordering device. It is, in Sartre's (1976) terms, a series, not even as structured as people waiting in a bus queue:

... seriality is fundamental to Fromanger's sense of the drift and displacement at meaning's most general level, and also to the drift of what we might, in a certain vulgar nominalism, call a painter's style. For as Félix Guattari has remarked, Fromanger's work is a synchrony of differences rather than a development, defying and denying any descriptive judgement of the kind early, late, mature, typical or whatever: 'He is the painter of the act of painting'. Seriality orders his elaboration of the multifarious parts of a whole that these same parts can never come fully to compose. At the same time, it is inscribed in the flow of brushmarks on the surface of his works. Paint on Fromanger's surfaces is strangely centripetal in its application and its movements, always belonging where it is and somewhere else in meaning. But it escapes us without in the least expressing a strain or anxiety of precipitating towards or beyond some determined edge, of the canvas or meaning's limit. As Deleuze insists in his essay:

> what is revolutionary in this painting? Perhaps it is the radical absence of bitterness, of the tragic, of anxiety, of all this drivel you get in the fake great painters who are called witnesses to their age.
>
> (Rifkin 1999: 28–9)

As also noted in the same essay, Fromanger as subject fades from the painting, thus his work uncovers a 'strange being without a subject'. It is almost the definition of the Lacanian unconscious as an 'it thinks' rather than an 'I think', a place where the subject disappears. These are places where meaning is displaced, ex-centric to the material substance, the ink, paint and so on that is its vehicle. In the Fromanger works it results in a 'drift', a sense of parts that do not compose a whole, a banality of the crowd and the scene that counters the staged spectacle of, for example, a military parade, a millennium celebration, a football match. It is a kind of non-witnessing. Yet, of course, there is a frame, a canvas upon which the painting is staged, and the very banality or triviality becomes the spectacle, the drift of meaning becomes the meaning. Between the hanger (see earlier discussion of Tschumi's Fresnoy project) as cover for events and the canvas as a frame and a surface staging representations, witnessings, meanings, are the 'gifts', the surprising spaces, the non-senses that are the preconditions for sense emerging, for creativity, for seeing anew.

Seeing anew is discovering a viewpoint not contained in the old spaces, orientations and events. The categories through which a world is inscribed lose their hold. If the subject is the product of language, then the subject also loses hold. There is no longer a hierarchy of perspective, a privileged point from which to act and witness. All is drift, a levelling of elements; nothing stands out, discourses lose their formal functions and fail to connect with meanings, producing only banalities at best or the incomprehensible nonsense words and images of the dream where the key to understanding has been lost or repressed.

Drift seems to connote the ultimate in a loss of agency, in particular of political power. Standing at the edge between the glorious dreams of Modernism and its apparently sickly offspring, the postmodern world, desiring agency, what other choice is there than to return, violently if need be, to a fundamental set of values, beliefs and Order; or to play the postmodernist game, floating from one 'style', image or belief to another, indifferently, shiftily, as the subject fades? However, choosing one of these is to lose an opportunity. It is to place Modernism (or some other stable order of beliefs) into a binary relationship with the Postmodern. Rather, drift, stability and fading are experienceable states or dimensions in a process of change, that is, the emergence of difference.

Reframing catastrophe, drift and order

Methodologically, language provides the metaphorical frame for all representations of the personal and the social. Semiotics provides a means of locating language within a debate about the use of any kind of sign to produce meanings as a basis for attempting to order or bring about social action. Hence, methodological interest returns to the evolving edge between the absence of meaning and the emergence of meaning as individual interacts with individual by employing a process of signing that always implies the agency of a 'third' element that stands between the individuals and defines them as a 'subject' speaking to another 'subject'. This 'third', as Pierce (1931) called it, can be defined in many different ways. Whether it is the Name of the Father which Lacan describes as being imposed between the Mother and the Child or is language with its dictionaries and codes of correct usage, the third acts as the fixing agent countering the drift of signifiers and thus limiting the flux of meaning. Rather than proclaiming a specific or totalizing 'third' as the agency to guarantee the 'truth', 'solidity', 'reality' of a given world view, or indeed *the* World View, methodologically more interesting, to me at least, is the shifting edge between 'thirds' as world views come into collision, contest, collusion or dialogue. It is here that the 'new', the 'novel', the 'innovative' can be glimpsed.

The researcher then can explore any text for what it reveals about the movement of the edge between 'thirds', that is, the bringing face-to-face of one authority structure with another. Each represents the dangerous Other to the other, that is the negation, indeed potential annihilation, of the desired world order in the other. The edge of the one as it slips side by side over the other either negotiates a 'point instant of change'

(Schostak 2000) or erects powerful defences to keep the other out of sight, out of range, out of existence. For example, consider this description of adolescence by an interviewee of Logan's in his 1988 doctoral thesis:

> Sixteen is no joke, whether you're leaving school or staying on to do 'A' levels. There are so many conflicting emotions; you're torn between the adult world you're entering and the childhood you're clinging onto so desperately as you see it being left behind you – happy secure memories vanishing into the mists of the past.
>
> 'What do YOU have to complain about?' I am asked so often; 'you've got everything that you could possibly want.' An unperceptive outsider can often see so little apart from the heavy webs of deceit which cover up one's actual self, which protect one's fragile emotions from the world.
>
> (Meehra (16))

In this 16-year-old's own words, there is a sense of flux and fading as well as something emerging. Signifiers are on the move. In this circumstance the signifier is a person who feels the wrench as what used to be held in place now drifts out of touch. The individual as a text to be read by others and by self finds that the way in which she used to 'read' her self in order to arrive at content composed of happy memories is now vanishing. Childhood slips away and the emergent yet uncertain signifiers of adulthood have not yet fixed upon any secure content/signifieds that would then provide her with a new sense of security (securing/fixing/ anchoring). During the slippage, deceits (signifiers which misdirect) are set in place to manage the threats. This process of misdirection problematizes her sense of self and in turn paves the way, through a series of studies of adolescents, for Logan to postulate the need for a sense of an authentic self (see Chapter 7). It seems, then, that an affective and desiring dimension fixes signifiers to signifieds and in the process a sense of self is constructed or protected, that is a self is at stake, or, perhaps, being staked out. However, in the 'new' social conditions of the postmodern, the world provides no anchorage.

Both personally and methodologically drift erodes any hermeneutical strategy to discover and fix an essential meaning. Adopting a methodology to represent, analyse and understand this process of drift leads either to the use of social theory to explain drift and argue for strategies to deal with drift, or the development of new methodological approaches that articulate drift in their very methodology. These latter, however, do not escape the hermeneutic circle from fragment to whole if they can only be 'seen' as drift by a backwards reference to a previous order of fixity, or non-drift. If there is 'escape' then it is to a 'point' where neither drift or fixity have any meaning, that is, the Real. This gives, as

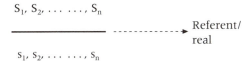

Figure 5.3 Signifier and signified

it were, a negative meaninglessness (drift) and a positive meaningless-ness (openness to the Real).

Returning now to the sign, it may be redrawn to illustrate first, the drift of signifiers (S_1, S_2, ..., S_n) over a flow of possible signifieds (s_1, s_2, ..., s_n); second, the separation of these two orders as represented by a bar; and third, the problematic relationship as a broken arrow search-ing for some referent (meaningful object, or Real) (Figure 5.3).

There are two ways of reading the figure. The first posits a meaningful referent as the outcome of the signifying process. The second aims fruit-lessly to find Meaning in terms of the Real; an impossible task rather like the quest for the Meaning of Life, or the Meaning of the Universe, that is, an impossible referent. This split parallels that of the split subject described in Chapter 2. Where the subject appears to consciousness in the real (whether as imaginary or symbolic), it fades in the Real, in effect being the equivalent of the impossible referent. Methodologically, the choice is not between the one and the other. Nor is it an illusory mapping of the one onto the other. The human is constructed as a play of emergence into meaning (that is, existence in the real worlds of everyday life) and a fading into the Real (non-sense, the impossible referent).

Drifting and fading between 'real' and 'Real'

Projects can be designed to collect data to explore the multiple dimen-sions of the 'human' by, for example,

1 focusing on signifying systems, their referents and the processes of constructing the multiple realities or worlds of everyday life; for short, analysis of real–Other systems or constructs;
2 the collection of accounts of drift and fading experiences and the exploration of strategies for representing drift and fading;
3 collecting accounts of eruptions of the Real through the surface texts of the real; e.g. traumas;
4 exploration of novel constructions emerging 'between' the fixity of the real and the impossible spaces of the Real.

None of the above are mutually exclusive choices for the researcher. Rather, they may be a choice of focus. But the one has the others in shadow.

A real–Other system is dominated by the Law whether as Rationality, Tradition, Religion or some other Power that becomes the principle of order. It coexists with others as possibility, as evils to be destroyed, as problems to be resolved or as the repressed, hidden, forbidden. To believe in the System (whether as Reason, Law and so on) is to subjugate oneself to its Principles. To do this, one must override feelings to do otherwise. Whether this is the 'objective' stance of the scientist or judge, the cold duty of the bureaucrat, the fierce pride of the traditionalist, or the fervent faith of the religious, there is a suspension of feeling or an a-pathy (non-feeling) in the midst of all these acts that enables reason to prevail, and justice and duty to be dispensed. The parallels between each real–Other system may mutually reinforce, overdetermine in Freud's sense, the actions of individuals, locking them into fatal strategies, that is, strategies that seem like 'destiny' and at the extreme permit the most terrible of actions. Indeed Baas (1992) has shown the role of a-pathy (non-feeling) in the ethics of Kant, Sade's philosophy of the libertine and Lacan's analyses of his patients. In fact:

> The whole of Kant's analysis is thus founded on the subject's iden-tification with the law and on his 'a-pathy', what Lacan calls the 'radical rejection of feeling' (in the sense of logic of feeling). Reject-ing all sentiment, the subject escapes the whole logic of sensory interest and can identify with the law while affirming oneself as legislator of this law to which one submits.
>
> (Baas 1992: 33; my translation from the French here and in
> the following extract)

The Law arises from the Other rather than the self as initiator. The subject, to be ethical, is to act as if he or she were the legislator of the law while suspending all interest in the pleasure of sensation. Purity for Kant is stripped of all empirical matters and resides in an *a priori*. How-ever, Lacan compared this position with that of Sade whose Libertines drew upon the Law of Nature conceived of as cruel and indifferent to human interests. In adopting this law the subject of the libertine is divided between the sensation of the body in itself and the demands of the law and in this division it fades, loses feeling.

> So as not to have to put up with his/her division and the cruel pain implied by it, the sadien subject, meaning also the sadistic and per-verse subject, vanishes and projects on to the Other the cruel effect of the law and so reduces itself to being only the a-pathetic (non-feeling) agent of the law – that is, the objet *a*.
>
> (Baas 1992: 44–5)

The objet *a* (often translated as little object a) is meant to contrast with the real–Other as 'agency of pure semblance' (Zizek 1992: 40), the *Autre*, Other. The objet *a* is the missing something in the life of an individual or group that is experienced as being lost (and at the same time unnameable) when alienated under the law of the Other, the Codes of Language, the Symbolic. It is often defined as the 'cause of desire', in the sense that a given object of desire (money, sports cars, chocolate . . .) is not necessarily desirable in itself (could be a piece of rubbish), but for the individual who sees it, it somehow calls up the sensation of completing something missing. Thus if only he or she can get enough of this object, a sense of satisfaction, of fulfilment, might be attainable, indeed, the sense of drift may be halted as a sense of Meaning is realized. As such it is the cause of desire in the person.

What all this suggests is: to create meaning, a sense of the Real, a sense of authenticity instead of alienation and continual chasing after the objet *a*, there must be a return to feeling (that is, the logic of feeling, taking into account rather than suspending what feeling reveals to be the case); otherwise, in place of this, some powerful ruling order, whether Sade's cruel indifference of Nature (Airaksinen 1995), Kant's categorical imperative or Lacan's *Nom du Père*, is the focus for the willing submission of the subject and the condition for the development of fantasies of fulfilment defined in terms of the objects that take the role of the *petit a* in the life of the individual or group. Thus the code and the command welds the subject and the objet *a* together in some fantasy about reality. The fantasy provides the motivating imagery through the control of appearances, melding fear and desire with objects in the world, and so provides a sense of there being a possible fulfilment that completes the self currently alienated in the social world. As an example of the power of fantasy sustained through the control of pure appearance, Zizek describes the fall of Ceaucescu:

His crucial mistake, probably the immediate cause of his downfall, was his decision, after the slaughter of Timisoara, to organise a gigantic old-style rally of support in Bucharest to prove to the 'big Other'[12] that the appearance was still maintained. The crowd, however, was no longer prepared to play the game and the spell was broken . . . The usual explanation, according to which Ceaucescu was a megalomaniac who lost contact with reality, was sincerely convinced about popular support for his regime and *therefore* organised the rally obviously falls short. As if the ramified network of the Securiate is not evidence enough for that, for years, he was systematically preparing to crush popular revolt against his rule! Ceaucescu definitely did not believe in the support of the people. What he did believe in was the big Other. Moments like the mass rally in

Bucharest when 'the spell was broken,' i.e., when the 'big Other' disintegrated, exemplify perfectly how we can *lose something we never possessed*. Was not the crucial turning point in the decomposition of Eastern European 'really existing socialism' the sudden awareness of the subjects that, in spite of the tremendous force of the apparatuses of repression, the Communist party is actually powerless, that is only as strong as they, the subjects, make it, that its strength is their belief in it? And is this turning point not best rendered by the paradox that the Party thus lost what it never had?

(Zizek 1992: 40–1)

The real–Other as a focus for belief is to be found in many different guises. It is to be found as discussed earlier in Hegel's trans-subjective observer–thinker that comes into being in terms of the Other as Reason which takes on its sinister dimensions in the invisible hand (Smith [1776] 1961) of market economics (Benhabib 1986: 31). As Haseler (2000) has argued, with the globalization of capital the power of Nation States (the big Others in Zizek's terms) to control the flux of capital has diminished; their agency is fading as spin doctors play seductive games to give the illusion of power while daily losing it.

Although it can be argued that the conditions for globalization have existed for centuries, indeed millennia, cyberspace has given globalization an impetus, the logic of which has barely begun to reveal itself (cf. Jameson and Miyoshi 1999). There is a considerable project to be undertaken here, in exploring the impact of cyberspace and globalization on the life of the individual in relation to others. For the researcher what is 'new' is first, the exploration of contemporary conditions framing subjectivity and the possibilities for action and the allocation of resource to need, second, the development of methodologies appropriate to exploring these conditions, and third, the promotion of strategies to augment the agency of the individual in relation to the global.

The urgency of the impact of globalization on local communities and the individual is well illustrated by Haseler (2000) in his book detailing the accumulation of wealth and the control of resources by what he sees as a new class of super rich who no longer have any commitment – that is, there is no logic of feeling that commits them – either to 'nations' or to the general well-being of people in 'society'. Without a commitment to a given nation state, the power of the super rich to influence the global allocation of resources is increasing as that of the rest is decreasing. Haseler argues that the conditions are new, albeit the problems of inequality of opportunity, wealth and quality of life remain. The nation state can no longer be seen as a vehicle, through democracy or the development of an enlightened welfare state, to resolve issues of poverty and social injustice. The inhumanity that results from global power untempered by any form of countervailing power is described by Scheper-Hughes (1992) in her book on the poor of Brazil. For example:

> ...perhaps it was the words of Terezinha's seven-year-old son, Edilson, that reminded me that I could still feel something in the face of death. Edilson, who more than once had been given up for dead, continued to surprise everyone with his persistence in holding on to life. Edilson, had survived, but he had not thrived, and he existed in a liminal space midway between death and life. No one, especially not his mother, expected Edilson to survive his next crisis, his next uphill battle. He was very small and without strength. Terezinha showed me Edilson's latest affliction: a tumorlike growth on his neck that made it all but impossible for the child to swallow.
>
> 'Now the little critter (*bichinho*) eats nothing at all,' she said with pity. 'He's not going to live long. Soon he will join the others' (i.e., his dead siblings).
>
> 'Don't talk like that in front of Edilson,' I said to his mother, trying to protect the boy, forgetting that he had walked in a liminal space on the edge of death since his birth and that he was *bem conformado* (well adjusted) to his ghostlike social status. And so it was Edilson who silenced and corrected me so as to protect his mother. He tugged at her skirt anxiously to get her attention, and he said of his own death, 'Hush, Mãe, hush. I'm not afraid; I'm ready to go there.'
>
> (Scheper-Hughes 1992: 141–2)

Braving the postmodern, broaching the new is to readdress many old questions concerning freedom, rights, and the allocation of resources to opportunities for people to explore their own creativity and develop their own well-being in the production of the 'good life'. This project of exploring the complexities of contemporary life begins not by trying to grasp the totality, but by trying to see what is at stake for individuals and groups in their everyday lives at home, in the workplace, the street corner, the classroom and to address the problems they face. It is here that the individual faces two ways: one way towards the real–Other and the other towards the Real. And between there are all the possibilities of drift, fading, the concealed, repressed and forbidden. The researcher, in collecting the accounts of everyday experience, contributes to the processes of critical reflection on the impact of social conditions at local and global levels on the double lives of people as 'ghosts' who face one way under the real–Other but must face from time to time the Real, whether fearfully or, like Edilson, 'ready to go there'.

6

Being shy of the truth

Projects are haunted by questions of validity, reliability, truth. Are these interpretations of what my interviewees have said valid? And if they are, are they going to be valid for other people in similar situations? Did they lie? What if I only saw what they wanted me to see? Did I look in all the wrong places and listen to all the wrong people? How can I know the truth? Each philosophy, each methodology provides its answers. For some there is a Truth to be found if the correct procedures are applied. For others truth is a chimera and there are no correct procedures. For yet others truth is not found in the rational forms of science but in faith, intuition, the 'body' rather than the 'mind', or in a deep harmony with the universe. There are the truths of the real–other, the fading of truth in drift and the return of truth in facing the Real. In each of these, 'truth' is being used somewhat differently.

Under real–Other systems 'truth' often refers to checking a particular statement against an observable event. In this case, the statement 'it is raining' is true only if it is actually raining. A set of consensually, bureaucratically or dictatorially driven rules about how statements can be checked against observation is sufficient to 'prove' the truth within the system. What now of the statement 'it is raining in our hearts'? Its truth does not reside in the physical event of it raining, but in its expressiveness of a state, perhaps of sadness, gloominess that the audience shares with the speaker. There is no verifiable observable event. Rather, its truth depends on the assent of each individual who recognizes that the words fit a particular feeling. Of course, a dictator can 'prove' to the world that the nation is in mourning for some 'loved' hero of the State by compelling mass parades with streets full of wailing mourners. But only if one can peer into hearts can the Truth be known. Failing that, if circumstances permit, through interviews people can be asked to provide accounts of the reasons why it feels like it is raining in their hearts.

They can give examples of situations when that feeling arises. These accounts can then be compared and contrasted with each other. Then when all the analysis is completed, conclusions can be drawn about the social circumstances, structures and processes that generate the feeling expressed by the statement 'it is raining in our hearts'. But what if they were lying, mistaken or just trying to please the researcher? If the interviewees were accurate judges of situations, if they were telling the truth, and if they hid nothing, then the conclusions are 'true', 'honest', 'complete'. Rather than guaranteeing truth, honesty and completeness, the researcher can make clear what was done by the researcher to increase the reliability of the data and of its analysis in each case. The acceptance of the truth of a statement or conclusion then depends on the nature of the supporting arguments developed by the researcher.

In logic, the more that truth is exhausted of meaning the more it can deliver on its promise. Truth achieves its greatest triumph in the mechanical operation of truth tables. A truth table, in logic, defines the conditions under which a proposition or a series of propositions are true or false. It depends on a series of assumptions taken as axioms. For example, a proposition 'A' cannot be both true and false. If 'A' is true and 'B' is true, then a proposition 'C' composed of both 'A' and 'B' is also true. However, if 'A' is true and 'B' is false then 'C' is false in those circumstances when 'C' means both 'A' and 'B' (A & B) are required. Otherwise, if either 'A' or 'B' (A v B) will suffice, then 'C' is true because one of them being true is sufficient for 'C' to be true. The truth table for each case is as follows, where T = True and F = False:

A	*B*	*C = A & B*	*C = A v B*
T	T	T	T
T	F	F	T
F	T	F	T
F	F	F	F

In the truth tables all content has been excluded. Its power is in the very lack of content. It is through the power of truth tables that our computer-based society functions. It enables the circulation of any kind of content, whether the referent is real or virtual. The binary structure of truth tables enables the complex operations of computer systems to take place, indeed making possible artificial or 'intelligent' decision making by machines. However, the quality of decision making is not necessarily increased. Garbage in, garbage out (GIGO), say computer programmers. Truth tables thus do not solve the problem of Truth. In this sense, truth remains an embarrassment. That is why it is often clothed in inverted commas – to hide its shame.

Nevertheless, Truth plays at the edges of any discussion of validity, Reality or the subjective and intersubjective realities of people's everyday lives, and the media-controlled realities of 'pure appearance' (Zizek 1992), as well as discussions of essence or necessity or simply 'being right'. Rather than attempt what could only be a sketchy review of this vast area I want to focus on truth as a social project in itself. What I mean by this is truth allied to feelings, wilfulness and purposes, not a subjectless 'objective' truth that churns through its calculations. This latter is important for the social project when it impacts upon the truth of the subject, splitting the subject between Being (in-itself) and Thinking reduced to representation, analysis and calculation rather than Knowing (as in lived experience, carnality). The social project of truth is a question also of rights. If it is true, do I have a right to it? The question I want to explore then is: can discussions of truth offer a critical edge to the researcher to explore and challenge prevailing social conditions as a basis for framing personal and social action?

What's right?

Rights pass from one generation to another, from premise to premise to conclusion. Their truths are contained in the rites of the law, part of the texture of property power and consumer sovereignty. Rights are the product of social collusions and jealously guarded from acts of treachery by the machineries of the law. Whether hammered home by accounts that are founded on Reason or on a religious Revealed Truth, or on the terror of naked Power, 'my rights' in a given situation are secured by an Other whose will cannot be denied. What if the power of that other crumbles, drifts like smoke, vanishes? It would be a betrayal of cosmic proportions for those who once believed with all their heart. In face of this there is only panic. Panic is everywhere:

> Last winter we received a letter from an American friend who had this to say about the prevailing obsession in the USA over *clean bodily fluids*:
>
>> Do you remember loyalty oaths? When I was growing up in the US teachers were required to sign them to affirm that they had never been communists. Some, on principle, refused. That, it seemed to me at the time, required courage in the prevailing hysteria over bad attitudes and disloyal ideas. I remembered loyalty oaths last week when I read an article in the *New York Times* about the latest twist in the anti-drug hysteria. Since

quite a business has developed in the sale of drug-free urine, now there's talk of compulsory drug testing requiring urination under observation. Well, it seemed to me only a matter of time, given the contemporary crisis over clean bodily fluids, until someone will decide teachers have to take urine and blood tests to keep their jobs. Aren't we, after all, the guardians of the good health of the young? But can one as a matter of principle, refuse to piss in a bottle? It does seem ridiculous. The refusal to sign a loyalty oath was quite dignified; to refuse a common medical procedure would seem silly.

(Kroker and Kroker 1987: 10)

What nowadays can still be refused without falling into 'silliness'? Whether it is panics over youth and drug taking, lack of exercise in the information technology age, the spread of AIDS or the falling standards of spelling, who can refuse to agree with the common concern to save our youth from their worst selves? Although there is little to refuse as such, there is little also to embrace with passion. At stake in talking of the postmodern is the status of eternal truth, the final guarantee of there being some sense to life.

The postmodern scene begins and ends with transgression as the 'lightning-flash' which illuminates the sky for an instant only to reveal the immensity of the darkness within: absence as the disappearing sign of the limitlessness of the void within and without; Nietzsche's 'throw of the dice' across the spider's web of existence.

(Kroker and Cook 1986: 8–9)

What sort of 'truth' does this express? To glimpse the postmodern scene is to peer behind the triviality of what cannot be refused to find the immensity of what cannot be grasped. How then does one deal with this 'insight'? What are the available contemporary positions that define the way to be 'right'?

Anderson (1995: 111) describes four ways. These four ways follow from adopting one of four world views or paradigms:

(a) the postmodern-ironist, which sees truth as socially constructed; (b) the scientific-rational, in which truth is 'found' through methodical, disciplined inquiry; (c) the social-traditional in which truth is found in the heritage of American and western Civilisation; and (d) the neo-romantic in which truth is found either through attaining harmony with nature and/or spiritual exploration of the inner self. Each of these has its own set of truths, and its own ideas about what truth *is* – where and how you look for it, how you test or prove it.

The postmodernist, seeing that all is but an appearance, a fabrication, can either adopt an ironic position (hence opening the way for Derrida-like deconstructions of any position claimed by its adherents to be 'given', basic, foundational) playing with appearance, use it as a player in a game of power or scorn all as being ultimately valueless, empty, thus adopting a nihilistic attitude. The scientific–rational world views 'are conservative attempts to pull back from postmodernity'. They have their variants in secular humanism and sceptical views of all kinds that seek to apply forms of logical analysis and rationality to clear up the woolly, liberal, lefty forms of thinking of others (see for example Bloom 1987). At their extreme, as values slide into the fluid calculations of the global market place, some yearn for the old certainties of Nation, God, Race and Family. Alternatively, as technology rushes ever faster to an electronic, globalized, virtual net, increasing numbers of people yearn for Nature, feelings, the flesh.

Handling the truth

In contemporary societies many if not all the different forms of establishing the 'truth' coexist. The researcher can explore the different ways in which people handle the 'truth' and the impact of these on their own lives and those of others. In doing this, critical researchers must also make known their own ways of constructing the 'truth' of their own project and the 'truth' status of what it says about the worlds of others. Hence, there are many layers involved in researching the 'truth'. There are many ways of falling into self-delusion about the 'truth', hence the wariness of most experienced researchers in making claims to have discovered the 'truth' of something.

This wariness is of both the truths of the logicians whose tables are constructed to ensure a kind of hygienic passage of truth-value from one sentence or proposition to the next and the kind of truth that is felt in the bones. Nevertheless, sometimes 'common sense' or deeply held beliefs compel us to proclaim the truth. For example:

> Chomsky went to the dentist, who made his inspection and observed that the patient was grinding his teeth. Consultation with Mrs Chomsky disclosed that teeth-grinding was not taking place during the hours of sleep. When else? They narrowed it down quickly enough to the period each morning when Chomsky was reading the *New York Times*, unconsciously gnashing his molars at every page.
>
> (Cockburn 1992: xi)

It was due to the keenly felt anger, frustration and hurt experienced by Chomsky about the 'abuses, cruelty and hypocrisies of power'. Truth, in this context, is not an attribute of sentences (although that is tactically important); it is existential, a gestalt that gathers up within itself a whole world view as well as the flesh of the subject, rendering the subject vulnerable to its life or death grip. Truth is what binds individuals to their circumstances. In a sense, it is the truth of the individual as a human being who engages with and feels strongly about the world. It is expressed in Chomsky's interview with Barsamian:

> If you suggest things should be reformed in this or that fashion and there's a moral basis for it, you are in effect saying, 'Human beings are so constituted that his change is to their benefit. It somehow relates to their essential human needs.' The underlying concept of human nature is rarely articulated. It's more or less tacit and implicit and nobody thinks about it very much. But if we were ever to achieve the state – and we're very far from this – if the study of humans were ever to reach the point of a discipline with significant intellectual content, this concept would have to be understood and articulated. If we search our souls we find that we do have a concept and it's probably based on some ideas about the underlying and essential human need for freedom from external arbitrary constraints and controls, a concept of human dignity which would regard it as an infringement on fundamental human rights to be enslaved, owned by others, in my view even to be rented by others, as in capitalist societies, and so on. Those views are not established at the level of science. They're just commitments.
>
> (Barsamian 1992: 2)

There are many problems with this passage. It assumes an 'essentialism', a truth as to the essential nature of the human being. It assumes also that this essence is knowable, and explicitly places 'establishing the truth, facts' and so on, on the side of science but relegates 'human dignity' and 'freedom' to the level of 'just commitments'. Many professionals, like Chomsky, start from certain premises about 'human nature' that they hold dearly. There are many stock phrases that reveal their basic commitments, for example:

'All children need "x".'
'Teachers will instinctively "x".'
'I am doing "x" in their best interests.'
'Parents want "x".'
And so on.

In research terms these are all formulations that can be rendered problematic, that is, the historical, political and social circumstances that underpin these formulations become subjects of inquiry. The 'fact-like' qualities of the statements are cracked open to reveal how and in whose interests they were constructed. Whether it is the motives of politicians to create a compliant citizenry or those of the wealthy to skill their future workforces can underlie such imperatives as 'All children need', say, 'to achieve certain standards of reading, writing, arithmetic and obedience.' This can be explored in the statements of politicians or industrialists as well as legislation or the official curricula of schools.

From the preceding discussions two ways of generating a project framework emerge:

1 A project can frame its aims based on assumptions regarding human nature and the commitments of the researcher. These will not be rendered problematic. The object will be to map the circumstances and problems that need to be understood in order to formulate strategies that will achieve the aims. The aims will be realised employing the appropriate research methodologies. The critical focus of the project will then be reserved for the methods employed, the processes of data analysis and 'consistency' of the conclusions generated with the original assumptions.

2 A project may be conceived that critically reflects upon its key assumptions and commitments. As a result of this critical reflection a researcher may first, proclaim some 'truths' and 'commitments' as being those chosen on the basis of careful self-examination and critical discussion of philosophies and beliefs; second, proclaim that all is relative and no certain truth or unproblematic commitment is possible; or third, that uncertainty means never formulating anything but provisional statements and strategies. Hence, the methodologies chosen will reflect the positions adopted. They will be subjected to continuous scrutiny concerning what they imply about 'truth', 'essence', and value commitments.

Each approach will result in very different projects. Each clearly set up their game rules concerning how they approach 'truth' and 'commitments'. Each can therefore be judged according to the extent they fulfil their stated game plan. Is this sufficient? In my view, no. Projects of each kind will be found in the research literature as well as in successful doctoral theses. Nevertheless, it seems to me that the second kind is preferable because it allows for the possibility of alternatives, differences and errors that could challenge established conclusions. Human dignity, freedom, and human rights are all powerful concepts, but none are unambiguously defined nor 'scientifically established'. What they mean in the lives of individuals cannot be assumed, but may be discovered if the researcher retains a critical stance on all versions of taken-for-granted, assumed or 'revealed' truth.

Truth, witnessing and revelation

Perhaps the paradigm case of revealed truth is that of religious truths. It is the 'road to Damascus' experience. On this road there are plenty of St Pauls. Some are accepted as founders of major world religions, others are ignored or locked away. However, other forms of revelation are more mundane, personal, yet no less decisive. Take for example Denzin's (1989: 17) focus on the 'epiphany' experience in everyday life. An epiphany is a life-changing experience. Denzin sees four kinds:

> In the major epiphany, an experience shatters a person's life, and makes it never the same again. Raskolnikov's act of murder is an example. The cumulative epiphany occurs as the result of a series of events that have built up in the person's life. A woman, after years of battering, murders her husband, or files for divorce. In the minor or illuminative epiphany, underlying tensions and problems in a situation or relationship are revealed ... In the relived epiphany, a person relives, or goes through again, a major turning point moment in his or her life.
>
> (Denzin 1989: 17)

What is the truth status of such epiphanies? There are two directions in which to go: first, the truth revealed to the person who experiences the epiphany; second, the facticity of the account (made either by the interviewee or by the researcher representing the interviewee's account) as an accurate representation of the experience. The first of these seems to move towards a sense of 'authenticity'; a sense of having touched Reality. There is the 'aha' experience of sudden realization when all the bits and pieces suddenly come together to make a full, or at least fuller, picture. Thus for example, Denzin comments on an alcoholic's realization of his own incapacity to say that he *is* an alcoholic that, although his understanding is cognitive, it is not emotional and so he 'dissociates himself from the negative experiences he creates when he drinks'. In that case his understanding is neither 'true' nor 'authentic' (p. 122). Denzin goes on to comment that *'Stated succinctly, the goal of interpretation is to build true, authentic understandings of the phenomenon under investigation'* (p. 123, original emphasis). Yet this authenticity can only be mediated by words, by the accounts given.

> A thick description creates verisimilitude; that is, truthlike statements that produce for readers the feeling that they have experienced, or could experience, the events being described. Thick descriptions are valid experiential statements, if by valid, or validity, is meant the ability to produce accounts that are sound, adequate, and able to be confirmed and substantiated.
>
> (Denzin 1989: 83–4)

All takes place in the imaginative theatre willingly established in the mind's eye of the reader. No real contact can be made with the authentic experience of another. What is being revealed is yet another surface in the textuality woven through language. Being ever tightly imprisoned in the webs of language may delight the spider but not necessarily the fly. No matter how 'thick' the description in terms of details the depth attained is no deeper than the word. But words cut deep, creating painful surfaces as they slide. Representations and the theory built from them may falsify:

> At any level, we could be capable of false witness, because the therapist does undertake a form of witness, witness through the patient's or client's own pain and death equivalents, let's say especially if they are survivors. What becomes false witness, for instance, is the all-too-frequent experience in therapy of people who have undergone extreme trauma of having that trauma negated, as the source of psychological importance or significance. And I've heard accounts of this again and again in which the therapist insists that the patient look only at his or her childhood stress, or early parental conflicts, when the patient feels overwhelmed by Auschwitz or other devastating forms of trauma.
>
> (Caruth 1995: 142)

There is a double witnessing involved here, a kind of first order witnessing that led to the trauma, and a witnessing by the professional who negates that trauma that in turn traumatizes and leaves the act unwitnessed. Whether professional or researcher, or professional as researcher, do their actions constitute the cause of the problem, its cure, or a neutral representation of the 'truth' of the situation or 'case'? For the Real of the trauma, the researcher who simply insists on his or her truth, theory, interpretation instead of maintaining an attitude of continuous, careful, critical reflection on methods, interpretations, theories implements their power rather than seeks to contribute to understanding.

Witnessing truth, interest and power

Staging the truth employs appropriate strategies and tactics to produce the appearance, the belief, the commitment that 'this is the truth'. Staging is about the construction of the stage, the props, the script, the scenes, the performance. Its purpose is to bring about the effect of 'reality'. The power of the modernist project was to tear Truth from its grip by Kings, Tradition and Religion. In doing this it bore witness to another kind of truth that promised to liberate people from slavery to vested interests, myths and superstitions. However, the promised liberation was in subjugation to Absolute Truth and idealized forms of subjectivity that left no place for feeling, particularity, individuality. Its projects involved the factory organization of education, health and work that violated the sense of individuality and self of those who were not the beneficiaries of the system (Schostak 1983, 1986, 1991, 1993). Can one witness differently?

> Though empirical, our work need not be empiricist. It need not entail a philosophical commitment to Enlightenment notions of reason and truth. The history of Western philosophy, thought, and science has been characterised by a 'refusal of engagement' with the other or, worse, by an 'indifference' to the other – to alterity, to difference, to polyvocality, all of which are levelled out or pummelled into a form compatible with a discourse that promotes the Western project. And so the 'Enlightenment,' with its universal and absolute notions of truth and reason, may be seen as a grand pretext for exploitation and violence and for the expansion of Western culture ('our ideas,' 'our truths'). Ideally, anthropology should try to liberate truth from its Western cultural presuppositions.
>
> (Scheper-Hughes 1992: 23–4)

What Scheper-Hughes offers is to show the constructed nature of the project work that results in descriptions and analyses. She wants to show her own doubts, fumblings and misconceptions. It is a kind of building of trust. And by that route it is a return to a form of truth building that is not about sentences but about the author revealing something about his or her interests, values, beliefs. There is something of the confessional about attempts such as these. It is the 'truth' of the project and researcher as much as or perhaps more than the 'truth' of those represented. It moves towards the project conceived as a process of continual critical reflection on the researcher as well as others who are the focus of the researcher's project. Thus, the focus is on the role of being with others in the textual staging of truth.

Textual staging of truth

The text is a product of being with others who are capable of signifying their presence, their absence and wiping their traces from the page. It incarnates a play of face and facelessness where recognitions are organized narratively, meaningfully, deceptively, elusively, stealthily, poetically. No longer seeing the face the prisoner is executed. Shielding the face behind a mask, the terrorist commits atrocities. Becoming impersonal is the way in which bureaucracies can commit crimes. Having a face is being vulnerable, whether to pain or blame. Telling the story is a way of placing a face on those who would hide. With face comes a kind of truth: it was he/she who did it! Or, that's her true self. The text incarnates that which is proximate or local with that which is distant, global. To read a text there must be access to language which is both everywhere and nowhere. The place where language resides cannot be pinned down to a physical location since it is freely available to all the speakers, writers and readers of that language. Its codes and regulations are not possessed alone by any one individual; rather, the codes pre-exist the individual. In that sense language is global – it is everywhere. Yet to speak it incarnates it and renders it local. To speak at all requires first the recognition by another that what is uttered is meaningful. Without recognition by an other and without the recognition that self is an other for that other within the same linguistic community there can be no basis for interpretation, nor negotiation on what is 'true', or 'authentic'. To recognize oneself through language is to place language as the Other that guarantees possibilities for interpretations being made of one's own and others' identities, intentions, actions, meanings and relationships. A given text is a framework for reducing, opening up, concealing, and/or disclosing possibilities for interpretation, for staging the truth. The status of interpretations may then be disputed through dialogue that circles a given text, exploring it, deconstructing it, critiquing it. Projects are framed through which 'truths' may be sought, denied, abused. A project moves then from the realm of 'truths' guaranteed by a system of calculation or of proof to a realm of action, of work, of 'praxis':

> If, for animals, orientation in the world means adaptation to the world, for man it means humanising the world by transforming it. For animals there is no historical sense, no options or values in their orientation to the world; for man there is both an historical and a value dimension. Men have the sense of 'project', in contrast to the instinctive routines of animals.
>
> The action of men without objectives, whether the objectives are right or wrong, mythical or demythologised, naïve or critical, is not praxis, though it may be orientation in the world. And not being praxis, it is action ignorant both of its own processes and of its aim. The interrelation of the awareness of aim and of process is the basis for planning action, which implies methods, objectives and value options.
>
> (Freire 1970: 21–2)

Take, for example, Rosenberg (1997) who for his doctoral project studied the right-wing onslaught on UK education in the 1980s fomented by various articles in the *Salisbury Review* by a Bradford head teacher called Raymond Honeyford. In one such article in 1983 he wrote that education needed to be rescued from those who

... teach all our pupils to denigrate the British Empire ... the multi culturalists are a curious mixture; well meaning liberals and clergy-men suffering from a rapidly dating, post-imperial guilt; teachers building a career by jumping onto the latest educational bandwagon; a small, but increasing, group of professional Asian and West Indian intellectuals; and a hard core of the left wing political extremists often with a background of polytechnic sociology.

(Rosenberg 1997: 219)

This was a time when the right-wing government under Margaret Thatcher had passed the 1981 British Nationality Act following riots in many of the major cities across Britain, had sought to undermine the trade union movement, brought unemployment to over three million and had consistently attacked 'trendy lefty' progressive education (Schostak 1993). Rosenberg wanted to study the Honeyford Affair, employing it as focus for social critique. It was to be a complex study:

The 'Honeyford Affair' is examined in depth against the backdrop of seminal texts from jurisprudence, psychology, Enlightenment philosophy, politics, literature and social history. It includes readings and counter-readings of primary and secondary sources and reflects upon the iconographic and mythical foundation of the truth status we ascribed to knowledge. The cultural tensions and contradictions of identity formulation in a pluralist society are explored: their cause and consequence.

(Rosenberg 1997: 27)

It is clear from this passage that there was to be a focus on attempting to uncover something that might be called 'truth'. This is not simply a relativist position, as made clear in the following:

'Racism is as human as love', Keneally suggests ... So it might be, but it is a false credo, illiberal, unfair, indecent and unacceptable on any grounds known to the author. That it is a common political, cultural, economic and psychological weapon and a convenient tool of social engineers is beyond dispute. It provides spurious refuge for the alienated, the disenchanted, the aggrieved. It legitimates many violences with licence to revenge.

(Rosenberg 1997: 20–1)

This is a powerful, unyielding statement of the author's position. There is no relativistic position here. There is the ring of absoluteness. Yet the author does not present a simple version of examining truth statements, nor resting his judgements on an Absolute that is beyond scrutiny:

In the crisis of authority which characterises post-modern times such studies as these are extremely complex. If as is argued, racism is a product of cultural socialisation the dilemma at the heart of the work is the efficacy of using Institutional State Apparatuses in the service of anti-racism in the knowledge that their statements, texts and philosophical underpinnings serve racist interests.

(Rosenberg 1997: 32)

Having adopted a position he sees that that position is itself caught up in the very means of social reproduction he wants to attack. Thus, in order to generate a methodology that will help him examine the truth-status of the texts he is studying and the text he is writing, he sees three consequences of the complexity of his chosen research field:

1 The need to go beyond the school gates to explore the structures, layers of experience, nuance and patterns of power which make their impact upon the lives of children and their teachers (p. 22).
2 The realization of the inescapable contextuality of texts and the discourses they inform . . .
3 Textual contextuality is a concept which might provide a useful model for the analytical deconstruction and realignment of texts, and the understanding of their endurance through endless modification. The notion of all texts being located in a social dynamic is fundamental to this research. Contexts are, in their turn, perpetually reconstructed and modified through the interplay of the power orientations, policies, ecclesiastical and philosophical presentations, the way there is always a residue of previous attempts to articulate the significance, teleology and social consequences of patterns of power, emerges as an unexpected (to the author), feature of this work (p. 23).
4 The impact of technology upon the manufacture and dissemination of knowledge, the increasing power of the messenger over the message.

Rosenberg is broadly writing from a postmodernist standpoint that recognizes the constructed nature of social life. However, the position is more than a gentle reminder that 'all roles are reified social behaviours' (p. 115) that can be discarded. There is within it a highly committed social project, passionately delivered. If people are to recreate and discard their everyday roles there have to be reasons to do so. These reasons will go to the bedrock of 'truth', the examination of beliefs, values, notions of freedom, dignity and the 'good' society. But the barrier to this is the mundane performance of business as usual.

The mundane performance

There is nothing trivial about performing the mundane business of everyday reality. It has a solidity, an inertia that little seems able to budge. It is this very inertia that totalitarian regimes as well as Western democracies have employed to carry out the unthinkable. Is truth powerless against it? To understand its power, projects have to reveal the stickiness of the everyday web. It is found in accounts by individuals of the 'facts' of busy-ness. Take, for example, this account by a ward manager in a busy hospital:

> No they're not trained . . . there was a further three came on. Well there was four originally then one got moved to another ward because they didn't have any staff either. So we ended up with, um, six staff, five of which could work on the ward. Um, so you do your drug round. Then once the drugs are done, the trained staff then obviously peel off. They . . . ideally, khuh, if you've got the correct amount of staff before you start your drugs you prioritorise [as pronounced] the care for your team so you have a little team meeting and say that needs doing, this needs doing da di da di da . . . Then you go back into your team, um, carry out care that needs doing e.g. dressings, removing drains things like, anything that you feel that you need to do, the patient's personal care, feeding them . . . anything like that that needs doing. You do that, that takes up predominantly most of the morning.

The truth-value of the statements in this extract can be analysed in a variety of ways. They can be placed into a propositional form that can be judged as either true or false when correlated with other sources of information (a correspondence framework). For example, it is true that some staff were not trained; it is true that originally there were four; and it is true that the sequence of events is . . . Each of the statements can be tested against the statements of other people or against one's own observations. Here truth is being employed in a relatively simple and unproblematic way typical of those approaches to doing empirical research within a positivistic tradition. However, whatever counts as truth in a passage like the above does not reside at sentence level since an appeal has to be made to the intersubjective nature of the context within which the statements are made meaningful and truthful. The truth has to be recognizable by others if we are creating methodologies appropriate to subjects and their worlds and not non-subjects.

When such interview extracts as these are placed in a report, as they were (Phillips, *et al.* 2000), they have the 'ring of truth' for the reader. The validity generalizes through the reader's own experiences. The professional group who commissioned, read and accepted the report did so because the report echoed their own experiences and took those experiences into a variety of analyses that helped them see new possibilities for action. Part of the 'truth' of that reading, that acceptance of a report, lay in the stickiness, the inertia of the everyday realities being portrayed.

The mundaneness of everyday reality resists the individual's attempts to 'wish them away', to 'act differently'. You follow the routines, you respond to the interruptions and the problems because there is no other choice at the individual level.

This mundaneness has a terrifying quality. If you're not up to it, it can roll over you, crushing you:

> R: What do you think of your chances when you qualify?
> S: I'm absolutely terrified. I'm frightened of being qualified, there's so many things we're not competent [at]. I do know basic things but that's not enough. I know to go to others and say, 'There's something wrong.' But I should be able to do more than that. I feel I should be able to formulate . . . to think, 'Right, that happened, what I need to do now is a, b and c' and I may need someone to watch me do that but I should be able to work out what plan I need to remedy what's happening. In some situations I can but in a lot of them I can't. The thought of wearing a blue dress and people, as soon as they see you, saying 'Oh, she's a nurse, she knows what she's doing.' And I feel I'm going to be putting people at risk once I qualify.

The statement 'Oh, she's a nurse, she knows what she's doing' constructs a kind of truth that the individual feels unable to meet. It is more than the truth of a given proposition; it is the truth of an identity, the truth of the trust that is placed in that identity as promising 'competence', as promising 'knowledge', that goes well beyond any easy definition of what a nurse is. There are normative dimensions to the truth being expressed here. These, in a sense, lie in wait for the individual who then has to 'measure up'. As a researcher, in the field, there are likely to be similar expectations of competence, knowledge, sophistication. Or, indeed, in some contexts, there may be assumptions that the researcher is 'out of touch', a bit 'strange', or thinks of himself or herself as 'superior', or 'posh'. However, adopting the role of expert, I believe, defeats the objective of engaging in dialogue with others whose knowledge, beliefs, values, experiences are the subject of the research. It is the other who is 'expert' in the context of their lives. Researchers, I believe, need to prove nothing other than their interest in the other, their willingness to listen, not pass judgement in the context of the conversation, and to accord the other the dignity and status of 'expert' reporter of their own experiences and knowledge of their world as it impacts on their lives. The researcher then is in the role of student learning about the mundane truths experienced by those who are insiders and who must live according to the mundane truths in which they believe. Learning the mundane truths impacts upon the sense of self in relation to the world about:

I: I guess if you feel that hospital, certainly in some posts, is about survival, you must develop a sense you can survive anything?

T: Yes, that's what I think now.

I: Oh right.

T: That's what I think now.

I: (Laughs) So that the preparation isn't just 'Wow! What a wonderful clinical preparation', it's 'I can take what's thrown at me.'

T: Yes. I mean it's dealing with uncertainties, it's dealing with your non-existing knowledge, knowing what to do, dealing with that situation, dealing with, er, yeah, getting your own adrenalin levels down again, and just being quiet if there's a volcano erupting next to you, just give confidence to other people in a situation where you're maybe not that confident but that's what you need at the moment, doing things that you've never ever done before, but they are life-saving so you just do it.

Here is a truth about oneself in relation to a truth about the world as a place that always exceeds what is known personally. Here is a medical trainee who spoke of her difficult first three months of a six-month placement in Obstetrics and Gynaecology. She has just spoken about her inner conflict over medical terminations. Although she would not contemplate a termination for herself, she 'would not deny it to anybody who wants to do it. I would not judge about that person, because they have their reasons.' However,

T: Sometimes I felt quite angry when I was working in that job because I had women coming in for their fourth, fifth termination. I could not understand this. I mean in England the pill is free, there's such a lot, there's good access to family planning . . . and sometimes I got really angry. And then I got angry because I was pushed in that situation to do something I really, and when I felt that anger, I thought oh no, you should not do that, you should not start judging, but I did. And, um, that was a difficult situation because I thought that the patient may realize that, they feel my anger, which I did not want because that is, that's my personal opinion. And sometimes I had difficulties dealing, to deal with that.

The expression of the truth of one's feelings becomes further problematic in situations that reduce the sense of the human:

T: . . . and the other thing is like, you're in a big machinery, you have, you have to function well, so you and your personal needs, they sometimes, um, yeah, put apart, put aside, or I don't know how to say that.

I: Suppressed?

T: Yeah, they're suppressed. But they build up and build up and you have to get rid of, of them somehow.

But with the, I mean, with the Thursday release course, and, you, you know you get a feeling and you do your exercising and you know that you have to do a kind of a house-cleaning, a house-keeping in your self, so you know, so you get a bit of an inside of yourself and you know what to do. You get an idea of how to handle the problem and how to go with it.

Truth may under these circumstances involve gaining freedom from alienation in the 'big machine'(Zizek's big Other). Such truths, if they may be called that, do not exist as attributes of sentences but rather as ways of being. As such they go beyond knowledge and representation and are rather found in the black hole of the eye through which a sense of subjectivity as other than the subject of language is constituted. The black hole of the pupil of the eye is a metaphor for the radical uncertainty of the life looking outwards from some indefinite inside always vulnerable, because always mortal.

Beyond consensus

The promise of truth, that there is something solid, something constant, has eroded throughout these discussions. Consensus in contemporary circumstances is little more than a collusion maintained under some circumstances but betrayed as circumstances change and consensus truth drifts from convenience to convenience. The truth promised by the modernist project has too often proved to be a double cross where the powerful, the rich, the deceitful retain their privilege and rights of exploitation. However, there is a truth yet to be considered. It seems to be implicit in the recognition by a subject of another subject. Intersubjectivity has too often been slanted towards consensus and the collusive production of realities. However, intersubjectivity that does not reduce the subject to a position of likeness, but rather entertains difference, produces the possibility of dialogue. Dialogue is a way of deploying maps not to force consensus but to discover difference, the truth of the new, the hyperreal of the postmodern age. The hyperreal is where the map has in a sense fused with the real in such a way that the map precedes the real and 'it is the territory rather than the map which is now rotting and decaying' (Perry 1998: 69). It produces a method where fantasy maps can be employed to explore realities produced in other ways. When a mathematician lays a logical structure over the world the fictional points deduced through calculation enable bearings to be coordinated. What is looked for is not so much the truth of the world but a better or different fiction by which to guide action in new ways and thus produce new effects. Feyerabend (1975) alarmed the scientific world when he claimed 'anything goes' and supported his views from the ways discoveries have been made in science: whether this was Kepler placing the sun at the centre of the solar system because of his belief in the sun god, or the road to the discovery of the structure of DNA from a dream. Dialogue, like the coiling strands of DNA, twists subjects into a mutually creative relationship, not producing consensus but producing a world of differences continually mapping self onto other and other onto self. Self and other pull themselves up by their bootstraps. It is a mutually sustaining intentional structure where no one point penetrates another. Each look glances off the surface of the other. The truth shimmers across the mirror never grasped. The textuality of the surface resides in the webs of intentional networks where subjects write up their projects like graffiti sprayed or cut into walls, windows, mirrors in order to repossess them, haunt them.

7

Framing texts and evidence: con/texts, intertextuality and rhetoric

Just look, it is self-evident! I am an open book! Evidence is always fatally compromised. Nothing is ever transparent. No one is ever simply naked. Something stands in our place, covering us and the world about with categories. Before birth, a linguistic cot was already being prepared for us by anxious, loving or hateful parents. In the womb our lives were already being measured out by health professionals. Princess or bastard, love child or heir, gift or curse – the unborn is already framed and clothed by texts. Texts are anything that can be 'read', that is, something that is coded in some way. Body language can be read. Indeed, a body is categorized and coded in many ways. So are the clothes worn, the way of walking, the look of the street. Being streetwise in dangerous company is necessary or else the wrong signals may be given out. It is difficult to distinguish between the textuality of the object and its 'thing-ness', that is, what it is outside our grasp of it through language. Indeed, because appearance is woven textually, all is spectacle: 'the language of the spectacle is composed of signs of the dominant organisation of pro-duction – signs which are at the same time the ultimate end-products of that organisation' (Debord 1994: 13).

Consider the difference between employing the terms 'flesh' and 'body'. Flesh, of course, has the connotation 'sins of the flesh' and the 'flesh trade' that can code this word for uses in talk about illicit sex. It also has more mundane meanings which code it to refer to the meat of an animal or the softness or fullness of a part of the body as in 'fleshy lips'. However, apart from such meanings the term flesh is unspecific about the parts of the body. It is tempting to use flesh to refer to the undifferentiatedness of the 'real' or material side of the body. Body then can refer to something quite different, its textuality. Flesh does not become a body until it is mapped into zones, parts, structures. A body has arms, legs, a head, a brain, insides. Flesh does not. In permitting people to name something, a body is created out of what was previously just undifferentiated flesh. It is for this reason that Lacan gives precedence to the signifier (agency of the cut) over that which is signified (the meaning content that is cut out). However conceived, through the body flesh makes a spectacle of itself.

> The spectacle cannot be set in abstract opposition to concrete social activity, for the dichotomy between reality and image will survive on either side of any such distinction. Thus the spectacle, though it turns reality on its head, is itself a product of real activity. Likewise, lived reality suffers the material assaults of the spectacle's mechanisms of contemplation, incorporating the spectacular order and lending that order positive support. Each side therefore has its share of objective reality. And every concept, as it takes its place on one side or the other, has no foundation apart from its transformation into its opposite; reality erupts within the spectacle, and the spectacle is real. This reciprocal alienation is the essence and underpinning of society as it exists.
>
> > (Debord 1994: 14)

Every category creates a boundary (or, more dramatically, a wound) and hence a space for a specular/textual performance that can be claimed as territory whether 'real' or 'imagined'. A boundary exists, therefore, between 'hand' and 'wrist' just as it does between yellow and orange. However, when exactly does the incremental addition of red to yellow turn it to orange and eventually to 'red'? In one language blue is a particular range of colours; in another, although that range overlaps, it is not identical. Which one is right? Its truth, if that is the right word, resides in its relation to the spectacle performed by a given community as 'their' social world. To become a member of that world is not just a matter of looking. One has to learn to look and see properly. So, Patrick (1973) in his study of a Glasgow gang could not reveal his true identity and thus had to 'pass' as a member. To fail could be very dangerous. He had to learn how to dress, speak and act appropriately. To do this it was important to learn in context from an 'expert'. There was no other way of learning than by becoming a member. Usually, there is a choice between making it clear that one is doing research and attempting to become 'invisible' or passing as a member as did Patrick. For Patrick, there was little choice if he wanted to be unharmed. Whether one adopts an undercover or an open stance one has to learn the worlds of the other. In each case, there are different discourses that articulate the different worlds of experience of different groups. These different discourses provide the vocabulary through which their worlds may be represented and the evidence fabricated.

Evidencing the 'realities' of the Other

Evidence and representation are two sides of the same mirror. On the mirror's surface reality seems to emerge as an image of a reality 'out there'. In the mind of reader the text evokes its referent as either a reality 'out there', 'in here' or as an illusion, dream, fiction and so on. Evidence is thus intentional in structure. That is to say, it appears only as the object of consciousness: evidence is always evidence of something for someone. The status of this something as 'real', fiction, 'dream' is constructed through a complex of intentional acts. Chapters 4, 5 and 6 have provided the basis for discussions of the complex relationships between data, meaning, reality, and truth in terms of 'intentionality', both in its strict phenomenological meanings and in its wider pragmatic meanings to do with motives, purposes, wishes. The next step is to utilize these in developing an approach to analysing the relationship between text and evidence.

In its relation to evidence intentionality provides a subjective bridge between the materiality of existence (as in-itself, the Kantian noumenon), its appearance to consciousness as 'phenomena' that is then constituted into 'data' about some entity and the representation of this in text. Intentionality does not occur as some clinical set of operations; rather, as described by Levinas (1998: 132), it has a remarkable relationship to the reality of the world:

It promised to formulate the relation between man and world in new terms. For to affirm intentionality does not reduce to giving another name to the relation between subject and object. Intentionality does indeed indicate, in the first instance, its relationship focused upon 'intentionality' both in its strict phenomenological meanings and in its wider pragmatic meanings to do with natural causality. But intentionality indicates more. General ideas, relation-ideas, do not flow on like dreams in the depths of a blind soul; they blaze paths that open onto being; they have an ontological import. Henceforth, contrary to all positivisms, ideal structures determine the real world. The intentionality that runs through our affective and active lives confers the dignity of objective experience upon all our concrete engagements; values belong to the real just as do ideal structures. The real is human and inhabitable. But above all, Husserl has shown that the intention of consciousness that intends an object belongs in fact to a context of thoughts that at once exceed the theme intended and confer a meaning on it. Their latent presence is indispensable to the intention that forgets them but that they subtend. These 'thoughts' keep open a horizon in which our preceptual, scientific, and even affective and active life is already situated. These 'thoughts' are not necessarily judgements or perceptions in their turn; they are prepredicative engagements of movements that necessarily precede our experience of the outer world, but that cannot be considered to be physical events, for they, too, are 'intentional'. The fact of having a hand, tensing one's muscles, walking, settling on a land, the sedimentation of a certain history in the thinking Ego, were necessary in order for the representation of a space, a time, and a physical causality even to be formed. Thus we would be wrong in placing this prepredicative work into representation, for which it is a condition, and from which the thinking subject is already nourished before representing the world to itself. Intentionality indicates not only a direct relation between reason and things, but the horizon in which the flow of things supports and carries along legislative reason itself.

For Levinas intentionality is not some abstract concept but is the very process through which reason and the material world is humanized and made evident. This humanization is essential to an understanding of the construction and use of evidence in qualitative research. Evidence is pointless unless it is a way of 'returning to things', a way of thinking about the Real and the realities of self in relation to others.

In Levinas's reading of Husserl, Husserl's demand for a return to things 'means vision of essence – Wesenschau. The Real sets the vigorous structures of its solidity against the faint movements of history. Truth is not a work of the subject' (Levinas 1998: 133). Evidence is the work of the subject as it deals with the Truth that is outside the endeavours of the subject. Intentionality seems then to provide two ways to evidence Reality and the realities of others: first, as the ground for the construction of meanings, and second, as the point of resistance where self meets the absolute difference of Otherness. In a useful parallel, Tragesser (1977), reflecting upon mathematical 'realities', defined the real or the objective as that which resists arbitrary wishes and desires that it should be otherwise. Mathematicians are continually faced with the sense that there is a solution to some complex problem, but without there being at this stage any such proof. Tragesser asked why. It was, he concluded, because mathematical objects stood before the mind in non-arbitrary albeit partially comprehended ways, ways he called 'prehensions'. Our grasp of the world may be incomplete, but it is not arbitrary. Each resistance, each prehension, each incomplete grasp, evidences the non-arbitrary nature of the thing that stands beyond a full comprehension. The task then is to build increasingly complex understandings of the complex called 'world' or any object within that world by collecting the evidences of resistances. Objects, whether those of mathematics, the material or social worlds, stand in our path, resisting attempts to push them aside.

Illustrating this from a doctoral thesis Ratnavadival (1995: 308) described the process of dealing with Otherness as follows:

> Although I conducted the majority of my interviews in English, the cultural factor was ever influential. Although the interviewees responded in English, the context of interaction was set in the Malaysian culture. So, there was still a degree of formalities. There were certain formal structures to the conversation, there were certain unwritten but well understood cultural norms about what is permissible to say and what is not permissible to say. In so far as that, for example, severely limits criticism or negative comments or the expression of a personal point of view, I had to find some way of getting around that.
>
> In those instances my intuitive judgements of what I had to do was to employ intuitive strategies such as reading between the lines and then say to the interviewee, 'right, I think of course what you are trying to say is . . .' That, I realised, was very dangerous because when we offer people alternatives, particularly in fairly even balanced power situations or in situations where I had more authority either as the evaluator or because of my known position there was a strong tendency for people to agree irrespective of whether they do in fact agree or not.
>
> So in my later interviews, I used what the interviewee had said literally, to ask the person to say something more about it. In prompting I tried not to put new content into what the respondent had said. This is quite different of course from replaying what the respondent had said, in my own words, where there is a real danger of me introducing extraneous material or where I ended up at least offering the opportunity that they might prefer my explanation to their own, or my words to theirs, and that is one step away from reading between the lines. I had to say, 'yeah, I understand what you are saying', and then I may say something that is actually different from what they had said.

At first, the researcher sought to overcome what he saw as obstacles to 'get around', to 'deal with' and thus 'overcome'. He was then tempted to add in content by 'reading between the lines' in order to get at the 'real' meaning at the back of what is being said on the surface. The result is that useful data is overlooked by filling in the perceived gaps; his data derived more from the researcher than the interviewees. Each obstacle, however, through its very resistance, can provide insights into the non-arbitrary structures of ways of thinking and social interaction that are tacitly held. The following passage by Tsai (1996: 28) is another attempt to handle 'Otherness':

On the date of 25th October 1993 I did not set my clock an hour back for the British winter time, and unconsciously I arrived at CARE an hour before the methodology course. As I entered the empty room, I encountered a shock of silence because I was there alone and surrounded by the quiet but powerful atmosphere of the CARE Teaching Room. I found myself confused by a cross-cultural puzzle and trapped by a cross-cultural dilemma. I was becoming increasingly aware of a cultural lag which would challenge me in the process of my research. Furthermore, I was struck by an enduring dilemma of a cultural borrower: can an investigation in the UK inform or solve curriculum problems in the Taiwanese context? What are the limits of such transfer of learning?

The questions point to the limits of both translation and representation. To speak to another, the other has to translate what is being said according to the codes of decryption at his or her disposal. A code is both out there and in here. It cannot be taken for granted that the code as I experience and use it is identical in every way to the manner in which you experience it and use it. Yet, whatever is real is mediated always through the codes used. The codes are like reference points on a map to guide attention, inform judgement, and coordinate the acts of people who learn to use the 'same' code in relation to each other. The code organizes the web of signifiers thrown across the complex object of our attention. Even though the complex object may not be fully comprehended in all its detail, a close focus on the intentional structures of sentences or utterances provides the framework for analysis of the way we consciously seek to grasp and complete the picture of these partially understood – or prehended – objects.

Taking a given text one can create an intentional map of these 'objects', where the referent is the 'reality' or 'object' to which the text 'refers'. The text is the work of evidencing, or making real the prehended object. Indeed, triangulation (described in Chapter 3) can be thought of as the successive acts required to prehend or grasp 'objects' in the process of framing evidence in qualitative research. Smith and McIntyre (1971) provide an example of the intentional analysis of the relation between the object as real referent in the world and the meaning, or 'noema', as they call it, carried or produced by a signifier (through an act of signification) in the following description:

Consider what happens when I walk around the tree I am seeing. As I do so, my original perception is replaced with new ones in which the tree is presented to me in different ways with somewhat different properties. I now see, for example, that there is a bit of moss clinging to it which I could not previously see, and so on. In short, what I see to be true of the tree changes as I move round it.

Now, it is the content, the predicate-meanings, in the noema that account for what I see of the tree. Hence, as I walk round the tree, my original noema is replaced by a sequence of new noemata, each with slightly different noematic content corresponding to the different perceptions that I have. Even though this is so, there is nonetheless something that is common to every act I perform as I perceive the tree from different perspectives: every such act is an act of perceiving that *same tree;* they are all acts directed to the same object.

The act of triangulation described above is that of changing perspective on the 'tree' (the referent, the Something, the Other to language, the X in Figure 4.1) in order to produce the 'meaning content' or 'signified' that both prescribes what is seen and individuates it. It is objective only in the sense that by taking multiple subjective perspectives that which is common to all possible variations of subjective position 'stands out' or 'exists' as an individual entity. As each perspective adds new information, initially there may not be the sense of a 'whole' but rather a listing or adding of dimensions, qualities or associations (having the structure 'a and b and c and . . .'), a process captured in the rhetorical figure of asyndeton. Grasping the tree as a 'whole' requires an imaginative leap, then part–whole relations between, say, 'twig' and 'branch' or 'tree' are permitted. The tree loses its concrete nature as it becomes 'tree', that is, a concept to be applied to all possible variations of a tree. However, a particular tree may be an index for the individual, evoking a whole range of experiences undergone when seeing that tree (e.g. fond memories of a first kiss). Davies and Harré (1990: 51) define the progressive accumulation of such experiences as 'indexical extension':

'Powerlessness', for example, might be grasped in terms of what was felt on past occasions when a person took themselves to be powerless. With respect to this particular attribute we have observed that women in industrial societies tend to make such extensions of the significance of the concept.

Another form of generalization they call 'typification extension' where

we think, metaphorically of a person scanning their past experience for a concrete occasion on which to build an interpretation of the position they have been assigned (whether they accept it or reject it) until they encounter the record of a typified occasion such as 'nurse/patient'. Through these kinds of extensions gaps in knowledge are 'filled in'.

Hence, if a thousand years ago a million people believed the world was 'flat' then what was common was that the world was flat. To that extent the flatness of the world is 'objective', 'true' and, indeed, generalizable. Although all the world cannot be seen immediately, experience 'fills in' the missing bits. The 'grasp' of the object is a leap of imagination, a leap limited by the 'thinkable'. It will take another kind of technology available only to people of different time and place to 'think' otherwise. The language of my time and place, then, 'gives' me a world that has meaning to me and to others who share my time and place. To learn my world, the Other will have to walk with me while I point out the trees that I see and the flatness of the world upon which I walk. Only then will that world begin to appear to the consciousness of the other and the Other will be drawn progressively into membership, reduced from Other, to the other-who-sees-like-I-do, the other who is a being like me, with me. It is a world made word, a world that can only be evidenced through the word. Validity of evidence, in this sense, is equivalent to being a validated member of a world made word.

A world made word

Whole worlds can be caught up in a word, not a word that stands in a one-to-one relationship with all that matters, but a word that signifies more than it can ever capture. Something of this is expressed by Ted Hughes (1976):

> If the story is learnt well, so that all its parts can be seen at a glance, as if we looked through a window into it, then the story has become like a complicated hinterland of a single word. It has become a word. Any fragment of the story serves as the 'word' by which the whole story's electrical circuit is switched into consciousness, and all its light and power brought to bear.
>
> As a rather extreme example take the story of Christ. No matter what point of the story we touch, the whole story hits us. If we mention the Nativity, or the miracle of the loaves and fishes, or Lazarus, or the Crucifixion the voltage and inner brightness of the whole story is instantly there. A single word of reference is enough – just as you need to touch a power-line with only the tip of your finger.

A word is not reducible to the signifiers of which it is composed. Rather it is compacted at an intentional level as described above by Levinas, and by Smith and MacIntyre. Each perceptual variation, each act of consciousness towards objects in the world, each experience of subjectivity is worked into a chord like structure strung out on a music score:

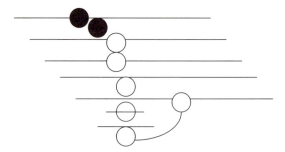

Figure 7.1 Music of meaning

The word is uttered and its chord-like ring evokes a world, complex, rich with connotation, denoting real objects and the realities that give them a sense of substance, hardness, reality. There is nothing arbitrary about this complex when its music sounds in the flesh giving it shape and direction. To take on the world of another is to learn its music, its legislation that places notes above or below the shifting, contextually bound bars of openness, legitimacy, decency and the forbidden, criminal, and sly. Context is built through connotation, juxtaposition, contiguity, and all the other possible relationships that may be composed, a world made visible and symbolic through text – a world with text. As a mirage is a trick of the light, the world of meaning is a trick of the text, a con/text. The researcher who attempts to gain access to the connotations (the melodic or dissonant structures) of a given individual or group's use of terms has in some way to find strategies by which to represent these. Fundamental to the process of representation is what I call referential rhetorics.

Referential rhetorics

Referential rhetorics, as defined here, underlie the textual strategies involved in creating a sense of the real, organizing desire and weaving the real and desire together into discourses evocative of realities. These are deceptive contexts that can fascinate, dupe, appear to inform and seduce or compel action to produce real outcomes for the benefit of a winner. This means that what is absent is the Real itself (the X, the Something, the Other), that is, the Real beyond all linguistic reference and rational calculation. The Real in the Kantian sense exists in a way which does not depend upon language or the symbolic more generally for its being. In the obliteration of the Real by the realities of the symbolic and the imaginary, referential rhetorics draw on the intentional networks that construct the relations between subjects and their worlds. It is the process through which a sense of self, position, agency, strategy and objective reality is constructed in the minds of individuals. For example, if, from a given perspective, life is seen as a competitive struggle, then controlling the sense of reality through rhetoric is critical to the processes of winning and losing. Referential rhetorics are the means by which such game-realities are created, negotiated, contested, distorted, subverted and so on.

Linguistically, a rhetorical framework organizes subject positions for people to inhabit and construct identities, by placing face-to-face relations within the realm of first- and second-person accounts and relations with the Other as society, law and so on as third-person accounts:

> In first-/second-person accounts, we think of ourselves as agents; in third-person accounts, we redescribe ourselves as others in terms that cut across the action vocabulary of the agent so that the agent's vocabulary is determined by forces of which he/she is unaware.
>
> (Steele 1997: 8–9)

There are thus two dimensions in the construction of game rhetorics. The first is organized at an intersubjective level, either as an intimate face-to-face network or as a local mutually interdependent cluster of such networks. The second is the third-person level that is either trans-subjective or globalized. In the trans-subjective there is only the Master with all individuals organized according to Absolute Reason (Benhabib 1986). To be a subject is to be subjugated. However, globally, there are many such trans-subjective contenders organized by religion, schooling, law and tradition. The global is a game of games. In short, it is learnt that reality is contested by alternative realities and that one has to learn the right moves to get what one wants by playing in the right game at the right time and place. For the researcher studying the role of referential rhetorics in the creation of a dynamic sense of reality for a given individual or group of people, this means mapping the interrelationships between game-realities held by different individuals and groups whether they are operating at local or global levels.

Global games run by quite different rules to that of locally enforced game rules. As Haseler (2000) argues, looking to the nation state as a safeguard against the global desires of multinational corporations is a big mistake. Indeed, global capital now treats nation states as pieces on a global chess board. Researchers and other professionals who do not recognize this are in the position of playing draughts at the local level yet serving the interests of others in a much bigger, more sophisticated game. Indeed, politicians seem only too cooperative in playing the game according to global rules while maintaining an illusion of local agency. For example, global capital and their political friends, whether nominally 'left-' or 'right'-wing

> have given up on the old-fashioned, Victorian–utopian idea of creating an 'educated population'. Thus although the rhetoric about

education remains, the reality of the global economy is that capital does not need educated people; rather it needs a local population that is trained and skilled.

This task of maintaining and enhancing the skills of local populations is conveniently not assigned to global capital itself, but rather to the public sector. British Prime Minister Tony Blair once went so far as to argue that such skilling and reskilling was nothing less than the 'greatest single priority' of government in the global economy. Global capital will of course play its part in this process – as a kind of umpire, picking and choosing between nation-states as to which ones have performed best, and rewarding the winners by investing, for a short period, in their local populations.

(Haseler 2000: 158)

Strategies for effective political action thus depend on deconstructing the referential rhetorics by which political realities are maintained at local and global levels. The scale of this task for any researcher, no matter how experienced, is daunting. It will be pursued in the discussions of Chapters 8 and 9 when focusing on the relations between action, ethics and politics.

To maintain the political realities subjecting individuals in their everyday lives involves the continuous manufacture, the kind of *bricolage* meticulously attending to the trivial that underpins the social order. By this I mean the moment-by-moment, barely discernible interactions that accumulate the 'weight', the 'density', the 'hardness' of everyday realities. Birdwhistell (1973), for example, analysed the incredibly brief interactions consisting of no more than a second or two between a mother caring for her baby. He argued that in this way the baby's behaviour was being shaped and, in this case, the interactions were producing situations where the child could not do anything right. Through millions of such interactions, consisting of seconds, the life of a child is indelibly marked. This is not to say that the researcher *must* record interactions in such detail, although of course, like Birdwhistell, there will be those who have this kind of research focus. Rather, the researcher can gain insights into the meticulous structuring of everyday life by attention to the ways in which behaviour is organized as 'right', 'proper', 'appropriate' and so on.

For example, on a long train journey during July 1999, a family of mum, dad and three children came to sit near me. Dad organized the children into place and then asked whether they wanted anything to eat. This involved describing the sequence of actions to be followed: 'First sit there, then I will check out the buffet and see what they have to eat. Then I will return and tell you what is on offer, and then . . .' As I listened to their interaction I began writing:

. . . there's an 'instructional mapping' before the event . . . Alongside this there's a continual surveillance.

Dad: Billy don't please, not on a train you don't. Joe, Joe, Joe!
Mum: Go and sit next to daddy.
Dad: Billy, don't!

I noticed that the strategy for handling their children was to map out the preferred sequences of events. Following this, the children were under constant attention and remarks were made as to whether they were behaving appropriately. The father knelt on the seat of his chair in order to see and speak directly to his children sitting behind him. I continued to write:

Mapping before the events sets out what is going to happen next, or going to happen if . . . ; the reasons why a particular sequence should be followed.
Mum (to the child beside her): Have you finished your chocolate bar then? Good. (Turning round to the two behind her): How about you two, how are you getting on?

This has a kind of time measuring effect, again reinforcing the 'proper' sequence.

The children frequently tried out or postulated sequences of events in conversations with mother or father who listened carefully and at the end, said 'good'. But, what am I doing at this point? I was doing what I had done thousands of times over the years on fieldwork, overhearing snatches of conversation, noting them, thinking about them, playing with the associations of ideas triggered off in my mind, mapping the intentional networks. In reports I might draw upon such musings under the name of 'theoretical' or 'analytic memos'. These are no more than data concerning my own 'thoughts in progress' capturing the little 'epiphanies' or gestalts. I use the term 'analytic memos' when I am focusing on possible ways of forming categories by which to describe what I am seeing. When I move towards attempting possible ways of explaining or forming theories or models concerning the focus of my reflections I tend to employ the term 'theoretical' memos. In this way I can reflect on how I am beginning to 'construct' what I am seeing and hence leave the way open for their deconstruction. Doing them, there is a sense of lived experience, of catching things in the flow. But is it research? As I write, what is it I am writing about? Is this a 'representation' of what happened? Is it data about the events as they occurred between the members of the family, or is it data about my observation and thinking processes? What, if any, is the nature of the relationship between the two?

The play of recording, analysis, associating with ideas and memories is a process of representation that draws out commonalities and differences between different contexts. It does not pretend to be a neutral one-to-one form of 'naturalistic' description that adds nothing to and takes nothing from the Real. It is a representation that goes beyond the misleading metaphor of the mirror that claims only to reflect what is there. Rather, the representational grasp is a constructive–deconstructive exercise.

What we have in the preceding narrative is similar to what von Wright called quasi-causal sequences composed of both a causal and intentional side where the 'events are linked . . . through practical syllogisms' (Howard 1982: 68). The fact of getting on the train next to the buffet car allows certain inferences to be made about obtaining refreshments. The father investigates and returns bearing factual information about what is available. The children are then invited to make choices. The father then goes and purchases chocolates according to the intentions of the children. None of this could take place without the sense of there being regularities that the actors think are true, that can be intentionally utilized by them to make a difference in the world according to their desires, needs, interests, whims. The researcher, thus, by identifying and describing such regularities can map the strategies of a given individual and group through which particular world views are maintained. Essential to this strategy is narrative.

Narratives describe the relationships between knowledge, interests and intentions within interlocking webs of evidence (Howard 1982: 64) and provide verification sequences (p. 63). In short, people need to 'want' the world to consist of immediately practical states of affairs. That is, they need to be designed into 'projects' for the accomplishment of cultural verities. If it is true that the world is 'like x', then people have to prove the truth of 'x' in their actions to ensure that their interests and orientations have been counterfactually designed, that is, worlds where people have been constructed into what is not wanted as an occurrence: thou shalt not . . . , on the one side, and future possible actions on the other (and your reward will be in heaven). We live and work in worlds predesigned in terms of counterfactuals and promises of reward (or punishment). Telling the story is then a major textual strategy for representing the worlds and lives of others. But how is it to be told?

Telling tales

Models for exploring the telling of stories can be found in novels, films, plays, biographies, documentaries. There is a particular power in the story that has its dangers.

> One of the most obviously artificial devices of the story teller is the trick of going beneath the surface of the action to obtain a reliable view of a character's mind and heart.[13] Whatever our ideas may be about the natural way to tell a story, artifice is unmistakably present whenever the author tells us what no one in so-called real life could

possibly know. In life we never know anyone but ourselves by thoroughly reliable internal signs, and most of us achieve an all too partial view even of ourselves.

(Booth 1961: 3)

In ethnography such omnipotence may reveal itself in the authority of the witness as writer who claims to know and to be the source and guarantor of evidence, a position critiqued by Geertz (1988). However, Scheper-Hughes (1992), tired of what she calls the obsessive debates of postmodernists and self-reflexive hermeneutics, defends a 'good enough' ethnography where 'we struggle to do the best we can with the limited resources we have at hand – our ability to listen and observe carefully, empathically, and compassionately'. Like Chomsky she is passionately committed:

I think of some of the subjects of this book for whom anthropology is *not* a hostile gaze but rather an opportunity to tell a part of their life story. And though I can hear the dissonant voices in the background protesting *just this* choice of words, I believe there is still a role for the ethnographer–writer in giving voice, as best she can, to those who have been silenced, as have the people of the Alto by political and economic oppression and illiteracy and as have their children by hunger and premature death. So despite the mockery that Clifford Geertz (1988) made of anthropological 'I-witnessing,' I believe there is still value in attempting to 'speak truth to power.' I recall how my Alto friends grabbed and pushed and pulled, jostling for attention, saying, 'Don't forget me; I want my turn to speak. That one has had your attention long enough!'

(Scheper-Hughes 1992: 28)

For her there is an intimate relation between the story, witnessing, the act of remembrance, of authenticity and of being an individual. Do not forget me!

Without such an approach that focuses upon the 'me's that clamour for attention, there remains the danger of an authoritarian[14] rhetoric where the author is the bureaucratic or committed overseer of analyses, interpretations and the production of theories that give the illusion of an ordered universe of explanation. As discussed in Chapter 6, it brings about what Benhabib (1986: 98) calls the trans-subjective subject as the 'third', that is the third person voice employed in its Absolute sense. There is no dialogue in this conception of the third because there is no intersubjective arena wherein differences are explored and celebrated. Rather, differences are to be resolved, homogenized under the gaze of the third, or in Lacan's terms the Other, where all falls under the legislative power of the Name of the Father.

The voice – first, second, third person – through which the story is told is a powerful rhetorical device framing the process of writing and of interpreting a text. The choice is political, ethical, educational. Each choice positions the text, the writer and the reader and gives a particular value to that position. Writing from the position of 'I' may connote personal opinion and therefore be perceived as of less value than the impersonal voice that connotes a legislative, objective stance. To write of 'I', 'you' and 'us' has the feel of a conversation between people who draw upon a set of understandings and experiences that assumes a value, a knowledge common to all and thus beyond dispute, or sufficiently non-threatening to bring about critical reflection upon personal experiences shared by many.

The researcher, whether doctoral student or highly experienced, needs to reflect on the 'voice' chosen for the thesis or report. In my view, whatever voice is chosen should be justified. As reader I may disagree with the choice but at least I can make my assessments according to the sophistication of the arguments provided concerning the choice. The thesis or report will enter into a community of conversation, dialogue, debate and will be judged according to how it engages with this community. Some will agree with it and some disagree with it. However, all should be able to judge the extent to which the thesis or report draws upon the different currents of argumentation, deploys its data in ways that adhere to, contest or develop from prevailing approaches, theories, 'knowledge' and 'beliefs'. A thesis is likely to be judged on how well it makes these relationships clear as it tells the 'story' of the project. The story, of course, can be told in many ways, some of which will be developed further in Chapter 10. Its narrative structure can either be broken up and rearranged to fit the development of the arguments of the thesis, or it can provide the underlying structure. Thus the narrative dimension of story telling can be employed either to reconstruct and represent events observed or, indeed, to frame the entire text of the report, thesis or publication. For example, the following vignette is employed to represent a 'typical' event where a trainee nurse is being assessed (Phillips *et al.* 2000):

> The general/genito urinary surgical ward is perpetually busy with four medical teams, daily theatre lists and emergency admissions. The staff feel over-stretched affording their patients of both sexes adequate care, observation and dignity in the separate bays and side-wards. The assessee (halfway through his adult branch programme) now has his third assessor in this single placement. His 'preliminary' interview occurred in week 3 and his mid-point assessment is deferred indefinitely. He needs this placement to acquire a range of clinical skills including oral and intramuscular drug

administration, but the pressure of work has repeatedly resulted in single nurse administration while he has maintained a basic level of care for the remaining patients. Today proves no exception.

Patients for surgery arrive before their beds are vacated by those awaiting discharge and the two emergency admissions are female when the only empty beds are in a male bay. The assessee moves beds and possessions accordingly, and as people go home, washes furniture and makes up the beds for the afternoon theatre list. In between, he assists patients to wash, where he can manage single-handed helps post-operative patients to sit out of bed, performs nursing observations and notifies trained staff when intravenous infusions require changing. Where pre-medication or post-operative analgesia is required, he is never free to be involved. His practical learning objectives are not being achieved and he fears this will affect his ultimate success. His sole ambition now is qualification before he leaves nursing.

(Micro-vignette Y – based on fieldnotes of observation in genito and genito-urinary surgical ward)

The function of the vignette is to provide concrete illustrations of typical aspects of a process both by indexical and typification extensions. These have been established through interviews and observations across a range of fieldwork sites around the country. The vignette, however, could be substantially expanded to provide detailed descriptions of the environment, the conversations that took place, the individuals. This in turn could be expanded to include descriptions and analyses of the wider contexts and implicit, although unrepresented, personnel of the organizations involved in running the ward, hospital, region and other national bodies. Or the focus could be on the biographies of the individuals involved – the stories of their lives and how these relate to their present actions. Or it could focus on the historical development of nursing, its philosophies, value systems and so on that are being articulated in some fashion in the vignette. The options for development are unlimited. This, of course, means that the researcher must make and justify decisions as to the prime purpose of the project and the likely concerns of the intended readership.

The narrative, in whatever form, is a powerful rhetorical device for representing the sense of 'reality', the sense of 'being there'. If practitioners are to be the audience (implicitly or explicitly) of a particular report, thesis or publication then the 'smell' of reality in the text is important. The reader can say, 'Yes, I recognize that. Yes, that represents the complexity of my experience.' This is a form of generalization that moves from the text to the experiences of the readers who validate not from some trust in the use of statistics but through the experiences of their everyday practice. How to develop the narrative device as a methodology that connects data to analysis and to lives has been explored in the literature (e.g. Schostak 1985, 1991, 1993; Haug 1987; Denzin 1989; Davies and Harré 1990; Samuel and Thompson 1990; Goodson and Walker 1991; Linde 1993) and is developed further in relation to 'writing up' (see Chapter 10). Recalling the stealth architecture described in Chapter 4, narratives can be composed from evidence relating to the public and private spheres by which individuals and groups enact their philosophies in their social practices, employ or subvert the mechanisms and procedures of a given organization and gain access to the resources. Narrative is thus a vehicle that represents the relationship between events, social and material arrangements, and the multiplicity of voices and multiple meanings that are bound chord-like or dissonantly through which everyday life is constructed.

Ambiguity and irony

Meanings rarely, if ever, are given all at once. Ambiguity is not, as it is in mathematics, a flaw to be repaired but a resource to be explored and employed (cf. Empson 1930). Indeed, it may be dangerous to reveal too much. Irony has often been used to present on the surface one meaning that covers up a hidden alternative and 'true' meaning of the text. One famous example is that of Swift's modest proposal on how to deal both with overpopulation and with the famine in Ireland. He 'advocated' cooking and eating babies. Booth (1974), drawing on this and other examples, described both stable and non-stable frameworks for ironic writing. In a stable framework the ironies constructed 'build back' to produce a stable meaning (as in the Swift example). However, in an unstable formulation like 'This statement is a lie', the truth of the statement cannot be established. Its value oscillates. If it is a true statement then it cannot be a lie. If, in literal terms, it is a lie then it must be false to state that it is a lie. These oscillations can operate like the double binds (Bateson 1972) or Catch 22s made famous in the title of Heller's book (1962) and explored in learning situations by Birdwhistell (1973). No matter what you do you will be wrong. The demand for novelty in a doctoral thesis is rather like a catch 22 in that if it is truly novel then it breaks with the previous frameworks by which it can be recognized as a doctoral thesis![15] To deal with this, the student will need to frame the novel against the background of the 'old', showing the 'novel' is not arbitrarily conceived, but has been adopted due to the failures or inappropriateness of the 'old' to deal with the project focus. Some approaches to this can be seen in Chapters 5 and 10, as well as through deconstructing the nature of the double bind.

The double bind constructs a fertile field for subjectivity to double-cross, masquerade, camouflage itself, seduce or all but disappear entirely from view behind facades that seem real, that produce reality and truth effects (Baudrillard 1990) that fool the eye and the mind. The stealth architextures described in Chapter 4 can be explored in terms of these ambiguous, ironic, seductive, deceptive textualities. It becomes a textual play of the legal and official as against the forbidden and repressed. This entwining of the open and forbidden I have elsewhere described as the forbidden discourse (Schostak 1993). Through it the textual subtleties of everyday life are fabricated and can be deconstructed in terms of its ironic and stealth structurings. Exploring the forbidden discourses of the everyday can reveal more than the researcher can cope with, or more than the powerful would wish to reveal. Either way, representing the forbidden discourses in a thesis, report or other publication can be problematic. The strategy adopted by the writer may involve a variety of stealth techniques, drawing, for example, on irony, or allegory. Here a 'surface' message occludes an alternative reading which can only be recovered through deconstructing the surface to see the traces that enable a reconstructed reading. This will be discussed further in Chapter 10 in relation to writing up where the possibilities of textual construction are exploited to the full.

The architecture of forbidden discourses and stealth strategies through which they may be expressed are constructed through the richness of the plurivocal:

Where the univocal constructs a linear melody, the plurivocal has its multiple layers of chords and discords. It is a multiplicity which never quite covers what it means to say. It is a place where fact, memory, imagination and desire collude in the fantastic production of the real, as reality effects in the way that a) a trompe l'oeil produces the effect of a real object on a painted surface, and b) the half light of dawn or dusk where nothing has a clear and distinct value and thus imagination works to fill in the gaps or draw the boundaries of objects which then emerge as fantastic beings. Upon the deceptive surface and in the half-light what can be witnessed and what can be taken as having been witnessed?

Such witnessing is dangerous, it releases too much of what can no longer be contained and yet entraps by other means:

J'attire l'homme vers plus de lumière; vers une zone frappée par un rai lumineux qui vient de la surface, traverse un soupirail et projette sur le mur la forme d'une grille. Nous allons jouir dans une cage fictive, une cellule aux barreaux seulement fabriqués par l'ombre et la lumière.[16]

Cyril Collard (1989: 89) writes of his life and of his impending death through AIDS through the light of fiction. He writes of the ambivalent pleasures in a world *'entre chien et loup'*[17] where in the shadows it is no longer possible to tell the difference between the dog and the wolf, between friendship and danger, a place, however, intensely seductive with intense emotions and uncontrollable drives, a place created through a dynamic of the fictional and the real. This place is the borderlands of the imaginary . . .

(Schostak 1999b)

The in-between of the chien–loup traces its lines according to a logic of betrayal, ambivalence, desire and anxiety. To have an identity at all, to be able to be represented is essential yet, as for Collard, open to betrayal. The story, as Zizek (1993: 11) comments, is critical for social existence:

Today, even the mass media is aware of the extent to which our perception of reality, including the reality of our innermost self-experience, depends upon symbolic fictions. Suffice it to quote from a recent issue of *Time* magazine: 'Stories are precious, indispensable. Everyone must have his history, her narrative. You do not know who you are until you possess the imaginative version of yourself. You almost do not exist without it.'

What many contemporary writers like Zizek are problematizing is the 'subject' presumed to be 'behind' the narrative, the story of one's 'self' and of others. What is being opened up here is not only that one may be mistaken about the 'subject' or the 'other' and not only that the subject and others may have no other reality than that of being 'possible selves' but that the possibility of identity is an illusion always open for reversioning for use in the next context.

New frontiers: virtual tracks in hyperspace

As a kind of chien–loup the world of cyberspace where differences between 'Real' and 'real' fade has become the site for identity play. One becomes whatever character one desires. This capacity is drawn from the role of language itself as promoting a kind of simulation of the Real in the mind of the reader or interpreter:

Subjectivity can never be real or full, as it is always based on simulation or what Algidas Julien Greimas calls the 'enunciative fallacy.' That is, 'I' and 'you,' 'here' and 'now' are *not* the subjects, place and time of the act of enunciation: these linguistic forms are 'shifters' and 'simulacra' within the discourse that *imitate* the act of enunciation within the utterance.

(Morse 1998: 11)

One way of exploring what is going on is through the Piercian semiosis. On the internet I found a series of communications between a student, a teaching assistant and a member of staff. The question concerned how to trace 'a line of semiosis' through a text. Although the exchange appears no longer to be on the original site it provided a useful discussion on the role of Pierce's conception of the 'interpretant', that is the act of interpretation, forming a meaning in the mind and its relation to a referent (that is the 'thing' or object that the sign refers to). A line of semiosis is constructed from the particular meanings that formed in the 'minds' of people or, in this case, the characters portrayed in a particular novel. Thus as a sign is read an interpretant of it is formed in the mind of the reader or character. This will be different from that of another reader or character and so on. As they exchange views further interpretants are constructed in the minds of each. Tracking the development of meanings in relation to signs thus becomes a line of semiosis. Through the work of 'shifters' (I, you, here, there, now, then and so on) the illusion of a reality is constructed; this illusion can be so firmly held by a given individual or group that it displaces all other possible realities, indeed, Reality.

This seems to me to evoke what takes place in making hypertextual links that jump from context to context and in so jumping make lines of connection in the mind of a given hypertext surfer. At the site that promoted the thoughts on lines of semiosis[18] there is a new hypertextual architecture where the tracks are of at least three kinds: those constructed by hypertext links; those formed in the pathways made by each jump from link to link; and those that are created in the *mind* of the reader who makes these jumps. This kind of structure seems to be typical of the representational realities emerging in cyberspace. Hypertext, as Moulthrop (1993) points out, has been around for a long time, indeed since the 1940s. It is 'a technology for creating electronic documents in which the user's access to information is not constrained, as in books, by linear or hierarchical arrangements of discourse' (p. 71). Its full implications await exploration.

Representation carried out in the new architectures of space, time and virtual realities perhaps finally loses the distinction between real/fantasy, true/false. Its importance for the project is that there are here new territories for exploration and for the allocation of resources to desire, opportunity and need. Far from excluding desire there are new opportunities for its articulation while at the same time reducing living flesh to obsolescence (cf. Kroker and Weinstein 1994). In cyberspace games there is always the possibility of reversibility through a replay; there's always the next game where fortunes may be reversed from penury to abundance and vice versa. Cyberspace and global realities are increasingly becoming one and the same. The world of the cyborg is no longer in the realm of science fiction. It is here and is the subject of an increasing number of studies (e.g. Gray 1995). The issue of the relation between the courses of action and games played in cyber–global realities and those transacted in physical and hence local domains is becoming increasingly urgent. It is a world where the maps and their referents (the real world that is the object of the mapping) have been displaced by simulacra, indeed where any map may be used as a means of 'navigating' another space (Perry 1998: 69–100). What is of interest in such a navigation are the surprises, juxtapositions, the collisions that might occur. When Gaad (see Chapter 1) constructed a map of the Egyptian educational structure in order to navigate in relation to the UK educational structure (and vice versa) she was doing just this, albeit not thinking in terms of hypertext, nor hyper realities. Here text and evidence have merged collusively, deceptively, ironically. Is research then just a double-cross with evidence the token purloined to be passed from subject to subject as they play out the possibilities for self-advantage? If there is an answer to this that is not just another ironic double-cross it is, I believe, to be found in discussions of the ethical and its relation to politics, dialogue and action.

8

Framing ethics and political issues

How can individuals overcome their existential solitude, anxiety and alienation? On the one hand, is it just a matter of finding the game to be played in order to draw profit from the system of legislating for value that is in play at a given time and place? Is the other just someone to use or double-cross? Or is it about trying to identify basic values of human dignity, freedom and justice? In thinking how to live with others and, in so doing, how to live with the consequences, ethical and political questions arise as solitude is replaced by the question of being with others in a common world of resource and action.

In carrying out a project – interviewing, observing, writing up analyses, views, arguments – there is inevitably some intervention in the life of another and with it both an ethics and a politics is projected having implications for how subjects and objects are valued, opportunities framed and resources allocated. Indeed, aren't ethics and politics simply two sides of the same coin? Where they differ is in what face is to be presented to the world. Yet there is a third, and perhaps binding side of the coin: religion, the edge that no matter how it is reduced, remains an edge – does one extend one's solitude to the point of death?[19] Or does one engage with otherness in terms of an Other that transcends time, place and death and whose judgement of our value must be sought and accepted? The fourth 'side' or dimension is the changing dynamic, the trajectory of the coin's circulation as value over time through which ethics, religion, politics appear in social life as history or, indeed, as biography. Ethics, politics/economics and religion, however conceived, implies a Good that is the object of action.

All projects are directed towards a desired state of affairs, whether these focus on describing states of affairs (truthfully, accurately, persuasively, ironically and so on), forming explanations, bringing about understandings, or engaging in actions. Focusing on individuals, on groups, on masses, on complex forms of social organization, projects set in motion interpretations, actions, debates. Again, as always, the question arises, upon what should I found my project?

Most if not all textbooks on research methodology include statements and discussions of ethics. Issues arise concerning the power of the researcher in relation to that of the research subjects. If there is here an echo of the Hegelian struggle between master and slave for supremacy it is not entirely accidental. The research subject is subjected to the gaze of the researcher, reduced to being of value as data to be drawn under the explanatory voice of the researcher's textual representations. The principles of ethics are set out in order to temper this power. Or does it merely reproduce or, indeed, inaugurate this power? Or, indeed, are protocols a way of bureaucratizing ethics, or of employing them stealthily to negotiate access at one level only to be abandoned at the point of dissemination? For example, in health contexts, what counts as 'informed consent' between doctor and patient? Or, how much does the interviewee or person observed by the researcher know about the risks of taking part in the research? How much will the researcher reveal of his or her purposes? These are all questions that cannot be settled in a simple act of obtaining assent whether through a signature or orally. The ethical and political issues need to be thought through in more detail.

Framing protocols

Take, for example, this extract describing an approach to two key research and evaluation issues:

reciprocity and equality of status
For the purposes of evaluation differences in power and risk should be minimised and political relationships should be subject to checks and balances. To this end relationships in and around an evaluation should be informed by the principle of reciprocity and equality of status. At a minimum this means that those persons who will be affected by an evaluation should be informed about how and why it is being done, should have opportunities to contribute to it and have access to its results. The procedures associated with this principle include:

1 the evaluators will attend to a wide variety of perspectives on the programme, to the diverse claims made about it, to its context and history;
2 there will be no *ad hominem* evaluation;
3 differences of opinion as to the conduct of the evaluation will, wherever possible, be resolved through negotiation. When this is not possible serious disputes will be resolved through arbitration;

4 the membership of steering groups or management committees should represent the major interest groups associated with an evaluation. The evaluation will have the right to be consulted about the membership of such bodies and to recommend at least one member.

openness

Openness is a necessary condition for the long term conduct of research since it provides the basis for public accountability and peer review methods, methodology and outcomes. Peer review is also important to the long term development of evaluation but in most cases it cannot provide the basis for a critical appraisal of outcomes within the timetable of programme decision-making. Evaluation requires other safeguards against bias and error and other forms of critical appraisal of its processes and products. For evaluation participant review is of more immediate value than peer review and requires that:

1 there will be no covert evaluation;
2 there will be no secret reporting, though some reports may be restricted;
3 the evaluation proposal, *modus operandi* and reports will be open to scrutiny by those whose work and lives are to be represented;
4 participants will have the right to comment on the fairness, relevance and accuracy of all evaluation reports.

(CARE 1994: 117)

Similarly principles of procedure can be elaborated for such issues as independence, impartiality, negotiation and confidentiality. But why do this? The object is to empower those who have traditionally lacked it, and to curtail the abuse of power of those who have traditionally been able to exercise it. But what sort of rationale is this? Does it have a democratic, social justice flavour? It apparently fits the social and political projects of those who agree with Mouffe (1993) that democracy is an unfinished revolution and who are committed to embedding it in all social practices in order to care for the freedoms, safety, humanity, dignity and so on of others. However, making such a statement and realizing it are quite different. It can so easily be reduced to a bureaucratic response satisfying demands, say from the supervisor of a thesis, that the student should indicate in the methodology section that ethical protocols had been made known to participants. Realization of such protocols in practice requires constant attention to the effects of the researcher's presence and methods and use of data on the people whose lives are under study. In the thesis the researcher can raise these issues and show how they were resolved or provide rationales for action taken.

Recall the stealth architecture of Chapter 4. Each passage from ideas to mechanisms, procedures or cultural practices generally, and each allocation of resources to the implementation of an idea, a value, a policy, involves both political and ethical choices. Rereading the stealth architecture as a framework for ethical and political choices identifies the decision points where self and other may adopt positions of mutual aid, competition, savagery or indifference towards each other in the allocation of resource to need, interest, talent and opportunities to enhance social justice, cultural change, human freedom and creativity. This point takes on greater force when read with those philosophers in mind who have recently argued, contrary to long-held dogma, that value statements can and should be drawn from statements of fact (Edgley 1976; Bhaskar 1986; Collier 1994).[20] In essence, the argument says that if a theory, say T1, correctly describes empirical reality then there is an implicit criticism of all other competing theories that do not agree with T1. If someone informs their judgement on the basis of a competing theory then they are not only mistaken, they *should not* act on the basis of it. If they persist in acting on the basis of the false theory then one *ought* to find out why. Is it a lack of knowledge? If so, then this knowledge *should* be provided to them. Is it some intervening illusion, procedure, or power structure that prevents them from acting according to T1? If this is the case, then that illusion, procedure or intervening power structure *should* be removed and/or replaced. Is it a lack of appropriate resources that is preventing people from acting upon correct knowledge? Then those resources *should*, indeed, *must*, be provided. Neither ethics not politics, therefore, can be removed from the practice of the researcher or other professional engaged in action in the world. However, in the social arena it seems to me that frequently there is no simple or unambiguous approach to ascertaining the 'truth' of a theory as may be the case in experimental frameworks of the natural sciences. The social world is not a closed system where all can be controlled (see Chapter 4). The social world can be described as an 'open system' where there is uncertainty, fuzziness, 'messiness'. It is important, therefore, for the stealth architecture to be reread in terms of the politics and ethics of generalization, validity and objectivity as research claims to inform policy and decision making. In this context it is particularly relevant to take into account Macdonald's (1984) argument that an evaluation may adopt one of three positions:

1 bureaucratic evaluation;
2 autocratic evaluation;
3 democratic evaluation.

These three positions frame data collection, analysis and interpretation and hence validity, objectivity and generalizability. Bureaucratic evaluation gives power to the policy maker, autocratic evaluation locates it with the evaluator and democratic evaluation locates it in the democratic code described in the principles of procedure of the project. The bureaucratic evaluator unconditionally 'accepts the values of those who hold office, and offers information which will help them to accomplish their policy objectives'. The autocratic evaluator offers 'a conditional service to those government agencies which have major control over the allocation of educational resources'. The conditionality is because its 'values are derived from the evaluator's perception of the constitutional and moral obligations of the bureaucracy'. Only in democratic evaluation are the powers of the different groups levelled to ensure that each has equal opportunity to provide their views, that no one view is given greater power than another and that all have access to the products of the evaluation.

Evaluations are typically wanted by policy makers when they need to have information about the success or otherwise of a programme, innovation, implementation of new organizational mechanisms or change in resource allocation. An evaluation can provide a range of information critical to successful implementation only if respondents feel that what they say will not prejudice their careers, life and liberty. This range can only be obtained if the evaluator listens to the different interest groups. The most powerful range of arguments and insights can only be generated if the evaluator gives serious critical attention to all sources of information, no matter how lowly their social or organizational status. Democratic procedures can then facilitate the gathering of alternative views.

However, powerful individuals and groups will often try to compromise the evaluator. There have been many occasions when students who wanted to carry out an evaluation in their workplace have been told by their superior that the evaluation could proceed only on the condition of revealing what particular individuals have said and done. The courses of action open to the researcher then are first, to identify the benefits that may persuade superiors that their best interests are served if they accept the protocols framing the research because these will provide the most useful information in anonymized form to facilitate policy formation and decision making; second, to leave and find another more cooperative organization; or third, to proceed either as an open challenge relying on the backing of a range of countervailing powers (the superior of the superior, powerful committees, or other allies) or proceed covertly, under the guise of doing a different project; or some combination of any of the preceding. All of these can be seen as the tactics employed to gain and maintain access in organizations – this is so of most, if not all – that to varying degrees want to control the research and the researcher. Each has to be handled with care and researchers would have to provide in their thesis the ethical and political rationales for their choice of action.

Carrying out any research in authoritarian contexts or those hostile to openness is a risk. Some who have tried it have had to change their careers or place of work. Research tends to reveal what the powerful would wish to keep quiet. It is important for any researchers to think carefully about the risks they are taking with both the careers, lives and liberty of others and also their own. Indeed, knowing all the risks is impossible. Often we are taken by surprise by those who we thought were allies who turn out to be a source of threat, or vice versa.

All research is thus political. Why? Because it is about entering the lives of others, making public what many may feel ought to be kept private or secret and, indeed, about making changes whether to perceptions, bodies of knowledge, beliefs, values or to the circumstances of lives. In practice all becomes confused:

> Despite the fact that the intention behind the use of principles of procedure is to ease potential problems for those who agree to take part in the research, when they are used for research conducted in hierarchical institutions like those in the Health Service they are not entirely unproblematic. Despite a principle of non-coercion, for instance, I cannot be one hundred percent certain that research subjects felt entirely free to refuse to participate. Some must have felt pressure, if only symbolic pressure, to be seen to be co-operating. And although there was a principle of confidentiality which helped to re-assure most of the people interviewed . . . , I was aware that the information I was being told in confidence would be 'used', in some form or another, in writing a report of the research. The aim of the interviewing and observation was to create a public account. A principle of control over release of the data operated and all participants were told that they had the right to say *'please don't include that bit'*, or *'please will you turn off the tape-recorder, I don't want you to quote me on this'*, or even, at the end of an interview, to ask to keep the tape. At the end of an interview I always checked to see if it was alright to use the material. I am aware, however, that I made my request hoping desperately that information would not be withheld, and I cannot be sure that some sense of this was not conveyed to the interviewees. The main purpose of the principles was to establish a trust between researcher and researched. If that trust was jeopardised the research too might well be jeopardised. This fact was a powerful practical factor in ensuring the spirit of the principles was upheld at moments when there might otherwise have been a temptation to operate according to the letter. As a consequence of these principles of procedure, the trustworthiness of the interview data was almost certainly increased.
>
> (Phillips 1995: 75, original italics)

The procedure adopted such as negotiation, or the method employed such as interviewing, or the resource used such as a tape recorder, all involve ethical and political choices that will differ from circumstance to circumstance. Even the choice of representing the researcher's own struggle has its political and ethical consequences. It generates a pervasive sense of strategy underlying the account of the researcher's application of principles of procedure. One explicit object of the passage is to persuade the reader of the trustworthiness of the data presented. One frightening question to ask a researcher is: how do I know you didn't make it all up? One answer is in the rhetorical style of telling: the air of continual self-critical reflection, and attention to the apparently trivial and, indeed, of ethical soundness evokes a relationship of trust, indeed a tryst between minds who meet at their appointed hour and destination. Politics, ethics, research and reporting are thus all intertwined in the desire to convince, to bring self and other together in agreement. The choices one makes matter.

How to choose? In the end the choices are those made by the individual. It is all bound up with the key theme: what is 'my' project? Whether the project is externally defined and funded or a matter of personal curiosity undertaken for private pleasure, a publication or a thesis the question remains. 'I' have to make choices about the underlying purposes of the project. Many different criteria for making choices have been discussed throughout the book. All have been rendered problematic as the values underlying those choices are put to the test of practice. It has been argued that one cannot just rely on something feeling right in the bones, or on deeply held personal opinions or, indeed, traditional verities or even 'scientific' procedures. It seems there is a fundamental catch-22 or double bind that underlies the research act. To do research at all, choices have to be made. Data has to be collected, analysed and made known. Who has the 'right' to say what should or should not be revealed or how it should be used? All the ethical protocols so far discussed have as a key objective: the protection of individual rights. Yet what if, for example, the respondent says 'No, I don't want you to use anything I have said, please wipe the tape!' What if that respondent had been acting fraudulently, was a child abuser, or was cynically employing organizational power? Indeed, if you were researching a violent criminal group, would you even let them know you were a researcher? What in general terms, to cover all possibilities, should underlie one's ethical concerns? Indeed, if protocols seem inadequate to handle all these possibilities, is it because to maintain an ethical point of view is just another form of self-delusion? Perhaps if the ethical is either too difficult to pin down, or indeed is a form of self-delusion, then a more practical approach is to explore the freedom to research in relation to the law.

The law

The limits to freedom are everywhere. In exploring the reaction of the West to the death threats made against Salman Rushdie for having written his book *The Satanic Verses*, considered at the time by many Muslims to be blasphemous, Webster (1990) examined the selective application of criticism by 'liberals'. Like the poet and novelist the researcher risks always upsetting the values and norms of others. Indeed, he argues that no civilized country would simply sweep away the laws surrounding, for example, libel in order to achieve absolute free speech:

> For words are not, as is sometimes claimed, neutral and harmless instruments. They can be as lethal, almost, as bullets and can cause great offence and personal distress. That is why absolute freedom to speech is ultimately no more desirable than absolute freedom to murder.
>
> (Webster 1990: 46)

Freedom, and hence the project, takes place not in the solitude of the individual's being but is staged, intersubjectively, historically. What is to be explored is freedom of selves among others within the context of particular historical circumstances. The law may be conceived as the necessary military and police force to prevent people from brutalizing and exploiting each other (Hobbes [1651] 1914) or as a way of maintaining and gaining the political power of the powerful (Machiavelli [c. 1515] 1976). Or it may be conceived as the exercise of reason over the uncultured, or animal side of human nature (Kant 1977; Locke [1693] 1989). Or as a guarantor of the rights of individuals in community with others (Paine [1792] 2000). These and other views on the role of the law in social life typically coexist throughout societies. A researcher may pursue the question: Which of these provide the greatest freedom for all individuals? For many, it is rationality that has seemed the most attractive and has indeed underpinned the enlightenment and modernist conceptions of social and political change. However, such rationality was defined in terms of the subjection of one's 'animal nature' to the civilizing powers of reason and resulted in distinguishing between those who are 'rational agents' and those who act within an 'animal state'. Thus, for example, the traditional distinction between male rationality and female emotionality was reinforced. It also became the basis of the professional justification for rational (or research-based) action that was 'in the best interests' of those defined as in some way incapable. Whether explicit or subtly implicit, there is a devaluation of the other as one who needs special treatment 'in their best interests'.

The research seeks to elicit the views of people with learning disabilities about aspects of their lives which they consider to be important, however a number of potential challenges exist in relation to involvement of individuals effectively, so that not only are people enabled to express their point of view, but their viewpoint is faithfully and accurately represented in subsequent reporting and analysis.

Some of the interviews were with people who have learning disabilities who have resided in institutional settings for the majority of their lives. During that time every day experience has emphasised limited opportunities for decision making. Thus the possibility of people becoming passive recipients of care is high. An examination of an average day in the life of a person with learning disabilities would reveal a comprehensive catalogue of events where little need to exercise responsibility is required. Thus it is that institutions reduce the capacity for choice and decision making and ultimately induce a sense of powerlessness in the people who reside in their structures. This phenomenon can be an obstacle in the research process if the goal of the research is to facilitate an atmosphere that does not place the person with learning disabilities within a net of coercion. As a researcher one has to be mindful of this possibility and try to reduce the likelihood of its occurrence.

(Shirtliffe 2000[21])

As a doctoral student, discussions with Shirtliffe have explored the need to build trust and openness with the families and the people with learning difficulties. This involves not only assurances of confidentiality and anonymization, but also requires the time, the openness and the care to listen, be with and take an interest in their lives. Just as important is the research attitude adopted where the researcher's own habitual ways of categorizing and interpreting are subject to scrutiny and made open to challenge by the ways others describe and account for their own experiences. Take for example Chow (1993), who in apparently different circumstances critiqued contemporary Western intellectuals in their concern to sanctify the victim and thus impose yet another view from the Western intellectual tradition as to how the Other should behave. There are:

the familiarly ironic scenarios of anthropology, in which Western anthropologists are uneasy at seeing 'natives' who have gone 'civilised' or who, like the anthropologists themselves, have taken up the active task of shaping their own culture. Margaret Mead, for instance, found the interest of certain Arapesh Indians (in Highland New Guinea) in cultural influences other than their own 'annoying' since, as James Clifford puts it, '*Their* culture collecting complicated hers.' (Clifford 1988: 232) Similarly, Claude Lévi-Strauss, doing his 'fieldwork' in New York on American ethnology, was affected by the sight, in the New York Public Library reading room where he was doing research for his *Elementary Structures of Kinship*, of a feathered Indian with a Parker pen.

(Chow 1993: 28)

There are ethical and political implications involved in a given research stance that in one context may seem not to be recognized, but in another can have dramatic consequences. Western forms of rationality that have underpinned Enlightenment and Modernist frameworks for doing science and organizing the political, social and economic worlds have, as discussed in Chapters 4, 5 and 6, a propensity for purifying and suspending the affective in the pursuit of objectivity. This play of purity and objectivity has left many washing their hands of the dirt of circumstances:

So Eichmann's opportunities for feeling like Pontius Pilate were many, and as the months and the years went by, he lost the need to feel anything at all. This was the way things were, this was the new law of the land, based on the Führer's order; whatever he did he did, as far as he could see, as a law-abiding citizen. He did his *duty*, as he told the police and the court over and over again; he not only obeyed *orders*, he also obeyed the *law . . .*

(Arendt 1963: 120)

Arendt described how Eichmann justified himself in terms of Kant's moral philosophy, but had twisted the message to become: 'Act as if the principle of your actions were the same as the legislator or of the law of the land' instead of: 'to (Kant) every man was a legislator the moment he started to act: by using his "practical reason" man found the principles that could and should be the principles of law' (Arendt 1963: 121).

In his own words Eichmann had distorted the message 'for the household use of the little man' (Arendt 1963: 121). Baas (1992: 34), however, pointed out that Eichmann did keep the appeal to the law and did carry out that law feelinglessly, reminiscent of Kant's insistence on carrying out the law without feeling. Unless the preceding seems like a rhetorical play with extremes, consider Milgram's experiments (1974) with individuals placed in the position of being asked to follow the instructions of a research programme to deliver electric shocks to 'students' who were being asked to recall some nonsense words. At each failure to remember the 'teacher' was asked to increase the shock as a punishment. Unknown to them the 'students' were actors and there was no shock. However, many delivered what could have been fatal charges of electricity – just because a person wearing the symbol of scientific rationality, a white coat, said that the experiment required them to do so. In a classic suspension of their 'animal pity' most delivered high charges and a few went all the way. This perhaps is the 'household science' of the 'little man'. It is the place where the 'ordinary' person may find the Eichmann within themselves.

Lacan's essay on *Kant avec Sade* set these same general principles in relation to Sade's philosophy of the libertine. Instead of the Führer there is the Law of Nature that governs the libertine's actions. This Nature is not the realm of the innocent, it is the jungle, the rage of the tempest, the terror of the earthquake, the savagery of the food chain. This Nature is utterly indifferent to humanity. In choosing Rawls as the model of the rational life plan to set into opposition with Sade, Airaksinen (1995: 97) sets up a similar opposition as Lacan's Sade with Kant. This opposition is worth exploring a little in order to deconstruct what is at stake in adopting an ethical point of view.

Rawls (1971) provides a theory of justice based on the idea that value is founded upon the individual's life plan chosen after having weighed up the alternatives. It is the rational life plan that determines the individual's 'good'. This seems to have some parallel with the choice of a project; indeed, doing a doctoral thesis can take anywhere between three years full-time and seven or eight part-time. It can become an obsession – either to finish, or to delay dealing with it. The project, however, can take on an even grander design if it refers not simply to the particular qualification or funded piece of research in hand but to a lifetime's ambition to contribute to some great movement like the globalization of democracy, the defeat of capitalism and so on. In this sense, the life plan integrates with the project to become the overarching ethical focus of all that is done. What are the implications of such a grand vision? As always, one approach is to seek its darkest contrast.

Now, Sade's master project can be understood as a baroque counter-argument against the view that identifies virtue with a coherent life plan, whether virtue is conceived in the Greek sense of the excellence of well-ordered habits or in the Roman and Machiavellian sense of virility, shrewdness, and strength of character. Coherence understood as order and strength is an undesirable quality for Sade, as for any anti-enlightenment thinker. It follows that their life plans cannot be modelled after a scientific theory. On the contrary, to them a person is an individual and his career is an expression of this mysterious uniqueness. The result is a kind of baroque view of thought. The good life and its values are founded directly on character, not on the explanatory coherence which hides individuality. This means that the life plan is neither seen nor accepted at the bargaining table; instead, it is displayed at once by the self-made hero for others to recognise. There is no guarantee that the plan is intelligible to the spectators. Still less probable is their willingness to share such one-sided values.

(Airaksinen 1995: 97)

There is an echo of Hempel's (1942) 'covering law theory' of scientific explanation in the adoption of a rational life plan. A human life is explained by the extent to which the observable events of life conform with the chosen rational life plan (similar to 'facts' being subsumed under a given scientific law – hence the title, 'covering law theory'). One becomes one's own research project and each action is just another datum to test the worth not only of the project but of one's life. The life plan, the project, is the explanation of the life that is being lived. What am I here for? Answer: to live this project. And this means:

Since explanations always generalise, a life plan does not individuate a person, but a type or a case. Therefore, if a person is perfectly moral, he is not an individual but is like any other bearer of these same values. It seems that Sade's counter-ethical point is that moral laws, and the principles of value derived from them, destroy personal identity.

(Airaksinen 1995: 98)

The irony in the Sadean universe is that orgiastic pleasure does the same. Sade faces a dilemma:

A person faces anonymous destruction within the bounds of ethics (that is, by reasoning like any other good person he loses his individuality); but the only way to avoid such a fate is to rebel and to break the laws of comprehensible thought and prudent action. Such mad rage is the person's only way out of the quiet death which is ethics. Nevertheless, by so doing he does not seem to be able to explain his life as his own. How can he individuate himself if he avoids all explanations?

(Airaksinen 1995: 98)

The answer, if there is such, is found in the style, the decoration by which the inexplicable and the meaningless are performed and adorned:

'My desires are a bit loathsome, I know, but you are intelligent. I have done you outstanding service; I shall do more: you are wicked, you are vindictive, – very well,' said he, tendering me six *lettres de cachet* which required only to be filled in with the names of whomever I chose to have imprisoned for an indeterminate period, 'here are some toys, amuse yourself with them'.

(Sade quoted by Airaksinen 1991: 101)

The purposes of the Sadean hero, like the will of the Divine, cannot be understood. They are essentially enigmatic, mysterious, awe-full. There seems to be an impasse. The discussion has returned yet again to the play between sense and nonsense discussed in Chapters 5 and 7. The tensions created by this impasse are powerful in their ability to deconstruct what has always been taken for granted. However, it provides no alternative answer as to what *should* be.

Returning to the research protocols discussed at the beginning of the chapter, what if the individual being researched is indeed a serious criminal, a Sadean figure? Researching the Sadean figure reveals the extent of social corruption through his or her social position, the structures and mechanisms that support that position and the values that enable that position to be guarded in secrecy. This is a hook that one does not get off very easily. One can adopt a position of covert research in the interests of making public what is secret. However, this conflicts with issues of trust, confidentiality, at least at the level of making individual commitments to the unsuspecting research subject. One can talk of the higher good, of actions that in the long term are in the best interests of all. That also is the way in which many tyrants have talked as well as those lesser 'tyrants' who have punished children in their best interests. Even compelling children to endure the coercive processes of schooling against their will 'in their best interests' does not escape criticism. However, if one cannot search for guiding principles in Rationality or Nature as Absolutes, where next?

Ethics and the individual

One answer at the extreme end of radical subjectivity says:

> Away, then, with every concern that is not altogether my concern! You may think at least the 'good cause' must be my concern? What's good, what's bad? Why, I myself am my concern, and I am neither good nor bad. Neither has meaning for me.
>
> The divine is God's concern; the human, Man's. My concern is neither the divine nor the human, not the true, good, just, free, etc., but solely what is *mine*, and it is not a general bone, but it is – *unique*, as I am unique.
>
> Nothing is more to me than myself.

The writer is Max Stirner whose major book *The Ego and His Own* still stands as a powerful landmark of anarchist thought. It was recognized by Marx as a counter-current and thus a threat to his own works. In Max Stirner's world, nothing is sacred except the 'ego'. It represents a complete overthrow of all morality, all religion, all traditional authority. The centre of the moral universe is no longer God, the State, Law and Order, but the individual. What sort of individuality is this? This is what

I tried to explore in my own doctoral thesis (Schostak 1985). Although I have 'moved on' since then, my concerns today still return to these themes expressed there as my departure point. Stirner to me remains a fascinating textural edifice for thinking. Why? Because in the debate about what is good, what is bad, what is worth striving for it demands one of the most radical steps back from the ethical and moral frameworks governing everyday life. It presents a powerful and radical alternative to the principles of procedure discussed above. Should it be taken seriously? If so, what are its implications?

Stirner provides an approach to the emergence of individuality. By this I mean not the mere individuality of the grain of sand on the beach or the individual in the mass, nor the individual as sovereign consumer of market economics. This was the individual who stood out (ex-sistere) from a background, from the mass. In that sense, it is a project that needs to be taken seriously if we are to take ourselves as individuals who, for example, seek to be free, happy and creative, and not just citizens of a politically controlled society in which we have little power to make decisions. What then are the implications of adopting a Stirner-style project?

In Stirner there is an Hegelian feel. There is a constant sense of attack and defence where 'because each thing *cares for itself* and at the same time comes into constant collision with other things, the *combat* of self-assertion is unavoidable':

Victory or *defeat* – between the two alternatives the fate of the combat waivers. The victor becomes the *lord*, the vanquished one the subject: the former exercises *supremacy* and 'rights of supremacy,' the latter fulfils in awe and deference the 'duties of a subject.'

Both remain *enemies*, and always lie in wait: they watch for each other's weaknesses – children for those of their parents and parents for those of their children (e.g. their fear); either the stick conquers the man, or the man conquers the stick.

In childhood liberation takes the direction of trying to get to the bottom of things, to get at what is 'back of' things; therefore we spy out the weak points of everybody, for which, it is well known, children have a sure instinct; therefore we like to smash things, like to rummage through hidden corners, pry after what is covered up or out of the way, and try what we can do with everything. When we once get at what is at back of the things, we know we are safe; when, e.g., we have got at the fact that the rod is too weak against our obduracy, then we no longer fear it, 'have out-grown it.'

(Stirner 1971: 43–4)

What sort of ethics is implicit in this? It is in effect the ethics of individuality that will not bow to the powers of others to proclaim what is good, bad, important, unimportant, meaningful, meaningless. In research and evaluation terms it places value on the ability of the researcher to maintain the standpoint of radical freedom. In the context of bureaucratic and coercive powers, to enact such an uncompromising approach, as previously discussed, may entail considerable risk. However, following Stirner's argument, what results from such a standpoint is 'mind':

> *Mind* is the name of the first self-discovery, the first undeification of the divine, i.e., of the uncanny, the spooks, the 'powers above'. Our fresh feeling of youth, this feeling of self, now defers to nothing; the world is discredited, for we are above it, we are *mind*.
>
> Now for the first time we see that hitherto we have not looked at the world *intelligently* at all, but only stared at it.
>
> (Stirner 1971: 45)

Is this an ethics of 'looking intelligently at the world'? If so, what does it entail?

> To bring to light *the pure thought*, or to be of its party, is the delight of youth; and all the shapes of light in the world of thought, like truth, freedom, humanity, Man, etc., illumine and inspire the youthful soul.
>
> (Stirner 1971: 47)

This, Stirner sees as specifically the project of youth: to chase ideals, to counter the stultifying moral powers of the old order. The role of the researcher and evaluator is thus clear: it is to critique the old order. The effectiveness of this critique in bringing about change will depend on the strategies employed in implementing (Chapter 9) and communicating it (see Chapter 10). Systematically 'looking at the back of things' the researcher finally begins to see what resides there:

> As I find myself back of things, and that as mind, so must I later find *myself* also back of *thoughts*, – to wit, as their creator and *owner*. In the time of spirits thoughts grew till they overtapped my head, whose offspring they yet were; they hovered about me and convulsed me like fever-phantasies – an awful power. The thoughts had become *corporeal* on their own account, were ghosts, such as God, Emperor, Pope, Fatherland, etc. If I destroy their corporeity, then I take them back into mine, and say: 'I alone am corporeal.' And now I take the world as what it is to me, as *mine*, as my property; I refer all to myself.
>
> (Stirner 1971: 49)

This can be read equally as an overblown statement of egoism as well as a statement of radical self-responsibility. There is no one else to blame.

Stirner goes on to summarize his developmental logic, detailing the phases by which his view of individuality emerges:

The child was realistic, taken up with the things of this world, till little by little he succeeded in getting at what was back of these things; the youth was idealistic, inspired by thoughts, till he worked his way up to where he became the man, the egoistic man, who deals with things and thoughts according to his heart's pleasure, and sets his personal interest above everything. Finally, the old man? When I become one, there will still be time enough to speak of that.

(Stirner 1971: 49)

What is going on here? Stirner is, in effect, defining a life plan, a project where only the experience, desire and interests of the self-responsible individual matter – all the good and evil refer back to the individual as perpetrator. This is a harsh court of self-examination indeed. It is an anarchist ethics that also evokes existential themes of solitariness.

Being with others and death

The existentialist thinks of the life plan in terms of rationality and solitude; Kant thinks in terms of the sovereign agents in their Kingdom of Ends, Hegel in terms of Reason equated with Totality. Levinas (1982) critiqued these positions and explained in an interview with Nemo why:

This history can be interpreted as an attempt at universal synthesis, a reduction of all experience, of all that is reasonable, to a totality wherein consciousness embraces the world, leaves nothing other outside of itself, and thus becomes absolute thought. The consciousness of self is at the same time the consciousness of the whole. There have been few protestations in the history of philosophy against this totalisation. In what concerns me, it is in Franz Rosenzweig's philosophy, which is essentially a discussion of Hegel, that for the first time I encountered a radical critique of totality. This critique starts from the experience of death; to the extent that the individual included within the totality has not vanquished the anxiety about death, nor renounced his particular destiny, he does not find himself at ease within the totality or, if you will, the totality has not 'totalised' itself. In Rosenzweig there is thus an explosion of the totality and the opening of quite a different route in the search for what is reasonable.

(Levinas 1982: 76)

To leave solitude, to explore one's own feelings rather than tame them, subdue them, is to move towards the other as person and the Other as revealed in anxiety about death or the Other as repressed, suppressed and rejected. For Levinas it is in being with others that the ethical takes its start.

The irreducible and ultimate experience of relationship appears to me to be elsewhere: not in synthesis, but in the face to face of humans, in sociality, in its moral signification.

(Levinas 1982: 77)

What are the plays of mutual recognition that take place when one looks at another? In such a play otherness is not repressed, the uniqueness of the other is recognized just as is the uniqueness of the 'me'. Indeed, society is a complex of 'me's where the uniqueness and the plurality is signified in the use of 'me's as the plural term. Although having an identity means being the 'same' over time and over place, this 'identity' will not be the same as that perceived by others, nor does the individual stay constant but changes over time due to shifting moods, new experiences and so on. To appear the Same for an Other is to allow the Other to enter, name and make comparisons. To be the Same for oneself is to recognize where the categories of the Other fail. According to Rey (1997: 39–40), 'social relations are the placing into relation and into society people who are incomparable' (my translation). For the researcher, then, it would seem the project is to be framed within an ethics and a politics of 'meeting' face-to-face with others, recognizing where categorization fails and secrecy begins. As Nemo comments on Levinas's ideas:

A society respectful of freedoms would thus not simply have 'liberalism' for its foundation, an objective theory of society which posits that society functions best when one lets things go liberally. Such a liberalism would make freedom depend on an objective principle and not on the essential secrecy of lives. Freedom would then be but entirely relative: it would suffice that one objectively prove the greater efficiency, from a political or economic point of view, of a given type of organisation, for freedom to remain speechless. To ground an authentically free society nothing less is necessary than the metaphysical idea of 'secrecy'?

(Nemo questioning Levinas 1982: 79)

There is an ethics founded on secrecy, the radical secrecy of a person's life. Secrecy is an existential limit, the other face of aloneness. It defines the essential humanity of the individual, an own-ness that is also an Otherness to Society, to others. This kind of secrecy is different to the secrecy of the stealth organization where openness and concealment are plays in a game of strategy and tactics. Existential secrecy is not a game. It cannot be absolved at will. However, concealment may well be a way of protecting this secrecy from hostile demands. How can or should this be handled? Glaser and Strauss (1964), for example, described the kinds of interaction that could take place between individuals from complete openness about each other's intentions through being in ignorance of the other's intentions and thus being fooled by them, to suspecting the hidden intentions of the other. A police officer doing a master's degree dissertation wrote the following:

> The observations were, as is frequently the case, a matter of notes made as soon as practical after the event. Hopefully the nature of my profession well equips me to undertake the task. Despite the covert nature of the observations, as far as was possible all notes were referred back to the relevant actors, and their consent was obtained to publish. In observations as well as interviews, and documentary evidence, all characters have been anonymised, although perhaps within such a small community the actors might still be identifiable within the group. However, whatever the pros and cons of the method adopted, none of those involved raised any objections to publication, nor did any request any alteration to the context.

In adopting a mix of covert and overt approaches it was necessary to provide a rationale for doing so. His rationale was in terms of gaining 'honest data':

> ... within this project an interview led to an adamant rejection of racist or sexist humour, on the grounds of 'political correctness' (Interview IV). This was so patently out of character, I could recall the person previously saying that he '... wasn't racist until I came into this job ...' Further I made a point of noting his comments about the opposite sex in the canteen the very next day. To say that his comments were 'politically correct' would be stretching credibility to unbelievable lengths.
>
> So my justification for covert research must be the acquisition of true data.

Reference was made to other studies where making one's presence as a researcher known 'skewed' or left in doubt the status of the evidence. One particular case the officer drew upon was Patrick's (1973) study of a Glasgow gang. To have revealed his identity (indeed the book is written under an assumed name) would have been dangerous.

Secrecy can serve many purposes and ethics cannot ignore it, nor can it arbitrarily rule that all should be open at all times. Ethics becomes in many research protocols, as well as in everyday life generally, a negotiation of secrecies and public accounts in the 'best interests of self and/or others'. As a final example, Shirtliffe (2000) quotes one individual with learning difficulties as saying:

> I'm never lonely because my mum and dad are always around — at the Training Centre scared me by saying they'd die one day because everyone dies. His dog died last week. My mum promised she would never die and so I don't have to worry. Even if she does die, it won't be forever.

What should carers or researcher reveal to the other, not other as generalized individual, but other as this individual in these circumstances?

Opening doors

Taking others into account has both political and ethical implications. To open a door into the life of another and portray them for all to see will have many consequences, the majority of which are unpredictable and never to be seen by either the researcher or the research subject. The little portrayal will be sent on a journey from reader to reader. Its power to act in the lives of others will remain largely unknown. The ethics and the politics of project work engages with the ethics and politics of everyday life. The intertextual plays that emerge as the messages are snatched from one set of circumstances and placed into others are beyond prediction. To ensure that each individual's life is valued equally with that of another is certainly an unfinished revolution started by the great philosophical, democratic and social reform movements throughout recorded history. To what extent can each project open a door to take the next step?

9

Framing ethical actions

Research, involving action, can be defined as a process of systematic reflection upon circumstances to bring about desired states of affairs. Reflection, whether it is critical of assumptions or simply based upon the acceptance of taken-for-granted presuppositions, aims to produce understandings, explanations, creative insights, syntheses, synergies, useful or delightful patterns as a basis for informing judgement, decision making and action. All research has implications for action. One's solitude and the duplicities of those who would exploit people and the resources of the world under cover of Rationality and Secrecy implies the need for action. Action research, as a 'movement' or form of research, explicitly draws individuals into researching their own practice to improve the quality of decision making and action in a given social circumstance and transform social practice to bring about social change (Elliott 1991, 1998). Action research, however, does not offer any easy recipe for bringing about change. Indeed, it can be employed for just the opposite.

I have elsewhere critically explored the nature of 'action' in action research (Schostak 2000). These explorations were set within the context of what I called the point instant of change, a term borrowed from a Buddhist logician (Stscherbatsky 1962). The point instant of change is the 'gap', the 'space between' that has emerged in earlier discussions (Chapters 4, 5, 6). It is the place where all the hard structures, the hard 'realities' of taken-for-granted life, traditions and sciences fall. It is a kind of death, a death of the ego as Boothby (1991) called it, that allows new structurations to arise. This chapter will in effect take action, the point instant of change and reflection, as its theme in amplifying the following along an ethical plane:

> Action research cannot just take on the role of the genteel terrorist, never wanting to do anything other than at most cause a little bit of

trouble in the hope that the discomfort will produce some sort of creative resolution. However, like any terrorist activity, all it produces is increasingly heavy handed responses by the agencies of policing backed up by the schooling of public knowledge. That is, any gaps to emerge, wherein creative visions may be developed, will be sutured over leaving the experiment sinking without trace, or at best with only a little marker reading, 'Here lies a brave effort, may it rest in peace and never trouble us again'.

Education has always been rather like viral action. It gets into the system and systematically subverts its genetic order. Schooling has always been the antidote to education, a pacifying of the masses. Both education and schooling have been frequently defined in terms of transmission. For schooling it is rather like the radio transmission of a message from sender to receiver, where the pupil as receiver is a good receiver only if the message is received exactly as sent. Thus the object of schooling is to ensure that nothing of essence is actually changed. The social order should always be reproduced in such a fashion that the basic inequalities of power are never challenged. For education the transmission is rather more like the transmission of diseases, where the disease continually adapts itself to new environments bringing about radical changes in states of affairs.

(Schostak 2000: 419)

The challenge that education research faces is to fall into schooling or to open into alternative visions for freedom. How may this come about? In another paper (Schostak 1996) I described a complex reflective process derived from a reading of Bhaskar (1993) that can serve as a basis for thinking about how different kinds of action serve the political, economic, social, cultural and ethical interests of individuals, communities, commercial and non-commercial organizations and nation states. I will rebuild this structure anew, piece by piece, in order to explore its ethical foundations and so derive principles underpinning projects for research that is educational, that is, that has as its overarching principle the cause of freedom. To do this the discussion of ethical action will go well beyond that of 'action research' in order to encompass technological and cultural change at global, local and personal levels. Its purpose is to facilitate the development of educational action.

The production of expert action

Imagine the process something like this. An individual starts from a position of not knowing, that is, not knowing what the expert knows. To become an expert knower requires the acquisition of knowledge and of expert ways of knowing and forming judgement for action. Before engaging in this process one lives in a state of pre-reflective theory (PRT), whether it is a position of taking for granted the ways of knowing, doing and thinking of everyday life, or the position of the newborn who has yet to engage with the social world in theoretical ways mediated through language. This is not to say that at some time in the past the ways of knowing were not produced from critiques of the taken for granted. It is to say that the dominant attitude is that of taking for granted particular ways of doing things, beliefs and knowledge. One draws upon the everyday traditional authority of one's family and community. That body of knowing and cultural practices were at one point taught to the individual by parents, other significant adults, older siblings or friends and so on as knowledge of how to behave expertly within the community. That is to say, the baby in growing gradually internalizes (i) the knowledge and practices of the adults and other teachers until understandings (U) arise of how the world works that become acceptable to the teachers and so the individual is then able to act in ways they consider to be expert (ea). The value of expert learning is thus that it enhances the powers of the individual and of the group or community to shape the environment to meet needs, interests and desires. Its drawback is that the very authority of 'expertise' too often inhibits the powers of critique and challenge if these arise outside the legitimated frameworks of critique and challenge. This process is summarized in Figure 9.1.

Of course it is a crude exposition. However, it can be made more sophisticated by exploring each of the key terms in relation to the various contemporary debates in philosophy, psychology and so on – a task not undertaken here. Rather, in the light of the previous chapters, I want it to stand as an indicator, a signifier, pointing towards that complex of everyday activities by which individuals are schooled into expertise, whether it is the expertise of the delinquent gang, or the much admired gangs of entrepreneurs, pop groups or politicians, or the expertise of

i = internalization
ea = expert action
U = Understanding
PRT = Pre-reflective thought

Figure 9.1 Expert action

medics, lawyers, school teachers and so on. It is a cycle whereby action is always monitored according to codes and standards of practice. There is in this cycle a 'right' way of doing things that can be argued about in the law courts. Recalling the Stealth Organization (Chapter 4) it can be made more complex by drawing a boundary between expert action as defined by audit trails and other public methods of accountability on the one side and expert action in terms of necessary compromises, short cuts and so on to make an ill-resourced and highly contested professional arena of action actually work (e.g. Phillips *et al.* 2000).

Schooling effectiveness is a late twentieth-century expression of the optimism[22] afforded to expertise to design the lives of young people through the agency of highly reliable visions of schooling modelled after aircraft engineering or airport flight controllers.

> The High Reliability Schools Project is an attempt to move beyond the goal of relatively successful schools towards the creation of schools which are absolutely successful and which have eradicated failure. Using the latest information from the study of highly reliable organisations such as air traffic controllers and nuclear power plants and from school effectiveness and school improvement programmes, an innovatory programme has been designed that aims to ensure high quality educational outcomes for all, in schools which set ambitious targets and which relentlessly push for success.[23]

I critiqued this approach in relation to the paranoid curriculum modelled after the experiences of Judge Schreber (Schreber [1955] 1988; Schatzman 1973):

> The paranoid curriculum is essentially about control for the purposes of 'rational' purification, that is, the construction of an order in the name of which individuals submit to reason and reject all that is inessential to reason. Reason is defined, like God, as a final court of judgement and reason itself is whatever is defined as such by the voice of reason. Reason here is whatever is ordered by the Dominant Other.

> (Schostak 2000)

Schreber's father was a renowned German nineteenth-century educationist whose works were translated into many languages and even influenced the British public school system. He in his way was also interested in producing high-reliability education and produced many pamphlets on how to raise children. It was a behaviourism pushed to its ultimate extremes. He controlled or engineered everything, eye movements, posture, bowel movements, eating regimes, study regimes and so on. This had various effects on his children: one son committed suicide; as one would expect for the times not much is known about the daughters but they were regarded as peculiar, and the other son – Judge Schreber – went mad. No doubt little would have been known about him had he not written a book on his mental illness that was subsequently analysed by Freud and Lacan among others. Schreber became a model for Freud's developing views on paranoia.

However analysed, Schreber's life is tragic in that it was designed by the expert action of the day. It is difficult to predict what contemporary expert action is doing to our children globally. Their salvation, perhaps, is that few fathers adopt the god-like (or, after Descartes, evil genie-like) position as systematically as Schreber's father. Hence, their well-being is founded more on incompetence than expert competence. Nevertheless, the genocides, the tortures, the starvations and deprivations experienced by millions of children around the world every day is enough to bring about the loss of faith in the 'expert' as politician, scientist, judge and teacher experienced by many and said to be symptomatic of the postmodern age. Yet this loss of faith coexists with a demand for expertise whether in the management of vast corporate empires, political systems, sophisticated technology, medicine, law or schooling and so on. Indeed, the rise of the expert, as manager, as scientist, as professional expert, seems fundamental to contemporary Western market economies (e.g. Perkin 1989). The demand is increasingly accompanied by audit, quality assurance systems, surveillance procedures through inspections, litigation and professional ethics committees (Power 1997). All are 'expert' instruments directed towards the control of the 'expert'. In whose name are these controls undertaken? There are many names of the father, the figure, like Schreber's father, who desires to control, design, engineer the lives of others.

The Father, of course, is not just the biological father of the child but the Our Father in Heaven, the Fatherland (or Motherland; same effect). It is the Head of the Family as State, Don, Pope, Captain of Industry. In everyday life identity and social structures mesh:

We were interested in the 'how' and the 'why' of the individual's relationship to the 'givens' of her everyday life, in the way in which she grows into the structures of society. We started from the premise that human beings, in the process of their socialisation, work at restructuring the given elements of their lives, until such time as their existence becomes relatively uncontradictory: in other words until social action becomes a possibility. Given that there is no such thing as an existence without contradictions – certainly not within social relations as they exist today, and above all not for women – we had to assume that the absence of contradictions in our self interpretations will to a large extent be constructed by us; contradictions are forgotten and omitted, left unperceived. While to a degree, it is our use of such constructions that enables us to get by in the world, they ultimately prevent us from gaining a proper grip on reality.

(Haug 1987: 40)

It seems, then, that the powers of individuals and their communities can only be discovered and exercised if the circumstances allow. A crude analogy can be made with Bhaskar's example of gunpowder used to illustrate the concept of causative powers in the natural sciences. Empirically one sees a pool of black powder lying on the floor. One can give many descriptions of it: its colour, taste, smell, as well as what happens if one adds water. However, its power to explode will only become manifest if a spark ignites it. The circumstances have to be right for its causative power of 'explosion' to be revealed. That causative power remains a power of gunpowder even if for that particular pool of gunpowder the right circumstances never obtain. Similarly for human beings, their powers of love, cooperation, caring for others, artistic creativity and so on may never have the right circumstances for them to be manifested. As in Haug's terms, how does one get a grip on reality when it is composed of imaginary relations? How can an identity be changed when it is composed of the givens of everyday life, when it is framed by the structures of social formations beyond the control of a given individual? The change if at all possible would consist in the dissolution of the structures internalized by the individual. It would have to involve some kind of dismantling or deconstruction.

Deconstruction, dilemma and reconstruction

Calling the taken for granted into question in some way, old forms of action become problematic.[24] They no longer provide the desired results, or are shown to cover over contradictions and unintended consequences. The world is no longer so certain as it seemed. The expert systems have been caught out. The understandings (U) taken as given under a prior age are collapsing under the weight of criticism, are being deconstructed (d-c), revealing their constructed or contradictory foundations.

Douglas, arguing for the need to refocus sociological theory, wrote:

Men of common sense frequently appeal to reason or rationality, saying 'be reasonable, man . . .' or 'Rationality demands . . .' Yet the one point about man that seems to pervade commonsense thought about human action is that reason is highly variable, undependable, and weak compared with emotions or feelings. There are many attitudes about the weaknesses of man, the inevitability of sin (generally related to sex and money), and the temptations of the world.

Practical men commonly view the rhetoric of rationality with great suspicion: 'Oh, yeah, what's in it for you?' Lust and greed, along with a host of lesser feelings, are assumed to be omnipresent and potent. Reason is seen largely as the handmaiden of these passions, the servant who caters to their interests, finding a way to fulfil them while hiding these realities from enemies. Morals were once thought to be powerful allies of reason, but today few men of common sense place much faith in morality as a dominating force in the world. Anyone who leaves his door unlocked is thought to be crazy, and people more commonly believe that everyone has his price (ultimately, everyone is greedy) than that the values on honesty will save his property and keep politicians honest. The man of practical wisdom is more likely to agree with Shakespeare that 'morals are as straw in the wind to the fire in the blood' than to share the value determinism of most sociologists.

(Douglas *et al.* 1977: 14)

When current forms of reason and tradition are no longer good enough guides, what then? It is necessary to reformulate according to another rationality (see Figure 9.2), a rationality that can grow from the contradictions employing dialectical reasoning (D), finding resolutions at a 'higher' level; or a reason that creates a paradigm shift so that all is seen new-born under some more powerful vision. For Douglas this meant a shift to an existential sociology. But what if no such vision or synthesizing rationality (R) is in sight? What opens up are the catastrophic spaces discussed in Chapter 5.

There are several options: one can repress all knowledge of there being a problem; one can look at the unfairness and fight it in various forms of 'criminal' or 'terrorist' action; or one can return burnt from the light of terror at there being no alternatives and adopt a new fundamentalism, a back to basics, saying the reason why it is failing is because corruption has set in. Get rid of the corruption, get back to first principles and all will return to normal (U). Any challenge to the taken for granted, any revelation that the founding illusions of reality are arbitrary, false, shaky, insubstantial, can be terrifying. At the most extreme, those who say differently are likely to be persecuted or treated as mad or bad by those who hold on for dear life to their founding beliefs and frameworks for knowing the 'truth', the 'real', the 'good'. For the researcher who wittingly or unwittingly makes the challenge, the reaction can be disturbing, frightening. However, action entails facing up to the problems inherent in creating the conditions for change. In requiring new ways of thinking, acting and allocating resources, change typically deskills or threatens the vested interests of individuals or groups as it empowers others, creating new benefits and opportunities. As argued

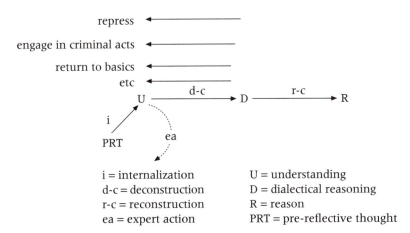

Figure 9.2 Repressive action

later, the researcher can look for ways of reskilling people and working with possible allies that may prevent or counter moves towards repressive action (Figure 9.2).

For those who do not want to change, the past can be seen as some kind of golden age, when things worked, when people knew their place, when you could leave your door unlocked at night. Such golden ages are regularly reinvented every twenty years or so as the ageing generation looks back on their youth, lamenting today's hooligans (Pearson 1983). The power of nostalgia is everywhere. Consider the following statement by a medical consultant lamenting the change in education for nurses:

> some of the old style nursing sisters, of which we are lucky to have some of the best, have maintained those skills despite the changes. I went onto a ward, yesterday, and I saw a patient without the nursing cover who was looking after that patient. And Sister was very cross, not with me, because I'd been there, but she was cross at the system that she had governed that she would be there, because she appreciates, not, it's, it's for the well-being of the patient over-all, but anything that the consultant or the team need to say about the management of that patient may be missed or may not be accurately reflected, so she was very cross with that system and they are worth their weight in gold.
>
> (Schostak and Schostak 2000)

What was at stake was not a lack of knowledge as such but that nursing now was organized in such a way that the profession was no longer conceived as being handmaidens to the consultants. The power of the consultant was under threat. The ward was no longer organized to fit with the consultant's diary. Nursing was now more focused around caring for patients rather than consultants. How then can change be managed so that consultants can formulate a new vision of their role and relation to other professionals that is as satisfying to them as it is effective for both the treatment and care of the patient? Research can contribute to mapping the prevailing relationships, roles and visions of the different professional groups, explore their constructed nature, identify contradictions (d-c), engage each group in thinking through their different ways of reasoning about their professions (D) and so reformulate their professions according to some more encompassing vision (R). However, the social and psychological forces against this happening are powerful. People want to take action in the midst of changes that are perceived as being out of control. Panic is symptomatic of the feelings of destabilization caused by changes perceived as out of control. There are panics everywhere and for everything (Kroker and Kroker 1987).

Change over the last fifty years has been so fast. And it is getting faster. Virilio (1996) described the impact of new forms of communication on decision making in terms of what he called the dromosphere (*dromos*, meaning course) where 'power is always the power of controlling a territory by messengers, the means of transport and of transmission' (my translation). Interestingly, one root of curriculum is *curricle*, meaning racing chariot. Young people can be imagined as racing along ever faster league table-defined tracks – becoming slow, medium and fast-track people. Knowledge, technological change and ethical values all change at different rates. Technology can outpace cultural and ethical practices. Progress, in short, may seem to take place without people. Noble (1995) advocates a new Luddism, not as an indiscriminate smashing of progress but as a way of ensuring that progress develops with people and not against them. Change is both at the global and the local – to what extent is a given researcher merely an instrument of change employed by global powers, or a change agent challenging global powers? How should qualitative researchers respond to global powers? For Noble it is war where 'capital is moving decisively now to enlarge and consolidate the social dominance it gained in the first industrial revolution' (p. 3):

In the face of a steadily declining rate of profit, escalating conflict, and intensifying competition, those who already hold the world hostage to their narrow interests are undertaking once again to restructure the international economy and the patterns of production to their advantage. Thus, with the new technology as a weapon, they steadily advance upon all remaining vestiges of worker autonomy, skill, organisation, and power in the quest for more potent vehicles of investment and exploitation. And, with the new technology as their symbol, they launch a multimedia cultural offensive designed to rekindle confidence in 'progress.' As their extortionist tactics daily diminish the wealth of nations, they announce anew the optimistic promises of technological deliverance and salvation through science.

It is perhaps a new scientific fundamentalism against which Noble fights. However, implicit in what he says is an ethics of 'progress' or at least 'change' *with* people. How can research be conceived as a way of facilitating human action in the midst of social cultural and technological changes that threaten to outpace people's capacity to handle them?

Speculative action

Working with rather than imposing on people brings research and action face-to-face with the circumstances and concerns of individuals in their daily lives:

> Perhaps it was the image of Terezinha carefully dividing four small rolls of bread into halves, one for each household member, regardless of age or size. What kind of blind justice was at work here, what radically egalitarian ethos? It was uncharacteristic behaviour in hungry Alto households and therefore disturbing. Ordinarily, the heads of the household would take a disproportionate share so as to be able to work. But on this morning Seu Manoel, the father, took his tiny share without comment, shoving it into the pocket of his baggy pants. He would eat his later, after a few hours of work cleaning out the clogged drains and recently flooded main street of Bom Jesus.
> 'Won't you be hungry?'
> '*Brasileiro ja se acostumou a forme.* [Brazilians have long since gotten used to hunger],' he said.
>
> (Scheper-Hughes 1992: 141)

This reported reflection acts like a kind of theoretical memo, a step beyond mere analysis towards imagining possible explanations, deriving possible understandings as a precursor to the different way of seeing and doing that is necessary if the social, cultural and political dilemmas, contradictions, discriminations and exploitations are to be resolved. Speculative action begins in 'wondering if' in the presence of others. It has an ethical basis:

> Anthropologists (myself included) have tended to understand morality as always contingent on, and embedded within, specific cultural assumptions about human life. But there is another, an existential philosophical position that posits the inverse by suggesting

that the ethical is always prior to culture because the ethical presupposes all sense and meaning and therefore makes culture possible. 'Morality,' wrote the phenomenologist Emmanuel Levinas 'does not belong to culture: it enables one to judge it' (1987: 100). Accountability, answerability to 'the other' – the ethical as I am defining it here – is 'precultural' in that human existence always presupposes the presence of another. That I have been 'thrown' into human existence at all presupposes a given, moral relationship to an original (m)other and she to me.

(Scheper-Hughes 1992: 22–3)

The vignette of an incident observed by Scheper-Hughes thus acts as an illustrative instance of being in the presence of another that generates the conditions for ethical action. If such action is not to impose but work with the other, then speculation on possibilities for action based upon a mapping of issues can through dialogue provide the basis for generating action.

Exploration of an instance of 'being in the presence of another' brings into focus an ethically defined case study that is not frozen, nor arbitrarily categorized, but is an instance of individuals in action having some regard for the action of the other; this regard is intentional in structure. The case, then, unfolds as an intentional network. There is a logic to it but it is more like what von Wright (1971) calls a practical syllogism. He considers these as fundamental to the methodology of the social sciences.

In this process an individual or group think they perceive a regularity which is believed to be 'true'. This regularity in social life is an intentionalistically generated regularity. Such regularities persist through time only to the extent that they are made to endure. When, as Zizek (1992) described, the fantasy of the power of Ceaucescu dissipated so too did his reign of terror. Such a fantasy seems to me to underlie a practical syllogism where any perceived circumstance is believed by one or more to demand a response. What response is chosen depends on the interpretation made of the circumstances. Following von Wright's example of the circumstance being the killing of a president then the purposes behind this action have to be considered. Was it an act of war carried out by a particular state, or was it the act of a lunatic or fanatic or criminal? In developing a response, would the purpose be to avoid war or engage in war? Whatever interpretation and purposes win out, possible ranges of action would be identified and discussed as for example in Figure 9.3.

In the simplified schema in the figure, the circumstances thus act as a necessary basis from which to make decisions. Each decision taken then becomes the circumstance which others have to interpret and on which courses of action are formulated. The decisions are not taken through an circumstance 1

| fact: the president is killed | + | meaning: war
purpose: avoid war | = | identify possible ranges of action |

circumstance 2

| hunt for the perpetrator | + | aim: avoid blame falling on the state | = | find possible scapegoats |

circumstance 3

punish the perpetrator

Figure 9.3   Practical syllogism

application of a scientific formula to produce the best possible response. Rather, what fills the gap is initiative, interest, purposes. Action in the world then is a mix between first, what is known about the physical world and particular social events or circumstances, second, people's meanings, interpretations, interests, wants, needs, purposes and, third, speculation as to possible actions and their outcomes. Consider the following vignette drawn from Phillips *et al.* (2000: 117):

A 65 year old builder is admitted to Casualty with severe lower back pain, after falling from a roof. The student (adult branch) works with his assessor to move the patient and position him for examination by the orthopaedic registrar; his first experience of the 'log-rolling' technique, performed under the explicit instructions of the assessor. Following this, he feels sufficiently confident to accompany the patient to X-ray where he now takes the lead role, transferring the patient from trolley to X-ray table and back. They return to Casualty where a diagnosis of fractured lumbar vertebrae is confirmed. The student completes the nursing record, assessing the patient for risk of tissue-damage and performing and charting baseline and neurological observations. The patient is to be admitted to the orthopaedic ward, having a CT scan en route. The student again accompanies him, providing sensitive care and directing the 'log-rolling' procedure required for each transfer. After giving ward staff a verbal hand-over, he returns to Casualty, up-dates his assessor and completes the departmental records. This entire episode has lasted $3\frac{1}{2}$ hours during which the student has been able to rely upon his assessor's support and guidance regarding learning opportunities presented.

In the report (Phillips *et al.* 2000) this brief narrative was analysed as follows:

Circumstances:
Place:
- Casualty
- X-ray
- Orthopaedic ward
- CT scan

Resources:
- Appropriate staff
- Time
- Equipment: X-ray, CT scanner, trolley, bed etc.

Dramatis personae:
- 65-year-old builder
- Student
- Assessor
- Orthopaedic registrar
- Ward staff

Orienting categories:
- Lower back pain
- Fractured lumbar vertebrae

Strategic level
- *Care principle:* implicitly – traditional nursing practice? Provision of 'sensitive care'
- *Education principle:* implicitly – see one, do one? Instructional teaching

Tactical level events/procedures/outcomes
Scene 1: Casualty
- Position patient for orthopaedic registrar
- Employ procedure 'log rolling'
- Show procedure 'log rolling'; give explicit instructions
- Outcome:
  - Performs procedure
  - Increased confidence

Scene 2: X-ray department
- Student takes lead
  - Transfer patient from trolley to and from X-ray table

Scene 3: Casualty
- Confirmation of diagnosis
- Completion of nursing record

Scene 4: Transfer to Orthopaedic ward
- Student accompanies
- Provides sensitive care
- Directs 'log-rolling' procedure
- Gives verbal handover

Scene 5: Casualty
- Updates assessor

- Completes departmental records

Overall tactical outcome: (a) care provided (b) support and guidance from assessor accomplished;

Overall strategic outcome: traditional nursing principle reproduced by student.

(Phillips *et al.* 2000)

A lot is left implicit and simply 'unknown' in such a short vignette. Nevertheless, it does provide in outline a framework for reflection upon key principles and how events relate to these principles. The analytic sketch of scenes and related strategies and tactics shifts attention from the 'doing' to the possible rationales implicit or explicit for why particular events take place. Such rationales can then be the object of critical study. Over the period of three and a half hours covered by this micro-vignette, what learning opportunities have actually been explored? What is missing from the experience? What can be said about the implicit 'level' of learning and achievement? Is such an experience appropriate for a budding professional? In what way is it appropriate and in what way is it lacking?

Each question reveals the problematics, the speculative work that may underpin the development of alternatives both for the professional and for the researcher who aspires to inform decisions about the possibilities for change and development. Each dimension of circumstance, principles employed, tactics and strategies adopted can be challenged and speculative 'what-if' games played in order to vary circumstances, principles, strategies, tactics. At each speculative variation, what is challenged, what resists the variation: what opportunities open up, or close down; who gains, who loses? In this way the researcher can draw from analyses of the data the possibilities for developing alternative visions, structures, roles, mechanisms, procedures, allocations of resources, cultural processes, and personal transformation. To continue the diagrammatic play already begun, speculative action results from an imaginative play that is enacted either in the virtual realms of the imagination or staged in material realities (Figure 9.4).

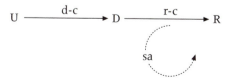

Figure 9.4 Speculative action

The understanding (U) that has been challenged through processes of deconstruction (d-c) demands some kind of dialectical reasoning (D) that plays on the tensions, the contradictions, the anomalies in order to formulate reconstructions that are not reproductions of what has gone before but which generate the possibility of grounding a new way of reasoning about the world. Here reason (R) is not reducible to the Reason of previous orders but is essentially a blank space, an x in some formula waiting to find its value. Rather than the totalitarian commitments of the New World Orders, speculative action (sa) is the result of the speculative enquiries that stop short of imposing a new Reality and New Order; they have the character of experimental world-plays that are fed back into the worlds of everyday pre-reflective life, the worlds of taken-for-granted rituals and experiences for consideration. The educational task of speculative action is to bring about the breathing space where not reflection but non-sense may tear asunder the taken-for-granted texts and allow a gulp of air. Speculative action is set within an ethic of being with others who each are unique, have their own viewpoint, their own horizon, their own 'case' to make and to project.

Speculative action suspends overeasy commitment to action (ca). Otherwise the totalitarian actions of new Revolutionaries and so on set about authoritarian conversion of all to the new way of seeing Reality, founding their purges and cleansings of the Old on the new foundational principles that must be challenged as described in Figure 9.5.

Overthrow when subjected to violently oppressive regimes may seem and actually be the only solution for its citizens who want a freer and happier life. It has been the favoured solution of modernist, rationalist thinkers who saw the only solution to the world's ills to be its total

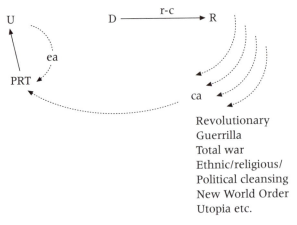

Revolutionary
Guerrilla
Total war
Ethnic/religious/
Political cleansing
New World Order
Utopia etc.

Figure 9.5 Overthrow

redesign either as socialist or as free market societies. These are the master narratives, the grand theories critiqued by Lyotard (1984) and others. The failures of both visions to bring the 'good life' are self-evident in a world riven by wars, genocides, famines, poverty and violence. Does this mean that researchers must give up the ambition of bringing widespread social change? It seems to me that, given the complexities of the global scene and its impact on the local communities of people rather than a 'one size fits all' theory, plan of action, or vision, the educational project is to draw out the multiple possibilities for critical review through speculative action. Both the deconstructive and reconstructive dimensions of the process leading to speculative action involve exploring the staging of truth.

Speculative action as the staging of truth

Truth can be staged because the world is nothing in particular. That is to say, it is 'no thing'. Things exist only because artificial boundaries are placed around them to make talking to each other easier. Thus:

> Were it not for appearances, the world would be a perfect crime, that is, a crime without a criminal, without a victim and without a motive. And the truth would forever have withdrawn from it and its secret would never be revealed, for want of any clues (*traces*) being left behind.
> But the fact is that the crime is never perfect, for the world betrays itself by appearances, which are the clues to its non-existence, the traces of the continuity of the nothing. For the nothing itself – the continuity of the nothing – leaves traces. And that is the way the world betrays its secret. That is the way it allows itself to be sensed, while at the same time hiding away behind appearances.
> (Baudrillard 1996: 1)

The work of the illusion is to produce the effect of truth (Baudrillard 1990). That is, while not true in itself, it has the effect of being true due to the belief that is projected onto it. Or in the words of Thomas (1928), 'If men believe it is true, then it is true in its consequences.' The fantasy dimension of time, for example, can be experienced each New Year. Indeed, at the advent of the year 2000, the world, according to the television coverage, the radio and the newspapers, partied. As midnight occurred at various time zones, fireworks were unleashed and champagne drunk. One BBC reporter took a ride in a fighter jet capable of chasing the sunrise in order to 'discover' the passage of time itself. Yet time is an invention. Its power is in ordering subjective experience in relation to intersubjectively agreed coordinates – datelines, the sectioning of a circle into hours, minutes, seconds and the steady movement of the two 'hands'. Time is staged. Its dates are arbitrarily started. Any moment will do for a year zero. Fixing it according to some culturally defining event, particularly a religious one, gives it a fantastic power, a truth-defining effect, a Beginning.

Looking awry can permit the researcher to see their own controlling fantasy. On the one hand, it is a process of staging as if real the theoretical perspective, on the other it is a catching sight of what lurks in the shadows of one's nightmares. In relation to the strategic interest it holds for the gaze of the project:

> What is at stake in the endeavour to 'look awry' at theoretical motifs is not just a kind of controversial attempt to 'illustrate' high theory, to make it 'easily accessible,' and thus to spare us the effort of effective thinking. The point is rather that such an exemplification, such a mise-en-scene of theoretical motifs renders visible aspects that would otherwise remain unnoticed.

Thus Zizek (1991) begins his book. Through studies of film producers he explores what is at stake in taking elements of philosophy and theory seriously. It works in the way that dreams do. In a dream acts of terror may be committed, but upon waking we can say 'it was only a dream'. Looking awry means that the dream, the fiction, the pun, the displaced image reveals something that we would rather keep covered, unexplored. It approaches the nonsensical world of dreams and nightmares.

Non-sense and the birth of speculative action

Non-sense is a condition of action, if by action we mean that which exhibits freedom rather than behaviour that is automatic because it is instinctual, or the result of habits, or due to the outcome of calculations. No action is possible unless it is ethical in the sense of being made under the gaze of others-with-me who demand, judge, consider or respond in some way to me. In this domain such action can only be speculative because it eschews commitment to anything other than 'play', 'potential', 'creativity', 'exploration'. This does not mean to say that the action that follows is unreal. Its reality, however, does not condemn; it releases. The individual who acts is acting not as a reproducer of outcomes but as one who initiates. In the Schreberian world where all is already prescribed, where the body is inscribed with the demands of an all-powerful other, there is no breathing space. To create breathing space the bounds must give way. The deconstructive approaches such as to be found in Derrida's works are examples of the way in which words may be broken up to reveal accidental yet creative and insightful plays of meaning.

This is the position of the creator of realities rather than the creature of pre-existing realities. It is the position of the creative artist or scientist. All such realities exist only as possibilities among others. They await to be explored through speculative actions; their virtues and dangers await description. Speculative action builds worlds and creates the conditions for the knowledge agencies through which these worlds will come into being and provide habitats for living. The worlds are built by setting into relationship the conceptual structures (ideas, beliefs, values, assumptions, axioms) together with the cultural practices (mechanisms, procedures, habits and so on) through which they are enacted and the resources (materials, tools, dramatis personae, time, space) appropriate to their realization.

The breath before the word

There are four strategies for speculative action: re-punctuating (such as stumbling, stuttering, making ironies, puns); creating the conditions for the cry which becomes the cr/eye of the witness (Schostak 1999b); dialogic action; and educative action.

It is not that language is the problem but that language when it becomes routinized becomes the problem. Human being has no way of articulating itself into existence without the word. There is no world, no world-play without word-play.

> The point for both Heidegger and Lacan is that the function of language comes into its own only when the droning-on of idle talk and empty speech is broken open in some way, only when it under-goes a kind of death. Yet Lacan might be said to give the better account of the process by which this death and rebirth of discourse occurs. It is not so much that empty speech *fails to say* what is required but rather that the subject *fails to hear it said.* It is not as if the new words must be found or that something different must be said but rather that the pat verbal formulas in which the imaginary order of the ego's defences are constantly rehearsed must be really heard for the first time, thus enabling something other to be regis-tered in the heart of what is most familiar. Accordingly, the function of the analyst is not to say something new or different but to respond to what is unacknowledged in what has already been said. The analyst's task is one of reflecting back the patient's own acts of signification, a task comparable to a re-punctuating of the patient's speech.
>
> (Boothby 1991: 213)

Thus the first task needed to bring about the breathing space is to allow something else to be registered by listening to and responding to the unacknowledged in what is being said. This is a stage that corresponds to the careful recordings and analyses of interview and observational records. It acts as a repunctuating which throws into light alternative readings or hearings of that which is so familiar it generally passes without notice.

However, there is a more radical stance yet. It is the emergence of the cry which refounds the eye of the witness (Schostak 1999b) and that becomes the 'I' of the ethical actor. In the case of a trauma, it is not that something that is said has to be listened to. Rather it is that something as yet is unsaid. Its expression is most likely to be a cry or a soundless utterance. Here, no accommodation to what exists can be made. No meaning can be addressed that founds itself on the prevailing patterns of social and discursive order. It is here that some neologism arises by which to recognize and affirm, providing an aye for that which cannot be fully said.

The gathering pace of meanings which outpace current dictionaries to contain them requires dialogue at an interpersonal level where:

> Human action . . . remains perpetually caught in a dialectic where the discrepancy between intention and consequence is never eliminated. This must be the case because the source of the discrepancy is not simply that the world does not permit realisation of our purposes. This may well be. More significant, the discrepancy between action and consequence arises through the misunderstanding, misinterpretation, and misconstrual of our acts by others. To be an acting agent is to live in this interpreted world where one's own understanding of one's deeds is but one point of view, one interpretive framework, among others . . . Human action, unlike objects and things, are not the property of their agents, or their 'work'. They do not embody or express a univocal meaning or purpose. Such a meaning or purpose can only be determined interpretatively; in this sense, human action is fundamentally indeterminate.
>
> (Benhabib 1986: 87)

Dialogic action repunctuates that which is given as 'real', as 'possible', as 'fantasy', as 'mad', as 'bad', as 'dangerous', as 'good', as 'evil' and as 'inevitable'. Every challenged reinterpretation and repunctuation reveals what is at stake for those who care, those whose realities are under threat. Through resistances and flows the lines of a world are drawn out. When someone says that is not possible, or that is the only way through which things occur, the hard and soft places are determined. What flows and what resists defines what is possible, what is real and what is fantasy. However, to reveal indeterminacy tears down the resistant structures and renders everything possible.

This indeterminacy is the precondition for educative action. Educative action is that process of drawing a world into being for creative action, interpretation and play for the identities, and dramatis personae yet to be born; it is that process where all worlds are also born to die, born to be suspended (*hors d'action*) in a playful, permissive, creative holding of the breath before the new word. And what of the ethics? That remains to be affirmed in the I's relations to others who together test the speculative in the hor'I'zon(e) of their own possibilities and consent with an inaudible 'aye'.

10

Writing it

A project is a kind of dynamic architecture of signs, symbols, meanings – an architexture as I have called it – intended to circulate among others to create a range of desired effects. These effects make writing a political, ethical act. How may ideas, implications and recommendations impact on people's lives? Always there are nagging questions leading to multiple drafts and redrafts. Rhetorically, as a writer, how do you want to play the text to achieve what purpose? In attempting to answer this question, writing becomes a project of rereading, a process of differentiating, making distinct, making stand out, inscribing, turning into signs, scratching with signifiers. Or, it becomes a process of subterfuges, making indistinct, tricking, seducing, compelling rereadings. In this project work, is the 'I' to stand out or fade before the readers and their readings? Should the 'I' be placed under the category of Expert, Author, Scribe, Ghost Writer or, as being elusive, shifting and shifty become the presumed agent who lurks but cannot be grasped? And what of the audience: who are they?

A first look at the audience

Some writers become terrified of losing control of their meanings as the text circulates among unknown readers. Others delight in the surprise their text may have in store for them as it returns by mysterious routes bearing new meanings and effects – some agreeable, and some not. Playing with imagined audiences is a way of elaborating and exploring the possibilities inherent in a text. Audiences are sometimes difficult to imagine. Initially they can be composed of friends, past teachers, colleagues and present supervisor and further sorted in terms of 'those I respect'; 'those I don't respect'; 'those who agree with me'; those whose views are fundamentally different'; and those whose views are socially/ politically powerful or dominant.

The extent to which any of the views are also respected or critiqued by the target communities of readers can provide ways of organizing the structure of a thesis. The substantive and methodological literature and data can be sorted and 'mined' to identify:

- What is at stake for the different camps? Should their views be threatened or supported?
- Which particular individuals, professions or parties wins or loses should one argument, course of action or world view prevail?
- In short, what and whose powers are threatened if one view were to take precedence over others?
- In adopting a particular stance, what powers if any could be deployed against the writer; in short, what's the personal cost of expressing a particular view?

By exploring questions such as these, writing, reading, rewriting and rereading is accompanied by an internal dialogue that helps to shape the strategy and the tactics in order to be sensitive to debates, circumstances, ethics and politics. It helps to shape the strategic rationale underlying the composition of the text. Often this rationale is covert. During a doctoral viva, as an examiner neither I nor my co-examiner could understand why the candidate had not explored certain questions, or made explicit certain implications. There had been no doubt about the quality of the thesis but we wanted to explore the issues to see whether we might ask for some minor additions to be made to clarify these points. The response both surprised and convinced us. The lack of explicitness was a deliberate rhetorical strategy. It was dangerous for a writer living in the country in which the research took place to speak or write too openly about certain issues considered by that government to be sensitive. There was the very real risk of imprisonment. What was to be said had to be said obliquely, under cover. In detail, the rhetorical strategy was then presented to us. What had seemed strangely incomplete suddenly appeared carefully structured, like a battle plan for a thoughtfully orchestrated campaign: it was a stealth architexture. Should a thesis be failed if it hides or censors what should be revealed? Yes. But, should a thesis be passed if it creates the conditions for increased openness? Yes. In this sense the thesis was performative; it was written as a blueprint for action within constrained local contexts. It could have been written fully for a British context and be left on the shelf in the UK university. Or it could be a stealth text for enactment in the student's home country where it could be used to facilitate action that otherwise was unthinkable. Rhetorically, it did all that could be asked of a British doctorate in terms of literature, theorizing, data collection, analysis and discussion of professional action. The stealth structure gave it an added quality to provide not closure but doorways to alternative readings that a home readership could take up. No additions were asked for. The thesis passed.

When writing there is a rhetoric of assessing one's own writing to address the 'checklists' and 'agendas', the wins and losses, the moves and counter moves held in mind by possible audiences. Rhetoric has had a bad press. Used pejoratively it implies something false, deceptive, shallow. However, there is no escaping rhetoric. It underlies all textual acts, all attempts to witness, to explain, to promote understanding, to persuade, to move, to inspire, to seduce and so on.

Rhetorical strategies and interpretation

Rhetoric creates effects, brings something about according to some rationale. It stages desire. Where Kant postulated sovereign agents acting in a Kingdom of Ends, few feel such fulfilment. However, they desire it. That desire is organized economically, politically, legally, religiously, ethically. To 'have it all' is a dream of millions in capitalist cultures, as to 'share it all equally' is a dream in socialist cultures. Whether seeing football stars or industrial leaders, religious gurus or members of communes as models of fulfilment, they are always distant from an audience, 'the mass' who strive to be like them – the fulfilled individuals. In their various ways they are the heroes of desire. Desire in this sense is about lack and it is through language that lack is manipulated. Each word is a signifier of what is absent. How these words and other signs or images that connote lack and desire are arranged is the work of rhetoric. What is evoked is what cannot be attained. The project either reinforces the illusion of possible fulfilment, or deconstructs it, or sets illusion and deconstruction in an ironic play in order to manifest the space between the lines.

To do this, rhetoric is made to operate at two levels: first, the rhetoric employed by those who are subjects of the study, and second, the rhetoric that comes into play in the author–reader relationship during processes of interpretation. Without some focus on rhetorical strategies and tactics, little or no understanding of the processes involved at any level or phase in the research project can be achieved. There are six strategies that I will explore here:

- narrowing interpretations to increase decidability;
- widening interpretations to play with undecidability;
- misleading interpretations;
- seduction;
- camouflage;
- playing the game.

The rhetorical motive behind narrowing the interpretations a reader or listener may make of an utterance or written text is to get one's message across. The principle is to 'mean what one says', to say it simply and clearly. It is what Hirsch (1967: 30) referred to as the Humpty-Dumpty effect: 'When someone does in fact use a particular word sequence, his verbal meaning cannot be anything he might wish it to be.'

> 'The question is,' said Alice, 'whether you can make words mean so many different things.'
> 'The question is,' said Humpty Dumpty, 'which is to be master – that's all.'
>
> (Carroll 1948: 114)

In Hirsch's view, 'A single principle underlies what we loosely call "the norms of language." It is the principle of sharability' (1967: 31). Despite the complexity and the variability of so-called language 'norms', Hirsch proposes that sharability, or reproducibility, is a vital factor in the communication of meaning. His point is that without some stability to meaning, communication is not possible. He is arguing against the notion that meanings vary so radically with each reader that there is the 'death of the author', that is, that the text can be interpreted in any way without reference to the 'real' meaning of the author. This, Hirsch says, confuses the mental acts of the reader with the 'meaning' that is independent of the acts. In defending a principle of sharability and the autonomy of meaning he has focused upon one rhetorical strategy implicit in most research, albeit not always explicitly stated. That is, the strategy of a 'naturalistic' recovery of 'real', 'authentic' meanings. If meaning is neither sharable nor reproducible there would be little point in maintaining the strategy of participant observation or ethnographic studies of particular groups of people. Given a principle of sharability, if communication fails, it can be argued that it is the fault of the writer who should have written more clearly, accurately, simply; or the fault of the researcher who failed to adopt appropriate research strategies. Much contemporary debate has been around whether or to what extent such a principle is attainable.

Hirsch, therefore, provides one approach to the formulation of the rationales that structure and justify a thesis. A rationale is a structure of reasons:

- I did this because . . .
- If you want 'x' then in order to get it you have to take into account 'a', 'b', 'c', and do 'y'.
- This is justifiable because . . .
- To find 'x' then you need to do 'y' for these reasons . . .

The rationale is revealed in the rhetoric of a thesis, report, or research-based publication when it attempts to persuade the reader of the veracity, justifiability, plausibility of the data, analyses, theories and models derived from them. Its purpose then is first, to narrow down the range of possible interpretations a reader might make of the final text; and second, to persuade the reader that the researcher had implemented a well-formulated methodology that would ensure a 'correct' and 'fair' interpretation of the meanings of those who were the subjects of the research. Recalling the stealth architecture of Chapter 4, the thesis can be constructed to narrow its meanings towards one clear publicly presentable 'message'. In this strategy the rhetorical task is to show that its conceptual structure is clearly derived from, or consistent with, the procedures and mechanisms by which data was collected, analysed and formed into explanatory theories or models that 'objectively' and 'validly' represent the 'case' as a basis for generalizable conclusions to inform judgement, decision making and action. The whole strategy of the thesis is to exclude or overcome anything that detracts from supporting the 'message'. This does not mean that any debate is excluded, merely that it is managed to focus attention down on the narrow range of interpretations the writer wants to 'prove', 'make convincing'.

By mapping the key 'sides' to a debate the writer can position the reader closer to one camp rather than another by a range of rhetorical strategies. Books on rhetoric describe sophisticated approaches to achieve such positioning through a combination of strategies that make an appeal to such factors as:

- authority;
- an individual's character;
- motives, desires, interests, curiosity;
- pragmatism;
- rationality;
- passion.

Authority dulls the critical senses of the audience. 'As Einstein said' prefixed before a short statement may well be worth a hundred pages of closely argued analysis! Hence, academic books are full of authoritative references to authors lined up in brackets, each with their pertinent page references. Of course, this can also be more than a blunt appeal to the power of the accepted authorities. Scholarship that reviews the 'authorities' of a given field is important if it contributes to, rather than stops, debate. However, positioning the reader into making particular judgements can also be achieved by drawing on the character or personal history of a given author. Some will point, for example, to the association of a philosopher with a reviled political movement, say Fascism, in order to undermine the standing of a particular philosophical contribution. Others will try to disassociate the mental state or bio-graphical quirks of an individual from the 'meaning' of the philosophy, rather in the way Hirsch disassociated the mental act from meaning. In this way it could be argued that the author did not understand or live up to, or misinterpreted or misused, their own philosophy.

Thus, rather than authority or character, the appeal to authors can be as contributors to viewpoints on the world. Engagement with those authors can sharpen an argument, clarify a distinction, or demolish an illusion. The principle of sharability is essential to debate, otherwise it would be noise without meaning. Yet, recalling the essential solitude of the individual, the limit to sharability resides in the existential difference between each individual. Meaning and sharability are constituted out of difference and can never erase that difference. This difference is not a mere mental act; it is essential to having a viewpoint at all, to being goal-directed.

A viewpoint entails interests, motives, desires if it is to be social. It answers the question, what is at stake in adopting a particular view? Rhetorical strategies are often adopted to appeal to particular motivations that audiences may have. What is it that a policy maker wants to hap-pen? If known then an appeal to that goal can be made when arguing for a particular strategy: to achieve that desired goal then 'x' strategy is the one to adopt. More generally, should the appeal be addressed to the baser or the higher motives? Advertising, of course, tends to focus on 'sex, drugs and rock 'n' roll' and so too does a considerable amount of research funding and the readers of research products. At its most cyn-ical, it is the presentation of 'juicy' extracts in order to 'sell'. A casual glance at the bookshelves selling sociology, psychology and cultural studies will reveal a considerable emphasis on these themes. And why not? They are fundamental to the social, political and economic interactions of everyday life. The curiosity concerning the lives of others, their se-crets, their fantasies, their loves, hates, ambitions, is at the heart of understanding people and society. However, also at the heart of this is some idea of the 'good life' and the 'good society'. Writing that addresses such issues will arouse attention. The ways in which appeals to various interests and motives are employed will colour the attitude of the reader. Is the text prurient, gratuitous, glib, hysterical? Inferences will be made about the character of the writer. Such inferences may reinforce or detract from the message the writer wants to present. It all depends on the underlying rationale, the writer's structure of reasons for writing.

To construct a non-emotional position, the 'objective' voice of the author has often been assumed. Such 'objectivity' draws on the author-itative power of either 'reason' , 'realism' or 'pragmatism' or some com-bination. Equally, passion has been drawn into battle as a counter to the dry neutrality of the rational or pragmatic voice. Rationality tends to reduce the visible role of the writer, apparently shifting agency as it were to the mechanical operations of logic. The rationale is constructed to get the reader to trust the logic, the procedures, the key assumptions. If the assumptions are not acceptable then the whole edifice falls (cf. Nozick 1981). As Harris (1980: 8) points out, the difficulty for researchers is in proving something not logically (deductively) but factually (inductively):

> Science has always consisted of an interplay between induction and deduction, between empiricism and rationalism; any attempt to draw the line on one side or the other conflicts with actual scientific practice. The main functions of these alternatives – besides giving jobs to philosophers – has been to provide ammunition for shooting down someone's theories or building up one's own. One's rivals have overindulged themselves with speculative, metaphysical assumptions or they have been obsessed with superficial empirical appearances, depending on which particular moment in the interplay one chooses to emphasise.

Considerations such as these bring rhetoric and theories of Truth into mutual play. A rationale may be entirely consistent or coherent in itself yet have no point of contact with people's experiences, desires, fantasies. If it does not in some way work in the world that people count as real, why bother? Hence rationality-based rationales often need to click with some pragmatic, empirical, utilitarian dimension. Such rationales concern what works and what does not within specific contexts. How people's ideas are connected to outcomes will vary according to social and material arrangements. The danger of such rational, pragmatic or realist accounts is that they can exclude or be interpreted as excluding the passionate, the playful, the mischievous and the celebratory in life. For this reason a rationale may be created to argue for more exploratory, speculative and experimental methodologies and forms of textual strategy in order to represent the dynamic, temporal and subjectively framed perspectives on personal and social life. Whatever rationale is constructed, the rhetorical strategy adopted inaugurates a viewpoint by which to canalize the reader's interpretational strategies.

Viewpoint

Viewpoint inaugurates a decisive organization of experience. Each individual's viewpoint is existentially unique; its horizon dies with the individual. Yet, this horizon is mapped according to the symbolic structures through which experience is ordered and made accountable. Individuals map the vista within their horizon utilizing the repertoires of discourses at their disposal. Thus a viewpoint is not just an arbitrary way of looking at the world. It is connected to the concrete experience of the existentially unique individual and the ways available to him or her of accounting for experience as 'real' or 'not real' through language. Being a subject of an account positions the individual in relation to others with whom viewpoints are shared, contested, denied, repressed. By varying and contesting viewpoints the non-arbitrary nature of an intersubjectively defined and experienced world is made manifest. Thus writing up such an account requires attention to the principles by which subjects mark their world with the status of being 'real' (Schostak 1985). The mark of reality, then, is a particular kind of signifier. It enables the ordering of experiences into distinctions between 'reality' and 'illusion', 'dreaming' or 'wishful thinking'. There are, of course, multiple realities:

> Our primitive impulse is to affirm immediately the reality of all that is conceived, as long as it remains uncontradicted. But there are several, probably an infinite number of various orders of realities, each with its own special and separate style of existence. James calls them 'sub-universes' and mentions as examples the world of sense or physical things (as the paramount reality), the world of science, the world of ideal-relations, the world of 'idols of the tribe', the various supernatural worlds of mythology and religion, the various worlds of individual opinion, the worlds of sheer madness and vagary.
>
> (Schutz [1945] 1967)

Some writing strategies erect a hierarchy whereby some chosen philosophical framework sits at the top as the criterion by which to judge other approaches to making sense of experience. Others may create a democracy of viewpoints to be placed into dialogue. And yet others nihilistically deconstruct all and find value in none. To take account of all these possible approaches requires at least a method able to dialogically engage with otherness. In practice the researcher, whether beginner or highly experienced, will discover, one by one, the different viewpoints and world views through an engagement with the data and the research and philosophical literatures. It is unlikely, perhaps impossible, to provide a complete account of all possible viewpoints. More importantly, the framework chosen for representation can remain open to alternatives. Thus, through dialogue the horizons of others can be represented as intersubjective experiences and leave open the space for the inclusion of as yet undiscovered others.

Writing an account of the worlds of others means engaging with their existentially defined horizons of experience. Reflecting upon this radical 'gaze' of the self as defining 'my' horizon opens up the possibility of a radical freedom to choose 'my' destiny in 'my' own interests but only in relation to how 'reality' is constituted as 'paramount'. The writing rationale thus needs to take into account dialogue, multiple possible worlds, radical freedom and a sense of there being a 'paramount reality', that is a reality addressed as something that cannot be overcome, something that provides a limit. Each cultural group or individual will have its own view as to what this is. The researcher can map the range of such views across an intentional network, that is, individuals and groups (or more generally, agencies) who take each other into account in some way in carrying out their everyday affairs.

To create an account appropriate to this multiplicity I argued that there are three other principles (Schostak 1985) underlying the construction of narrative case records. The second principle is: 'Preserve the ambiguity involved in multiple interpretations and levels of meaning.' This principle seeks to overcome the reductive tendencies of representations. In order to do justice to complexity it is important to preserve the ambiguities, the multiple levels of meaning and the plurivocity of social life. In writing up the project, data may be presented as 'juicy extracts' illustrating a favoured theme or interpretation; or it can be complexly related to the lives of those it is meant to represent or 'explain'. How this may be done requires consideration of the third principle.

There is always a multiplicity of voices each marking out their territory in the 'real':

> Identify the dramatis personae of the drama which occurs as desire meets necessity and life faces death. These may involve: characters, sub-personalities, masks and roles; and others which await empirical research and identification.

It is the dramatis personae who stage the dramas that are the subject matter of gossip, anecdote, biographies, scientific theories (as a particular approach to storying the world as being open to manipulation, explanation, understanding) and other tales of various kinds. The intentional networks they construct tie them lovingly, agonistically, hatefully, or indifferently 'as desire meets necessity and life faces death'. Necessity can be experienced in a variety of ways. There is the logical necessity of axiomatically defined systems, powerfully exemplified in mathematics. However, there is also the necessity of the powerful command, 'do this or suffer the consequences'. The powers that the state can range against the individual are overwhelming. To resist is to be defeated. In such circumstances the necessity faced is, effectively, the threat of death, a threat that can be carried out. Indeed, there is a kind of machinery of the state that rolls out regardless of individuals. It is the logic of that impersonal machinery that provides the sense of necessity: 'It has to happen this way, because that's what happens in bureaucracies.'

There are other kinds of necessities residing in the biological nature of the body and the materiality of the world about. Eat that and you die.

Touch that and you will be hurt. The dramatis personae in turn are organized biographically according to the history of their experiences as desire meets necessity and life faces death. The drama that arises in the various circumstances of life calls out its appropriate dramatis personae to play upon a stage, drawing from the biographical experiences of each individual who scripts it according to their available repertoires of ways of accounting for 'reality', for 'necessity', for 'what should happen next' and 'why it happened this way and not that'.

The entrances and exits of members of the dramatis personae may produce different chronologies of the events that compose the 'drama', thus leading to the fourth principle that I had expressed as: 'Identify the chronological order of members' engagement in the drama.' Sequences of entrances and exits are of course important. However, temporal ordering is not a single track defined objectively by the clock but is a subjective domain, experienced as duration, as 'what happened next', as 'just in time' or 'too late', as something I have no control over, that, regardless of my desire, passes. Hence chronologies together with the experience of time passing and timings are significant. The principle may then be modified to include temporal experiences and timings (as in 'not a moment too soon').

Being faithful to the range of viewpoints that together compose an intentional network that can be multiply accounted for is the key task of 'writing up'. The four principles discussed may help but are not exhaustive. More principles are waiting to be discovered, discussed and challenged. In particular, there are the principles of staging and of voice to be considered further.

Staging and voice

What is it that the thesis writer wants to stage? How may voices to be represented and heard? Each interaction on the stage, the ways in which accounts are made known, kept hidden or surreptitiously reveal themselves, implies an ethics, a politics and economics, in fact all the possible ways of presenting the subject with or without value. The drama takes place through time and over space. How should time and space be represented? And in these spaces, over these times, voices speak out alone, in a chorus, in a dialogue, as a blessing or as a curse, whispering or as an echo. How do the many individuals met during a research project speak their worlds into existence for us the researchers and for each other as they go about their lives? How are the stages and the voices to be represented within the architecture of the thesis?

Gaad (1998) simply made explicit (see Chapter 1) the many roles she felt placed into by those she met during her research. Ridley (1998), on the other hand, employed several such roles as deliberately chosen view-points around which to build the writing of her thesis:

> I originally wrote up this thesis in a five act structure, essentially to make clear the creative, fictional aspects of writing up research . . . It became apparent, however, that the 'I/eye' of the researcher and the 'I/eye' of the teacher, one and the same person, were not clearly differentiated; the first person pronoun used for both roles resulted in some confusion. Whose voice was speaking? I needed to clarify the text.
>
> First of all, I had to sort out my joint researcher–teacher position, so the next logical step, for me, was to move into the drama genre more fully, to change from writing in continuous prose to writing a playscript where the voices could be clearly distinguished. The voice of the researcher is indicated by the character Mariam Magnolia (a rather silly nickname I was once given); the voice of the teacher is shown as The Actress since I often felt I was playing a role, another thread I pick up later. Dialogue given to Mark and the Advocate are other voices of the researcher, adding comment, giving information and causing debate. Whenever one of the characters speak, their words are direct transcripts from fieldnotes or tapes; in other words, they speak directly for themselves. The only exception to this is The Director,[25] which is where I speak directly as the author to you the reader. This ploy is rarely used.

> (Ridley 1998: 2)

Then how were the locations for action to be staged? She began like this:

Sequence One: Setting up the situation

1. Exterior – promenade. Evening.

Mark Laurels walks briskly along the windswept promenade of Seaside Town, head down against the slanting rain, cursing under his breath as another drip slides coolly down his neck.

MARK *muttering* Some night off!

> (Ridley 1998: 6)

It was a risk to employ this strategy to organize her thesis. She would have to ensure that appropriate literature, critical discussion of methods employed, data analysis and so on were incorporated within her chosen framework. The multiplicity of voices and the 'staging' of the text as a play script sets into train complex possibilities for interpretation. It invites ironic play. In the thesis signifiers are woven to represent lived spaces where both stealth organizations and dialogic frameworks may equally evolve as the stages and machineries for action and interaction.

Ridley represents one model for thinking about the staging of a thesis in terms of voices, dramatis personae, locations and actions. It was presented for examination in a university department where innovation and risk taking are valued. Would it have 'worked' in a more conservative institution? It may never have been tried. Innovation in doctoral research depends as much on the individual as on the support of the supervisor and the research values promoted by the department where models of doing and writing research are limited only by imagination and a sense of the risqué. What is important in each case is to reflect critically on the processes of staging and the impact this has for issues in methodology, representation, and 'knowledge' in its modes of explanation and understanding. Like Ridley, many doctoral students have been frustrated by what they regard as the traditional ways of writing up a thesis and have increasingly turned to narrative, poetic and experimental forms. Here is the introductory scene of a very early attempt of mine at developing the elements of the case record:

Meeting Jacko

1 I lean against the ridged radiator, beneath a window pock-marked with rain. Casually glancing sideways, out there I see Jacko, cheeks swelled with laughter, mates small and thin dancing away from the swinging of his hold-all, a giant swotting flies. Only thirteen, but five foot ten and twelve to thirteen stone.

2 The five-to-nine bell goes. Jacko fills the open door of the office seeming in a hurry.

I ask yet again, 'Do you mind if I follow around with you?'

3 'No. Come on.' He's off. 'I want to catch up with my mates.' He runs. I run along behind, jumping puddles.

4 Jacko, his mates and I sink into the cross currents of pupils drawn to the teaching blocks, crushed at the entrance then spilt into the eddies of pushing shoving pupils, some moving toward the stairs, others to the several classroom doors of the ground floor.

5 We advance up the stairs past faces, some laughing, some serious. I barely see Jacko and his mates ahead.

6 A descending teacher, eyes alert, carries an empty space before and behind him. Unsure how to greet me. We pass.

7 Entering the tutor room, a chemistry laboratory, under the gaze of Jacko's mates, I feel inverted – watched, examined. Where shall I sit?

8 Carol, a girl I know, smiles, invites me to Jacko's group.

9 The tutor, a teacher I know well, enters. He ignores me.
'Jacko. All of you, come and sit at the front.'

No one moves. I feel uneasy.
'Come on now!'
'But there's gas taps at that table.'
'I don't care, I've told you to sit down here. Now do it.'
Carol moves, the rest follow and I am the last.
10 After the formalities of the tutor period – registration, reading a
pupil newsletter – the teacher approaches, smiling.
'So you're following Crawley around today?'
'Yes,' I turn away as best I can.
'Good luck,' the teacher retreats to the doorway where for the
remaining time he blocks the escape of three girls who push
against him.

Although memories fade, I can still 'see' Jacko, I can still 're-experience'
some of the feelings. It is to some extent an illusion, of course. Yet,
something of the sadness I felt then remains with me. Jacko, because of
his size, was the object of frequent teasing. By the end of the day he had
started a fight during a lesson when the teacher was out of the room.
The final paragraph of the account reads:

At the day's end I feel I have seen and heard too much. In talks
with the housemaster he begins to formulate the plan to lecture the
class on what had happened, to tell them he feels they were implicated as well. They set it up with their constant teasing of Jacko. He
feels I should not be around to witness the lecture. I agree. But in
the end he does not give the lecture. 'I chickened out John. Perhaps
it's best to let them sort it out themselves. They all seem subdued.
Perhaps they've learnt. I think life gives the lessons. Do you know
what I mean?'

I used the account for a CARE study group session in 1980 in order to
provide a piece of work that fellow doctoral and research associates
could explore with me. How does, or should, the narrative relate back to
the fieldnotes, the memories, the transcripts, the memos? How then can
an extended case record be employed as a basis for commentary, analysis and theory building? Such questions may suggest that there should
be an extensive, coded archive that readers can refer to, to check validity
and to inform their own judgement as to the interpretations being made
by the writer. In qualitative research this has always been a problem
since the data archives are likely to be extensive and difficult to append
to any thesis, let alone a publication. As technology and acceptance of
alternative forms of thesis presentation develop, data management techniques may contribute to the development of new ways of accessing
archives and representing research. Even then, the writer will need to
make clear and justify the criteria for selection for the extracts employed

in the thesis. In short, the principles underlying the relationship between extracts employed and the data collected need to be explored as a basis for the development of the arguments and textual strategies of the thesis.

In my account I continually made reference to the paragraph numbers that would support my analyses or arguments. Thus:

> As a researcher, through my time at the school, I have begun to earn the right to wander from group to group, clutching at 'data', ready to turn people's lives into explanatory types or illustrative anecdotes. I became a threat belonging neither to one group nor another. In one situation I am embraced by glances and friendly talk, in another I am rejected, pushed back, locked out by averted glances. There are degrees of permissible intimacy which mark the boundaries between acceptance and rejection on any particular occasion. Since teachers and pupils lock each other out of their private conversations they stand like hostile camps, sentries posted, 'Halt, who goes there?' And I must declare myself (12, 19, 21, 25), ask permission to be around (2, 8, 17, 18, 22), and justify myself (18, 21, 26).

I now have many criticisms of my approach. In many ways a hypertextual approach would serve the narrative record better than the flat sequentiality of the page. Somehow it would be better to have each word 'clickable' so that the reader could look through the rain-splattered window to see the school playground and other buildings. And at the name of Jacko this could be clicked to provide images, sounds of his voice, the comments of his friends and enemies describing their attitudes towards him, how he figures in their lives. The brackets lining up the evidence for comments provide a sense of being able to move across a text but also suture the gaps, the in-betweens that have found no 'voice', no place to be 'staged'.

Such an approach lends itself to creating models of typical narrative structures through which individuals organize their lives and the lives of others. By constructing analytic profiles (Schostak 1991: 145–53), the biographical accounts provided by individuals can be turned into more generalizable forms. As explored throughout this book an analytic profile is analysed

> in terms of its three interrelating and continuous aspects: the *self*, its *objects* and the *relationship* (ie, the *orientation* of self towards objects) which holds between them. These three aspects provide a first step towards analysing and thematising the accounts for curriculum or educational purposes. It is the sense of orientedness that renders the structure continuous and creates within itself what may be called an oriented space having boundaries separating it from other oriented spaces until some point of transition is reached . . .

In making analyses employing these conceptual ideas a number of key organising categories emerged:

5 Orientation;
6 Transitional events;
7 Career objects/aims/values;
8 Boundaries;
9 Encounters;
10 Decision;
11 Curriculum as a course of reflection and action.

(Schostak 1991: 145–6)

These general categories then become organizing devices for selecting data extracts and re-presenting the lives of others as vehicles for framing explanations and understandings.

There are dangers here. In presenting narratives and data extracts to support the construction of models, does the text flow too easily, betraying its fundamental allegiance to 'realism'? In its rhetorical appeal to a naturalistic flavour, an 'I was there and it happened this way', does it already bias, distort and mislead? How does one represent the 'in-between', the 'pause', the 'silence', the 'unutterable' which is in shadow but has no place to appear?

Against easy reading

In a thesis, not yet complete, being written by Jill Schostak, the sense of in-formation is continually the subject of play as she juxtaposes fashion, medical and social constructions of body and self. It is in the 'in-between' of these juxtapositions that novel meanings emerge, caught incompletely clothed:

What is the relationship of the 'I' in these contexts, mentioned above, to the particular 'I'(s) who made choices about the texture of the data collected herein; selecting these specific articles from newspapers, magazines, journals, books etc, and rejecting Others. Whether the choosing process was unconscious or conscious is a moot point, the 'I' that is research student can not delineate. This data gathering 'I' can only smudge the fine line by pencilling in the traces whereby I would agree I was consciously searching for 'interesting' data, knowing that I intended researching constructs of selves, but utterly un-knowing of the work-out shape of the text, yet to be constructed. At this point in time, this 'I' did not know how she intended configuring the text: what slant to take to cut the rhetorical texture in which to (ad)dress a fluent text, or which underwear of smooth silky arguments would be especially alluringly articulate to beguile and draw a reader into the corpus work.

(Jill Schostak 2000: 12–13)

Already the easy reading is disrupted as meanings try to peep through the skirtings of the text. It is more explicit in the puns, slashing and bracketings of words that erode the linearity of text and provide a multi-layered, multi-directional hypertextuality where readings are made counter to the surface structuring of the sentences and woven intertextually to voices elsewhere. If only meaning would always lie still, as nothing but surface, easy to decode instead of hiding, erasing its traces. If only meaning was not a work to be fashioned, wrestled into consciousness. If only it was always serious, never playful, childish, deceitful. If it is the task to explore the hinterlands, the in-betweens of sense and nonsense, how otherwise should this realm be represented? Her purpose is to 'seek out a form of pre-linguistic meaning' (Jill Schostak 2000: 44) until the thesis itself creates its own forms for making sense:

> Spiriting away that singular 'r', (a being rapidly and intriguingly becoming trickster), *le mort* is most powerfully transfigured to *le mot*. In an instant, the word is reborn of spellbinding through telling spaces and becomes flesh. In an effort to retouch up and flesh out my contours, I intend to utter(st)ance 'surface relation', wherein each 'mot', if subjected to the motif of deconstruction, enveloped within and of, those exquisite telling spaces, dazzles, at this instantiation, spark(l)ing off masked motives of flexing 'mot'-muscles, as in a flash, the 'r' is singled out from 'surface relation', and effaced from its subjective position at this precise point in the body of written words, revealing another social space that reads differently as 'us face elation'.
>
> (Jill Schostak 2000: 44)

What is being represented here is a mode of reflecting upon being, not as a passive describer of situations and circumstances but as a creative engagement. At the end of Chapter 9 it was argued that through a repunctuation of representations and texts it may be possible to create the conditions for a 'breathing space' for new meanings, new possibilities to arise. The method adopted by Jill Schostak seems a radical repunctuation where in a kind of reversal of the word as death-of-the-thing, death itself is transformed in the word and something, some meaning gets to be born. There is a kind of displaced stuttering, doubly read as (st)uttering, slipping to find its place, its stance as utter(st)ance. Now what did the writer intend with all this wordplay? Is there a stable meaning that lies (deceptively) beyond particular mental acts of the reading and writing of the words? Rather it is a framework for the evocation of meanings, a telling space for the playground(ing) of words and the spirited slippage of letters. Language provides the opportunities for analysis, explanation and understanding ranging far beyond the constrictive univocal categories, logics and procedures of positivistic forms of science. The choice of writing strategy is up to the writer's purpose and its desired effect on the audience, if any.

Telling the story of the project

There is a duplicitous relationship between representation and analysis. It would seem that some kind of faithful representation (re-presentation of 'what happened', what 'is') comes first, to be followed by an analysis that is a precursor for theory building, making explanations and generating understandings. However, rendering the world literally frames analysis within the logic of the letter, the signifier, the symbolic. There are both univocal and plurivocal strategies that can be employed. The univocal deployment of the letter is seen in both logic and mathematics where 'x' denotes a variable that has yet to find its value. The plurivocal exploits the rhetorical richness of language through metaphors, metonyms, puns, and all the other tropes of language as well as through deconstructions, deformations, neologisms and so on.

Telling the story of the project is a return to the beginning, a circling back like a bird of prey, or like the hunted who wants to confuse the trace. Telling the story of the project is critical. Is the story to be a history, focus for future action, a justification, an accusation, a confession, a celebration or a wake? The story provides a way of informing the reader how the thesis is to be judged. For example, in describing the journey undertaken it typically provides the initial circumstances of the writer in terms of an introduction that makes clear:

1 This is what I intended as aims and objectives, these were my beliefs that constructed my initial rationale.
2 These were how I conceptualized the structures, resources, mechanisms that framed my thinking and that of others.
3 This is how I conceived the structure of problems and opportunities that I faced at the outset.
4 And this was my initial methodology and chosen methods to obtain the data that I wanted.

However, after an exploration of the literature, or experience in the field of some combination of both I discovered:

5 More about my and others' ethical, political and so on value positions.
6 I discovered more about the implications of my theoretical frameworks.
7 I explored alternative methodologies, philosophies and theories.

And these are discussed in Chapter 'X'. Thus I needed to reframe my project in the following ways:

8 This led me to refine my data collection etc. according to new or modified rationales.
9 Which in turn led to innovative approaches to . . . , forms of representation of . . . and theories or models of . . . and facts or information, or findings concerning . . .

And what I finally learnt from reflecting back on all these substantive, theoretical and methodological investigations and experiences was . . .

The story creates an air of continuous critical reflection, debate and ethical soundness, and focuses on the agenda of concerns the writer wishes to emphasize.

Deconstructing the finality of the story

The manuscript is drawing to a close. It has been a long journey and it is time to say goodbye to it. But just one last look. How will it be read? What questions will the other hold in mind? Have I done enough? It is tempting to run through the manuscript once more ticking off the checklist of typical questions, engaging in an internal dialogue concerned with how risqué should this thesis, report, book be:

• How clear and significant are the aims/objectives/guiding questions? *Yet: how clear do I want to be? And for what purpose?*
• How clear and watertight is the description and discussion of the methodology employed and the data collected? *Yet: how watertight do I want it to be? And for what purpose?*
• How have changes in focus throughout the life of the project been handled? What impact has it had on methodology? What lessons were learnt? *Yet: how honest should this be?*
• Have ethical issues been properly addressed? *Yet: one does not tell the mafia boss that research is being undertaken . . .*
• How convincing is the way in which the data has been represented? *Yet: is this just a cop out, giving in to the demands of stale authorities more concerned with their own careers and protecting their own vested interests?*
• How should the literature be employed to support and contest arguments throughout the body of the manuscript? *Yet: don't the famous already have enough fame, and the others, why should their careers be supported? Aren't my arguments good enough without their authoritative words?*
• Is the conclusion really a 'conclusion'? How strong should any conclusions be? *Yet: are conclusions possible? Why not confusions instead, since all that is really left are more questions than I started with . . . ?*
• What is now 'known' that was not 'known' before? *Yet: what is ever really known?*

A cynical review of one's work is always possible, even useful. However, outside all rhetoric, if that is possible, what is the key idea, the key sentiment, the key attitude, the key response, the key action that makes doing the project worthwhile and that the reader should have ringing around the mind once the reading is over?

As a representation of the worlds and experiences of others, the text is a vehicle to voice their views, explanations and understandings about their worlds as they account for them. How this text is framed depends on the core values of the writer. As a political and ethical act, the text intervenes in public places where worlds are in contest. How this text is interpreted, used or abused can never be fully predicted. It will go far beyond the reach of the writer to claw it back to the 'meanings I really meant'. As a creative act, the text becomes an invitation for the creative play of others. The story of the project differs with every reading.

Conclusion

The project has to be teased. It cannot be pushed nor planned too much. To look for perfection results either in killing the research, or the re-searcher. In writing up one begins to inhabit one's text, exploring its corners, removing its cul-de-sacs and unwanted implications. A project is never ending. A piece of writing is never finished. It just stops. It has to stop sometime. New interests and demands arise creating the occa-sions for new journeys, new rationales, new messages.

The project, being framed by epistemologies, methodologies, politics, ethics and all the other ics, ists, isms and ologies leaves a trail of writ-ings, like the tracks and droppings of hunted creatures. What's the point of it? Of course, there is no final answer.

Between joy and tragedy there is an infinity of stories and possible projects. A project develops around the curiosities, needs and interests of the individual. It is unique to the extent that it derives from the existen-tial uniqueness of the individual. It transcends uniqueness and enters dialogue to the extent that it seeks out the viewpoints of others.

What then is the social, cultural, historical, political importance of the project? For me, it resides in the way in which it addresses the value of being with others. The social engineering project, for example, that seeks to produce outcomes and people (like any other raw materials) accord-ing to authority-imposed criteria, values people according to the extent to which they fit requirements. What sort of society does a given project imply?

Skinner (1976) told the story of his vision of the fully engineered life in *Walden II*. Schreber ([1955] 1988) described his vision of the world as he experienced it through his mental illness. This illness was the result of the fully engineered child-rearing procedures that he had received from his father (Schatzman 1973). Such a project produced the model for paranoia that Freud explored and can be expressed as having startling similarities with contemporary forms of schooling in its deployment of the techniques of surveillance and control (Schostak 2000). The techniques of surveillance and control are being made more sophisticated daily through information technology. It is a project that has its vision already framed by such novels as Orwell's *1984*, or Gibson's *Necromancer*.

Imagination is just as essential to the project as the empirical data collected by the researcher. Without an imaginative grasp the data fall dead. Without a vision there is no journey to project. The choice of journey depends on the individual. It returns to those questions that never cease. What do I really want? What sort of society do I want to live in? Each project is an answer to these kinds of questions.

Each project then is vital in the search for ways to enhance freedom, creativity and the quality of life. With the collapse of the great social and political projects of the twentieth century many are cynical of any attempt at large-scale change. Yet, as Chantal Mouffe (1993) has pointed out, it can be argued that democracy is as yet an unfinished revolution. The social and political project is to embed democratic processes and procedures into every institution of life. If this is so, then qualitative research, with its detailed focus on the complexities of social interaction, the collection of data and its interpretation, has a powerful role to play.

What for the individual and for society is a 'project'? The self in a state of aloneness faces others who position 'him' or 'her' within a social matrix of values. The project may be a bridge permitting 'reach', 'transactions', a passage or course of action that is either 'with', or 'against', or 'indifferent', or 'in ignorance' of others. For Freire (1970) a project is what distinguishes human beings from animals. It is a means of 'humanising the world by transforming it'. For Haug (1987, 1992) the project is a way of rewriting the self, finding one's agency. For many who have been influenced by Lacan, Derrida, Foucault and others, the project is a way of deconstructing repression and social power in order to open up spaces for creative growth. There is no limit to the projects that may be undertaken except those imposed by a failure of imagination or a lack of daring. Is the great social project dead? Only if challenging prevailing realities and improving the allocation of resources to need, interest and opportunities for creativity are no longer of interest to individual researchers.

Notes

1 Meaning 'whole'. In this usage it refers to the perceptual grasp of objects where the brain tries to create a holistic image from sensory data. With ambiguous data the brain tries to create a stable image. Once that image is created it can be hard to 'see' its alternative. Both images cannot be seen at the same time. However, for some people the images may oscillate from one to the other. See Köhler (1966) for an introduction to Gestalt psychology.

2 Ethnography is employed very loosely here to refer to getting close to the scene of action, focusing on the lives of people being researched. Ethnography was originally employed when doing very long-term fieldwork, living with the people being studied in order to be fully immersed in their lives. Many contemporary researchers now use the term more loosely as above.

3 Not used to imply unity.

4 The term is employed here not to imply length of time in the field, but as an approach that focuses on the ways people define and account for their experience and the use of these as key constructs for representing their worlds (cf. Fontana 1994).

5 Some may consider that this implies thought is independent of language. It seems to me that thought, in its broadest conception, is indeed prior to language. There are times when one struggles to find the 'right' word, when feelings exceed expression in language yet are an essential dimension to 'thinking', to determining what is 'right', 'true'. There are perhaps many modes of thinking and language supports only a particular range. Language may help clarify thinking, but may also misdirect it through an uncritical attachment to the categories, the grammars, the syntax through which thinking is canalized. This issue is picked up again in Chapter 10.

6 Copy hangs on wall in office to which he points at the moment of saying this.

7 By this is meant the source of authority in the 'Law', 'Code', 'Culture', 'Custom' and so on that sanctions action and 'fixes' the sense of the world's order for individuals, communities, or the 'mass'.

8 Semiotics, as the study of systems of signs and symbols modelled on language, would include such symbolic systems as dress codes, behavioural codes, the

ways in which space is organized in work and leisure areas as well as the particular discourses associated with particular groups. The context of cultural symbolic systems includes all such possibilities.

9 That is, a geometrical plane surface, like a mirror or a window that does not immediately reveal whether it is the one or the other and thus leaves one's perceptions in doubt.

10 That *nouvel* is one of the forms of the French for 'new' is perhaps a fortuitous accident in this context!

11 Of course, to build a design that includes so much fieldwork in terms of an unmanageable number of observations and interviews or so much reading that many years or a substantial research grant would not buy enough time to complete is not 'ambitious' in the sense I mean it, rather it is self-defeating. A design has to have a scope that can be brought into being during a reasonable period of time. See the earlier discussion in Chapter 1.

12 A version of what I call the real-Other. Here it is personified in the Dictator.

13 Rather like Ratnavadival's initial temptation discussed in Chapter 6.

14 There may be a fine difference between authoritarian and authoritative rhetoric. Rhetoric seems to me to be authoritative if it appeals to reason, justice and so on and gains assent only because of the convincingness of its arguments set into dialogue with others. Rhetoric is authoritarian if it depends on the exercise of coercive powers to bring about social order, thereby ultimately refusing any dialogue.

15 A double bind pointed out by Harry Torrance in his comments on the draft manuscript.

16 My translation: I attract the man towards more light; towards a zone struck by a ray of light coming from the surface through a basement window and projecting on the wall the form of a grille. We are going to come in a fictive cage, a barred cell made only out of shadow and light. (I have translated jouir as 'come' in its slang meaning of sexual orgasm which I take as the meaning intended by Collard describing a place where people go to meet partners for casual sex. His book is a story of a man in his thirties, ravaged by AIDS, torn between his desire for casual sex with men and his desire for a particular young woman).

17 'Between dog and wolf' – an expression employed, Collard tells us, in the jargon of film makers, and which Collard employs to announce the coming of night, the emergence of the wolf within the dog, perhaps.

18 The site is maintained by Earl Jackson and at the time of writing can be found at: *http://www.anotherscene.com/*

19 As in Chapter 4, the 'edge' here is the shifting negotiation between 'something' and 'nothing'. Religion provides the edginess of existence in the face of death. Beyond the edge, what is there?

20 Typically, the dogma is expressed as being that an 'ought' cannot be drawn from an 'is'. It stems from David Hume's arguments that empirical facts can only tell you what 'is', they cannot tell you what ought to be done.

21 Quoted with permission from an unpublished paper presented to justify the transfer from MPhil to PhD status.

22 I employ this term ironically. Many will consider it to be an expression of desperation while others will see it as a form of political cynicism where

governments compete with each other to convince global capital that they are indeed engineering children to be a relatively cheap skilled and compliant workforce; or at least, to convince their own populations to continue voting for them because they are securing their children's future by making them attractive to potential employers.

23 From a signed letter by David Reynolds sent to publicize 'The high reliability school: theory and practice' conference, 7 March 1997, London.

24 Research that stays within the schooled approaches of the expert seeks only Habermas's (1971) technicist solutions and instrumental rationality in order to 'improve' the workings of a system and dominate nature and the social world, rather than empower or liberate. It can be argued that all research inevitably challenges the status quo since it will eventually be faced with dilemmas irresolvable within the prevailing system or perspective. However, the researcher as individual may choose to ignore these or shy away from them, or confront them to seek the 'new'.

25 Interestingly, the voice of the Director is reminiscent of the position adopted by Hirsch (1967) discussed in Chapter 2. However, the Director remains somewhat ambivalent in status since the 'I' that claims authorship does so not in the voice of Ridley but as Director. Thus, it remains questionable that the Director can claim an authoritative position among the other voices of the thesis.

References

Airaksinen, T. (1995) *The Philosophy of the Marquis de Sade*. London; New York, NY: Routledge.

Anderson, B. (1983) *Imagined Communities. Reflections on the Origin and Spread of Nationalism*. London; New York, NY: Verso.

Anderson, W. T. (1995) Four different ways to be absolutely right, in W. T. Anderson (ed.) *The Truth about the Truth. De-confusing and Re-constructing the Postmodern World*. New York, NY: Putnam.

Arendt, H. (1963) *Eichmann in Jerusalem: A Report on the Banality of Evil*. London: Faber and Faber.

Baas, B. (1992) *Le Désir Pur. Parcours Philosophiques dans les Parages de J. Lacan*. Louvain: Peeters.

Bateson, G. (1972) *Steps Towards an Ecology of Mind*. London; New York, NY: Paladin.

Baudrillard, J. (1990) *Seduction*. Montreal: New World Perspectives.

Baudrillard, J. (1994) *Simulacra and Simulation*, translated by Sheila Faria Glaser. Ann Arbor, MI: University of Michigan Press.

Baudrillard, J. (1996) *The Perfect Crime*, trans. Chris Turner. London: Verso.

Baudrillard, J. and Nouvel, J. (2000) *Les Objets Singuliers. Architecture et Philosophie*. Paris: Calman-Lévy.

Bauman, Z. (1992) *Intimations of Postmodernity*. London: Routledge.

Benhabib, S. (1986) *Critique, Norm, and Utopia. A Study of the Foundations of Critical Theory*. New York, NY: Columbia University Press.

Berne, E. ([1968] 1975) *Games People Play: The Psychology of Human Relationships*. Harmondsworth: Penguin.

Berne, E. (1975) *What Do You Say After You Say Hello?* London: Corgi.

Best, S. (1994) Foucault, postmodernism and social theory, in D. R. Dickens and A. Fontana (eds) *Postmodernism and Social Theory*. London: Guildford Press.

Bhaskar, R. (1975) *A Realist Theory of Science*. Hassocks: Harvester.

Bhaskar, R. (1978) *A Realist Theory of Science*, 2nd edn. Hassocks: Harvester Press.

Bhaskar, R. (1986) *Scientific Realism and Human Emancipation*. London: Verso.

Bhaskar, R. (1993) *Dialectic. The Pulse of Freedom*. London, New York, NY: Verso.

Birdwhistell, R. L. (1973) *Kinesics and Context: Essays on Body–Motion Communication*. Harmondsworth: Penguin.

Bloom, A. (1987) *The Closing of the American Mind: How Higher Education Has Failed Democracy and Impoverished the Souls of Today's Students*. New York, NY: Simon and Schuster.

Blumer, H. (1969) *Symbolic Interactionism*. Englewood Cliffs, NJ: Prentice-Hall.

Booth, W. C. (1961) *The Rhetoric of Fiction*. Chicago, IL; London: University of Chicago Press.

Booth, W. C. (1974) *A Rhetoric of Irony*. Chicago, IL; London: University of Chicago Press.

Boothby, R. (1991) *Death and Desire. Psychoanalytic Theory in Lacan's Return to Freud*. New York, NY; London: Routledge.

Cannon, S. (1989) 'Social research in stressful settings: difficulties for the sociologist studying the treatment of breast cancer', *Sociology of Health and Illness*, 11, (1): 62–77.

CARE (1994) *Coming to Terms with Research*. Norwich: CARE, University of East Anglia.

Carroll, L. (1948) *Through the Looking-Glass. And What Alice Found There*. London: Macmillan.

Caruth, C. (ed.) (1995) *Trauma. Explorations in Memory*. Baltimore, MD; London: Johns Hopkins University Press.

Charraud, N. (1997) *Lacan et les Mathématiques*. Paris: Anthropos, Economica.

Chow, R. (1993) *Writing Diaspora. Tactics of Intervention in Contemporary Cultural Studies*. Bloomington; Indianapolis, IN: Indiana University Press.

Clifford, J. (1988) *The Predicament of Culture: Twentieth-Century Ethnography, Literature, and Art*. Cambridge, MA: Harvard University Press.

Coathup, G. W. (1997) Talking out: a search for empowerment. Unpublished PhD thesis, University of East Anglia.

Cockburn, A. (1992) Excavating the Truth: Introduction to *Chronicles of Dissent. Noam Chomsky, Interviewed by David Barsamian*. Vancouver: New Star Books.

Cohen, M. R. (1944) *A Preface to Logic*. New York, NY: Dover.

Collard, C. (1989) *Les Nuits Fauve*. Paris: Éditions J'ai Lu, Flammarion.

Collier, A. (1994) *Critical Realism*. London: Verso.

Cooley, C. H. (1902) *Human Nature and the Social Order*. New York, NY: Charles Scribner's Sons.

Cooley, C. H. (1956) *Social Organization*. Chicago: Free Press.

Danto, A. C. (1985) *Narration and Knowledge*. New York, NY: Columbia University Press.

Davies, B. and Harré, R. (1990) Positioning: the discursive production of selves, *Journal for the Theory of Social Behaviour*, 20 (1): 43–63.

Debord, G. (1994) *The Society of the Spectacle*, translated by Donald Nicholson-Smith. New York, NY: Zone Books.

Denzin, N. K. (1970) *The Research Act in Sociology*. London: Butterworth.

Denzin, N. K. (1989) *Interpretive Interactionism*. Newbury Park, CA; London: Sage.

De Saussure, F. (1966) *Course in General Linguistics*, edited by C. Bally and A. Sechehaye, translated by W. Baskin. New York, NY: McGraw-Hill.

Douglas, J. D., Johnson, J. M. and others (1977) *Existential Sociology*. Cambridge: Cambridge University Press.

Durkheim, E. (1964) *The Rules of Sociological Method*, 8th edn, translated by Sarah A. Solovay and John H. Mueller and edited by George E. G. Catlin. New York, NY; London: Free Press Collier-Macmillan.

Edgley, R. (1976) Reason as dialectic. Science, social science and socialist science, *Radical Philosophy*, 15: 2–7.

Elliott, J. (1991) *Action Research for Educational Change*. Milton Keynes: Open University Press.

Empsom, W. (1930) *Seven Types of Ambiguity*. London: Chatto and Windus.

Feyerabend, P. (1975) *Against Method*. London: NLB.

Fontana, A. (1994) Ethnographic trends in the postmodern era, in David R. Dickens and Andrea Fontana (eds) *Postmodernism and Social Inquiry*. London: UCL Press.

Frankl, V. E. (1963) *Man's Search for Meaning*. London: Hodder and Stoughton.

Freeman, R. (1998) The chameleon, the mirror, and the two-headed snake: a study of the development of mentoring in general practice. Unpublished thesis, CARE, University of East Anglia.

Freire, P. (1972) *Cultural Action for Freedom*. Harmondsworth: Penguin.

Freud, S. (1933) *New Introductory Lectures on Psycho-analysis*, authorized translation by W. J. H. Sprott. London: Hogarth Press, Institute of Psycho-Analysis.

Gaad, E. (1998) *The experience of education of a child with Down's Syndrome in England and Egypt*. Unpublished thesis, CARE, University of East Anglia.

Garfinkel, H. (1967) *Studies in Ethnomethodology*. Englewood Cliffs, NJ: Prentice-Hall.

Geertz, C. (1988) *Works and Lives: The Anthropologist as Author*. Cambridge: Polity Press.

Glaser, B. G. and Strauss, A. L. (1964) Awareness contexts and social interaction, *American Sociological Review*, 29: 669–79.

Glaser, B. G. and Strauss, A. L. (1967) *The Discovery of Grounded Theory. Strategies for Qualitative Research*. Aldine: Atherton.

Godelier, M. (1972) Structure and contradiction in *Capital* (from *Les Temps Modernes*, 246, November 1966), in R. Blackburn (ed.) *Ideology in Social Science*. London: Fontana.

Goffman, E. (1970) *Strategic Interaction*. Oxford: Basil Blackwell.

Goodson, I. F. and Walker, R. (1991) *Biography, Identity, and Schooling: Episodes in Educational Research*. London: Falmer Press.

Gottdiener, M. (1994) Semiotics and postmodernism, in David R. Dickens and Andrea Fontana, *Postmodernism and Social Inquiry*. London: UCL Press.

Gray, C. H. (ed.) (1995) *The Cyborg Handbook*, with the assistance of H. J. Figueroa-Sarriera and S. Mentor. New York, NY; London: Routledge.

Habermas, J. (1971) *Knowledge and Human Interests*, translated by Jeremy Shapiro. Boston, MA: Beacon Press.

Hammersley, M. (ed.) (1984) *The Ethnography of Schooling*. Driffield: Nafferton Books.

Hargreaves, D. H., Hestor, S. K. and Mellor, F. J. (1975) *Deviance in Classrooms*. London; Boston, MA: Routledge and Kegan Paul.

Harris, M. (1968) *The Rise of Anthropological Theory*. New York, NY: Crowell; London: Routledge and Kegan Paul.

Harris, M. (1980) *Cultural Materialism. The Struggle for a Science of Culture*. New York, NY: Vintage Books.

Hartley, J. (1982) *Understanding News*. London; New York, NY: Methuen.

Haseler, S. (2000) *The Super-rich. The Unjust New World of Global Capitalism*. Basingstoke: Macmillan; New York, NY: St Martin's Press.

Haug, F. (ed.) (1987) *Female Sexualization. A Collective Work of Memory*, translated by E. Carter. London: Verso.

Haug, F. (1992) *Beyond Female Masochism. Memory-work and Politics*. London; New York, NY: Verso.

Hedges, I. (1996) Special educational needs in the mainstream classroom, unpublished MEd thesis, CARE, University of East Anglia.

Heller, J. (1962) *Catch 22*. London: Cape.

Hempel, C. G. (1942) The function of general laws in history, *Journal of Philosophy*, 39: 35–48.

Hirsch, E. D. (1967) *Validity in Interpretation*. New Haven, CT; London: Yale University Press.

Hobbes, T. ([1651] 1914) *Leviathan*. London: Dent.

Howard, R. J. (1982) *Three Faces of Hermeneutics: An Introduction to Current Theories of Understanding*. Berkeley, CA; London: University of California Press.

Hughes, T. (1976) Myth and education, in G. Fox *et al.* (eds) *Writers, Critics and Children*. London: Heinemann.

James, W. (1890) *Principles of Psychology*, 2 vols. New York, NY: Henry Holt.

Jameson, F. (1984) Postmodernism; or, the cultural logic of late capitalism, *New Left Review*, 146: 53–93.

Jameson, F. and Miyoshi, M. (eds) (1999) *The Cultures of Globalisation*. Durham; London: Duke University Press.

Jencks, C. (1997) *Post-modernism: The New Classicism in Art and Architecture*. London: Academy Editions.

Kant, I. (1977) *Critique of Practical Reason*, translated and edited by Mary Gregor, with an introduction by Andrew Reath. Cambridge: Cambridge University Press.

Kosko, B. (1993) *Fuzzy Thinking. The New Science of Fuzzy Logic*. London: HarperCollins.

Kroker, A. and Cook, D. (1986) *The Postmodern Scene. Excremental Culture and Hyper Aesthetics*. New York, NY: St Martin's Press.

Kroker, A. and Kroker, M. (ed.) (1987) *Body Invaders. Panic Sex in America*. Montreal: New World Perspectives.

Kroker, A. and Weinstein, M. A. (1994) *Data Trash. The Theory of the Virtual Class*, Montreal: New World Perspectives.

Kropotkin, Prince P. A. (1904) *Mutual Aid: A Factor of Evolution*. London: Heinemann.

Kuhn, T. (1970) *The Structure of Scientific Revolutions, 2nd edn.*, Vols I and II. Foundations of the Unity of Science. Chicago, IL: University of Chicago Press.

Lacan, J. (1977a) *Écrits. A Selection*. London: Tavistock/Routledge.

Lacan, J. (1977b) The mirror stage as formative of the function of the I, in *Écrits. A Selection*. London: Tavistock/Routledge.

Lacan, J. (1993) *The Psychoses. The Seminar of Jacques Lacan*, Book III, 1955–1956, edited by Jacques-Alain Miller, translated with notes by Russell Grigg. London: Routledge.

Lash, S. (1999) *Another Modernity. A Different Rationality*. Oxford; Malden, MA: Blackwell.

Le Corbusier (1927) *Towards a New Architecture*. London: The Architectural Press.

Levinas, E. (1979) *Totality and Infinity*, translated by A. Lingis, Pittsburgh, PA: Duquesne University Press.

Levinas, E. (1982) *Ethics and Infinity, Conversations with Phillipe Nemo*, translated by Richard A. Cohen. Pittsburgh, PA: Duquesne University Press.

Levinas, E. (1998) *Discovering Existence with Husserl*, translated and edited by R. A. Cohen and M. B. Smith. Evanston, IL: Northwestern University Press.

Lévi-Strauss, C. (1969) *The Elementary Structures of Kinship*, translated by James Harle Bell, John Richard von Sturmer and Rodney Needham. Boston: Beacon Press.

Lévi-Strauss, C. (1970) *Introduction to a Science of Mythology, Part 1: The Raw and the Cooked*, translated from the French by John and Doreen Weightman. London: Cape.

Linde, C. (1993) *Life Stories. The Creation of Coherence*. New York, NY, Oxford: Oxford University Press.

Lindesmith, A. (1947) *Opiate Addiction*. Bloomington, IN: Principia Press.

Locke, J. ([1693] 1989) *Some thoughts concerning education*, edited with introduction, notes and critical apparatus by John, W. and Jean S. Yolton. Oxford: Clarendon.

Logan, T. (1988) Adolescent Schooling: Individuals, Institutions and Meanings in Transition. Unpublished PhD Thesis, CARE, University of East Anglia.

Lukács, G. (1971) *History and Class Consciousness. Studies in Marxian Dialectics*. Merlin Press.

Lyotard, J. F. (1984) *The Postmodern Condition: A Report on Knowledge*, translated by Geoff Bennington and Brian Massumi, foreword by Frederic Jameson. Theory and History of Literature, Volume 10. Manchester: Manchester University Press.

MacDonald, B. (1984) Evaluation and the control of education, in R. Murphy and H. Torrance (eds) *Evaluating Education: Issues and Methods*. London: Harper and Row (in association with the Open University); first published 1974 in B. MacDonald and R. Walker (eds) *Innovation, Evaluation, Research and the Problem of Control* (SAFARI), CARE, University of East Anglia.

MacDonald, P. S. (2000) *Descartes and Husserl. The Philosophical Project of Radical Beginnings*. Albany, NY: State University of New York Press.

Machiavelli, N. ([c. 1515] 1976) *The Prince*, new translation, introduction and annotation by James B. Atkinson. Indianapolis, IN: Bobbs-Merrill.

Malinowski, B. (1922) *Argonauts of the Western Pacific. An Account of Native Enterprise and Adventure in the Archipelagoes of Melanesia New Guinea*. London: Routledge; New York, NY: Dutton.

Marx, K. ([1867] 1970) *Capital: A Critique of Political Economy*, translated from the 3rd German edition by Samuel Moore and Edward Aveling, edited by Frederick Engels. Volume 1: Capitalist Production. London: Lawrence and Wishart.

Marx, K. and Engels, F. ([1932] 1964) *The German Ideology*. London: Lawrence and Wishart.

Matza, D. (1964) *Delinquency and Drift*. New York, NY; London: Wiley.

Mead, G. H. (1934) *Mind, Self and Society*. Chicago, IL: University of Chicago Press.

Meng, C. F. (1999) Angels with dirty faces: connecting pupils' views with curriculum in Malaysia. Unpublished PhD Thesis, School of Education and Professional Development, University of East Anglia.

Merleau-Ponty, M. (1962) *Phenomenology of perception*, translated from the French by Colin Smith. London: Routledge and Kegan Paul.

Milgram, S. (1974) *Obedience to Authority: An Experimental View*. London: Tavistock.

Mills, C. W. (1940) Situated actions and vocabularies of motive, *American Sociological Review*, 5(6): 904–13.

Morgan, G. ([1986] 1997) *Images of Organization*. Thousand Oaks, CA, London: Sage.

Morse, M. (1998) *Virtualities. Television, Media Art, and Cyber Culture*. Bloomington and Indianapolis, IN: Indiana University Press.

Mouffe, C. (1993) *The Return of the Political*. London and New York, NY: Verso.

Moulthrop, S. (1993) You say you want a revolution: hypertext and the laws of media, in E. Amiran and J. Unsworth, *Essays in Postmodern Culture*. Oxford; New York, NY: Oxford University Press.

Needham, R. (1983) *Against the Tranquility of Axioms*. Berkeley, CA: University of California Press.

Noble, D. F. (1995) *Progress Without People: New Technology, Unemployment, and the Message of Resistance*. Toronto: Between the Lines.

Nozick, R. (1981) *Philosophical Explanations*. Oxford: Clarendon.

Ortega y Gasset, J. (1957) *Man and People*. New York, NY: Norton and Co.

Owen, D. (ed.) (1997) *Sociology after Postmodernism*. London: Sage.

Paine, T. ([1792] 2000) *The Rights of Man and Common Sense*, introduced by Tony Benn. London: Phoenix.

Park, R. E. (1916) The city: suggestions for the investigation of human behaviour in the urban environment, *American Journal of Sociology*, 20: 577–612.

Parsons, Talcott (1949) *The structure of social action: a study in social theory with special reference to a group of recent European writers*, Glencoe, IL: Free Press.

Patrick, J. (1973) *A Glasgow Gang Observed*. London: Methuen.

Pearson, G. (1983) *Hooligan. A History of Respectable Fears*. London: Macmillan.

Perkin, H. (1989) *The Rise of Professional Society: England since 1880*. London: Routledge.

Perry, N. (1998) *Hyperreality and Global Culture*. London; New York, NY: Routledge.

Phillips, T. (1995) Changing nurse education: dialogue and discourse in the education of student-professionals. Unpublished PhD, School of Education, University of East Anglia.

Phillips, T., Bedford, H., Robinson, J. and Schostak, J. F. (1994) *Researching Professional Education. Education, Dialogue and Assessment: Creating Partnership for Improving Practice*. London: English National Board for Nursing, Midwifery and Health Visiting.

Phillips, T., Schostak, J. and Tyler, J. (2000) *Practice and Assessment: An Evaluation of the Assessment of Practice at Diploma, Degree and Postgraduate Level in pre and post-registration nursing and midwifery education*. London: London.

Piaget, J. (1970) *Structuralism*. New York, NY: Basic Books.

Pierce, C. S. (1931) *Collected Papers*. Cambridge, MA: Harvard University Press.

Power, M. (1997) *The Audit Society. Rituals of Verification*. Oxford: Oxford University Press.

Ragin, C. C. (1992) 'Casing' and the process of social inquiry, in C. C. Ragin and H. S. Becker (eds) (1992) *What Is a Case? Exploring the Foundations of Social Inquiry*. Cambridge: Cambridge University Press.

Ratnavadivel, N. (1995) The management of innovation: an evaluation of curriculum change in Malaysian teacher education. Unpublished PhD, CARE, University of East Anglia.

Rawls, R. (1971) *A Theory of Justice*. Cambridge, MA: Harvard University Press.

Rey, J. F. (1997) *Le Passeur de Justice*. Paris: Éditions Michalon.

Reynolds, D. (1996) *Making Good Schools: Linking School Effectiveness and School Improvement*. London: Routledge.

Ridley, B. M. (1998) The Cinderella service. The education of exclusions and refusers. Unpublished PhD, School of Education, University of East Anglia.

Riesman, D., with Nathan Glazer and Reuel Denney (1969) *The Lonely Crowd: A Study of the Changing American Character*, abridged edition with a 1969 preface. New Haven, CT; London: Yale University Press.

Rifkin, A. (1999) Introduction, in *Photogenic Painting. Gilles Deleuze, Michel Foucault, Deerard Fromanger*. London: Black Dog Publishing.

Rosenau, P. M. (1992) *Post-modernism and the Social Sciences: Insights, Inroads, and Intrusions*. Princeton, NJ, Oxford: Princeton University Press.

Rosenberg, A. (1997) Education and liminality in redressing racism: a cross textual analysis. Unpublished PhD, CARE, University of East Anglia.

Samuel, R. and Thompson, P. (1990) *The Myths We Live By*. London; New York, NY: Routledge.

Sartre, J.-P. (1964) *The Problem of Method*, translated by Hazel E. Barnes. London: Methuen.

Sartre, J.-P. (1976) *Critique of Dialectical Reason*, translated by A. Sheridan-Smith, edited by J. Ree. London: Verso.

Sayer, A. (1993) *Method in Social Science. A Realist Approach*. London; New York, NY: Routledge.

Schatzman, M. (1973) *Soul Murder. Persecution in the Family*. London: Allen Lane.

Scheper-Hughes, N. (1992) *Death Without Weeping. The Violence of Everyday Life in Brazil*. Berkeley; Los Angeles, CA; Oxford: University of Caifornia Press.

Schostak, J. F. (1983) Making and breaking lies in a pastoral care context, *Research in Education*, 30: 71–93.

Schostak, J. F. (1985) Creating the narrative case record, *Curriculum Perspectives*, 5 (1): 7–13.

Schostak, J. F. (1986) *Schooling the Violent Imagination*. London; New York, NY: Routledge and Kegan Paul.

Schostak, J. F. (1989) The play of education, *Cambridge Journal of Education*, 19 (2) 207–23.

Schostak, J. F. (ed.) (1991) *Youth in Trouble: Educational Response*. London: Kogan Page Norwich: CARE, UEA.

Schostak, J. F. (1992) Voices and visions; making sense of a large secondary school. Unpublished report, CARE, University of East Anglia.

Schostak, J. F. (1993) *Dirty Marks. The Education of Self, Media and Popular Culture*. London; Boulder, CO: Pluto.

Schostak, J. F. (1996) Teacher education: notes towards a radical view, in R. McBride, *Teacher Education Policy: Issues arising from Research and Experience*. Lewes: Falmer Press.

Schostak, J. F. (1999a) Action research and the point instant of change, *Educational Action Research*, 7 (3): 403–20.

Schostak, J. F. (1999b) Representing the cr/eye of the witness, in A. Massey and G. Walford, *Explorations in Methodology, Studies in Educational Ethnography, Volume 2*. Stamford, CT: JAI Press.

Schostak, J. F. (2000) Developing under developing circumstances: the personal and social development of students and the process of schooling, in J. Elliott and H. Altrichter, *Images of Educational Change*. Buckingham: Open University.

Schostak, J. F. and Schostak, J. R. (2000) Final report: a six month study of junior doctors' learning experiences. Unpublished report, CARE, University of East Anglia.

Schostak, Jill (2000) *[Ad]dressing Methodologies. Tracing the Self in Significant Slips: Shadow Dancing*, draft of doctoral thesis, CARE, UEA.

Schreber, D. P. ([1955] 1988) *Memoirs of My Nervous Illness*, translated by Ida Macalpine and Richard Hunter. 2nd revised edn. Cambridge, MA: Harvard Belknap.

Schutz, A. ([1945] 1967) *Collected Papers, I: The Problem of Social Reality*. The Hague: Martinus Nijhoff.

Schutz, A. (1976) *The Phenomenology of the Social World*, translated by G. Walsh and F. Lehnert. London: Heinemann.

Schutz, A. and Luckmann, T. (1973) *The Structures of the Life-World*, translated by R. M. Zaner and H. T. Engelhardt Jr. London: Heinemann.

Scott, M. B. and Lyman, S. M. (1968) Accounts, *American Sociological Review*, 33 (1): 46–62.

Sharp, R. and Green, A. (with the assistance of Jacqueline Lewis) (1975) *Education and Social Control. A Study in Progressive Primary Education*. London: Routledge and Kegan Paul.

Shirtliffe, D. (2000) Unpublished, untitled transfer paper for MPhil to PhD. CARE, University of East Anglia.

Silverman, D. (1993) *Interpreting Qualitative Data. Methods for Analysing Talk, Text and Interaction*. London, Thousand Oaks, CA, New Dehli: Sage.

Silverman, D. (2000) *Doing Qualitative Research: A Practical Handbook*. London: Sage.

Simons, H. (ed.) (1981) *Towards a Science of the Singular*, occasional publication. Norwich: CARE, University of East Anglia.

Skinner, B. F. (1953) *Science and Human Behaviour*. New York, NY: Macmillan.

Skinner, B. F. (1976) *Walden II*. New York, NY: Macmillan; London: Collier Macmillan.

Smith, A. ([1776] 1961) *The Wealth of Nations. An Inquiry into the Nature and Causes of the Wealth of Nations: Representative Selections*, edited, with an introduction, by Bruce Mazlish. Indianapolis, IN: Bobbs-Merrill.

Smith, D. W. and McIntyre, R. (1971) 'Intentionality via intensions', *The Journal of Philosophy*, 68 (18): 541–61.

Steele, M. (1997) *Theorizing Textual Subjects*. Cambridge: Cambridge University Press.

Stenhouse, L. (1975) *An Introduction to Curriculum Research and Development*. London: Heinemann.

Stinchcombe, A. L. (1982) The deep structure of moral categories. Eighteenth-century French stratification, and the revolution, in Ino Rossi (ed.) *Structural Sociology*. New York, NY: Columbia University Press.

Stirner, M. (1971) *The Ego and his Own,* edited and introduced by John Carroll. London: Cape.

Strauss, A. and Corbin, J. (1998) *Basics of Qualitative Research: Techniques and Procedures for Developing Grounded Theory.* Thousand Oaks, CA; London: Sage.

Stscherbatsky, F. Th. (1962) *Buddhist Logic.* New York, NY: Dover Publications.

Thomas, W. I. (1928) *The Child in America.* New York, NY: Alfred A. Knopf.

Thomas, W. I. and Znaniecki, F. (1927) *The Polish Peasant in Europe and America,* 2 vols. New York, NY: Knopf.

Thrasher, F. M. (1927) *The Gang. A Study of 1,313 Gangs in Chicago.* Chicago, IL: University of Chicago Press.

Tragesser, R. S. (1977) *Phenomenology and Logic.* Ithaca, NY; London: Cornell University Press.

Tsai, Ching-Tien (1996) *Approaches to curriculum development: case studies of innovation in the social studies curriculum in the UK and Taiwan.* Unpublished PhD, School of Education and Professional Development, University of East Anglia.

Tschumi, B. (1999) *Tschumi Le Fresnoy. Architecture In/Between.* New York, NY: The Monacelli Press.

Virilio, P. (1996) *Cybermonde, la politique du pire,* entretien avec Phillippe Petit. Paris: Les éditions textuel, Diffusion Le Seuil.

Vonnegut, K. (1965) *Cat's Cradle.* Harmondsworth: Penguin.

Von Wright, G. H. (1971) *Explanation and Understanding.* London: Routledge and Kegan Paul.

Weber, M. (1949) *The Methodology of the Social Sciences: Max Weber,* translated and edited by Edward A. Shils and Henry A. Finch, with a foreword by Edward A. Shils. New York, NY: Free Press.

Webster, R. (1990) *A Brief History of Blasphemy. Liberalism, Censorship and 'The Satanic Verses'.* Southwold: The Orwell Press.

Whyte W. Foote (1943) *Street Corner Society. The Social Structure of an Italian Slum.* Chicago, IL: University of Chicago Press.

Wrong, D. H. (1961) The oversocialised conception of man in modern sociology, *American Sociological Review,* 26 (2): 183–93.

Zevi, B. (1994) *The Modern Language of Architecture.* Seattle, WA: University of Washington Press; New York, NY: Da Capo Press.

Zizek, S. (1991) *Looking Awry. An Introduction to Jacques Lacan through Popular Culture,* Cambridge, MA; London: MIT Press.

Zizek, S. (1992) *Enjoy your Symptom! Jacques Lacan in Hollywood and out.* London; New York, NY: Routledge.

Zizek, S. (1993) *Tarrying with the Negative: Kant, Hegel and the Critique of Ideology.* Durham: Duke University Press.

Index